E-government in Europe

This book traces the development of e-government and its applications across Europe, exploring the effects of information and communication technology (ICTs) upon political action and processes.

The authors explore a range of concepts and topics underpinning e-government in Europe and assess:

- The degree to which e-government translates into genuine reform of government and public administration.
- Its democratic amelioration credentials in relation to citizenship and participation.
- The dual role of the EU as both a provider of e-government through its own internal activities and also as a facilitator or aggregator in the way it seeks to engender change and promote its ethos in member states across the EU.
- Cyberterrorism and its use both by terrorists and governments to pursue political agendas.

The book also features a number of in-depth case studies on the progress of e-government in the UK, France, Germany, Denmark, the Netherlands, Portugal, Greece, Slovenia, Hungary, and Estonia. Reflecting on the broader techno-cultural context within which the ICTs are utilized by governments in Europe, these case studies address the above issues while at the same time highlighting commonality and diversity in practice and the paradox between top-down strategies and the effort to engage wider civil participation via e-government.

This book will be of interest to students and scholars of public policy, politics, media and communication studies, sociology, computing and information and communications technologies and European studies.

Paul G. Nixon is a Senior Lecturer in Political Science at The Hague University of Professional Education, the Netherlands.

Vassiliki N. Koutrakou is a Lecturer in European Studies at the University of East Anglia, UK, and Director of the Centre for Research in European Studies (CREST).

Routledge Advances in European Politics

1 **Russian Messianism**
   Third Rome, revolution,
   communism and after
   Peter J. S. Duncan

2 **European Integration and
   the Postmodern Condition**
   Governance, democracy, identity
   Peter van Ham

3 **Nationalism in Italian
   Politics**
   The stories of the Northern
   League, 1980–2000
   Damian Tambini

4 **International Intervention in
   the Balkans since 1995**
   Edited by Peter Siani-Davies

5 **Widening the European
   Union**
   The politics of institutional
   change and reform
   Edited by Bernard Steunenberg

6 **Institutional Challenges in
   the European Union**
   *Edited by Madeleine Hosli,
   Adrian van Deemen and Mika Widgrén*

7 **Europe Unbound**
   Enlarging and reshaping the
   boundaries of the European
   Union
   Edited by Jan Zielonka

8 **Ethnic Cleansing in the
   Balkans**
   Nationalism and the destruction
   of tradition
   Cathie Carmichael

9 **Democracy and Enlargement
   in Post-communist Europe**
   The democratisation of the
   general public in fifteen Central
   and Eastern European countries,
   1991–1998
   Christian W. Haerpfer

10 **Private Sector Involvement
   in the Euro**
   The power of ideas
   *Stefan Collignon and
   Daniela Schwarzer*

11 **Europe**
   A Nietzschean perspective
   Stefan Elbe

12 **European Union and E-Voting**
Addressing the European parliament's internet voting challenge
Edited by Alexander H. Trechsel and Fernando Mendez

13 **European Union Council Presidencies**
A comparative perspective
Edited by Ole Elgström

14 **European Governance and Supranational Institutions**
Making states comply
Jonas Tallberg

15 **European Union, NATO and Russia**
Martin Smith and Graham Timmins

16 **Business, the State and Economic Policy**
The case of Italy
G. Grant Amyot

17 **Europeanization and Transnational States**
Comparing nordic central governments
Bengt Jacobsson, Per Lægreid and Ove K. Pedersen

18 **European Union Enlargement**
A comparative history
Edited by Wolfram Kaiser and Jürgen Elvert

19 **Gibraltar**
British or Spanish?
Peter Gold

20 **Gendering Spanish Democracy**
Monica Threlfall, Christine Cousins and Celia Valiente

21 **European Union Negotiations**
Processes, networks and negotiations
Edited by Ole Elgström and Christer Jönsson

22 **Evaluating Euro-Mediterranean Relations**
Stephen C. Calleya

23 **The Changing Face of European Identity**
A seven-nation study of (supra) national attachments
Edited by Richard Robyn

24 **Governing Europe**
Discourse, governmentality and European integration
William Walters and Jens Henrik Haahr

25 **Territory and Terror**
Conflicting nationalisms in the Basque country
Jan Mansvelt Beck

26 **Multilateralism, German Foreign Policy and Central Europe**
Claus Hofhansel

27 **Popular Protest in East Germany**
Gareth Dale

28 **Germany's Foreign Policy towards Poland and the Czech Republic**
Ostpolitik revisted
Karl Cordell and Stefan Wolff

29 **Kosovo**
The politics of identity and space
Denisa Kostovicova

30 **The Politics of European Union Enlargement**
Theoretical approaches
Edited by Frank Schimmelfennig and Ulrich Sedelmeier

31 **Europeanizing Social Democracy?**
The rise of the party of European Socialists
Simon Lightfoot

32 **Conflict and Change in EU Budgetary Politics**
Johannes Lindner

33 **Gibraltar, Identity and Empire**
E. G. Archer

34 **Governance Stories**
Mark Bevir and R. A. W. Rhodes

35 **Britain and the Balkans**
1991 until the present
Carole Hodge

36 **The Eastern Enlargement of the European Union**
John O'Brennan

37 **Values and Principles in European Union Foreign Policy**
Edited by Sonia Lucarelli and Ian Manners

38 **European Union and the Making of a Wider Northern Europe**
Pami Aalto

39 **Democracy in the European Union**
Towards the emergence of a public sphere
Edited by Liana Giorgi, Ingmar Von Homeyer and Wayne Parsons

40 **European Union Peacebuilding and Policing**
Michael Merlingen with Rasa Ostrauskaite

41 **The Conservative Party and European Integration since 1945**
At the heart of Europe?
N. J. Crowson

42 **E-government in Europe**
Re-booting the state
Edited by Paul G. Nixon and Vassiliki N. Koutrakou

E-government in Europe
Re-booting the state

**Edited by
Paul G. Nixon and
Vassiliki N. Koutrakou**

LONDON AND NEW YORK

Transferred to digital printing 2010

First published 2007
by Routledge
2 Park Square, Milton Park, Abingdon, Oxon OX14 4RN

Simultaneously published in the USA and Canada
by Routledge
270 Madison Avenue, New York, NY 10016

Routledge is an imprint of the Taylor & Francis Group

© 2007 Paul G. Nixon and Vassiliki N. Koutrakou for selection and editorial matter; individual contributors, their contributions

Typeset in Baskerville by Bookcraft Ltd, Stroud, Glos.

All rights reserved. No part of this book may be reprinted or reproduced or utilised in any form or by any electronic, mechanical, or other means, now known or hereafter invented, including photocopying and recording, or in any information storage or retrieval system, without permission in writing from the publishers.

British Library Cataloguing in Publication Data
A catalogue record for this book is available from the British Library

Library of Congress Cataloging in Publication Data
E-government in Europe : re-booting the state / [edited by] Paul G. Nixon and Vassiliki N. Koutrakou.
   p. cm. – (Routledge advances in European politics ; 42)
Includes bibliographical references and index.
1. Internet in public administration—Europe. 2. Europe—Politics in government—1989– I. Nixon, Paul, 1957– II. Koutrakou, Vassiliki N., 1962–
JN5.E46 2007
352.3'802854678–dc22   2006021373

ISBN10: 0–415–40186–0 (hbk)
ISBN10: 0–415–59948–2 (pbk)
ISBN10: 0–203–96238–9 (ebk)

ISBN13: 978–0–415–40186–9 (hbk)
ISBN13: 978–0–415–59948–1 (pbk)
ISBN13: 978–0–203–96238–1 (ebk)

To my son Patrick
  Paul G. Nixon

To my life-long friends Suzy and Tabatha
  Vassiliki N. Koutrakou

Contents

	List of tables	xi
	List of figures	xii
	Notes on contributors	xiii
	Acknowledgements	xvii
	Introduction	xviii
1	E-government and democratic politics MIKE MARGOLIS	1
2	Ctrl, Alt, Delete: re-booting the European Union via e-government PAUL G. NIXON	19
3	E-government under construction: challenging traditional conceptions of citizenship MIRIAM LIPS	33
4	Danger mouse? The growing threat of cyberterrorism RAJASH RAWAL	48
5	E-government and the United Kingdom NICHOLAS PLEACE	61
6	The digital republic: renewing the French state via e-government FABIENNE GREFFET	75
7	E-government in Germany TINA SIEGFRIED	90

8	Re-organizing government using IT: the Danish model KIM VIBORG ANDERSEN, HELLE ZINNE HENRIKSEN & EVA BORN RASMUSSEN	103
9	E-government in the Netherlands: from strategy to impact – the pursuit of high-volume, high-impact citizen e-services in the Netherlands MARTIN VAN ROSSUM AND DESIRÉE DREESSEN	119
10	The reform and modernisation of Greek public administration via e-government VASSILIKI N. KOUTRAKOU	133
11	'Alt-Tab': from ICTs to organisational innovation in Portugal GUSTAVO CARDOSO AND TIAGO LAPA	152
12	Estonia: the short road to e-government and e-democracy MARC ERNSDORFF AND ADRIANA BERBEC	171
13	This revolution will be digitised! E-government in Hungary KATALIN SZALÓKI AND PAUL G. NIXON	184
14	E-government and Slovenia's multiple transitions DARREN PURCELL AND AARON CHAMPION	196
	Conclusions	211

Tables

1.1	Internet access and usage by region, December 2005	8
1.2	Digital divide indicators within selected OECD nations	10
2.1	Investment in ICT research 2002	27
6.1	E-government ranking of France, 2005	82
6.2	Audience of the 10 French main public websites in December 2005	83
7.1	'Onliners' and 'nonliners' in Germany 2005	93
8.1	Classification of governmental actions related to e-government diffusion	107
8.2	International rankings on Danish e-government, 2005	110
8.3	Number of cases processed digitally in central government, 2002–5	112
8.4	Electronic procurement integration with accounting system or digital invoicing, 2003–4	114
8.5	Overview of the four cases with respect to means, audience, and mode of regulation	117
9.1	e-Citizen charter	125
11.1	Portuguese e-government initiatives: brief descriptions	155
11.2	Synthesis of the main indicators	161

List of figures

8.1	Take-up of digital tax form reporting, 1995–2004	115
8.2	Traffic at the MedCom network during the period 1998–2005	116
10.1	Greek attitudes towards the spread of e-government services	147
14.1	Selected countries' ICT access 2004	202
14.2	Household access to the Internet	203

Notes on contributors

Adriana Berbec from Romania studied European media and the European Union and is a graduate of the Master's Degree programme in International Relations and European Studies of the University of East Anglia, Norwich, UK.

Eva Born Rasmussen is the Head of IT Strategy Division for National Data Infrastructure within the National IT and Telecom Agency in the Danish Ministry of Science Technology and Innovation. She has a MSc in Computer Science and Literature (University of Roskilde and University of Copenhagen), and is currently completing a MSc in International Development Studies and Environmental Studies (University of Roskilde). Her specific research interest is policy development for data standardisation and advanced use of data both within the public and the private sector.

Gustavo Cardoso is an associate researcher at CIES/ISCTE and Professor of Technology and Society at ISCTE in Lisbon. His international cooperation in European research networks brought him to work with IN3 (Internet Interdisciplinary Institute) in Barcelona, and COST A20 and COST A24 projects. Between 1996 and 2006 he was adviser on Information Society and telecommunications policies for the Portuguese Presidency. Publications include 'Trends and contradictions in the broadcasting System: From Interactive to Networked Television' in Colombo, F (ed), *TV and Interactivity in Europe*; *Mythologies, theoretical perspectives, real experiences*, Milano: Vita e Pensiero (2004); 'Media Driven Mobilization and Online Protest. The Pro-East Timor Movement', in *Cyberprotest*, De Donk, Loader, Nixon and Rucht (eds), London: Routledge (2004); 'Feel Like Going Online? Internet Mediated Communication in Portugal', *Information, Communication & Society*, 6(1), London: Routledge (2003).

Aaron Champion holds a BA in Geography and is currently a Master's student at the University of Oklahoma, with interests in network analysis of human-environment relationships, including the use of computer-media communication systems.

Desirée Dreessen from the Netherlands studied European media and the European Union and is a graduate of the Master's Degree programme in

xiv *Notes on contributors*

International Relations and European Studies of the University of East Anglia, Norwich, UK.

Marc Ernsdorff from Luxembourg studied European media and the European Union and is a graduate of the Master's Degree programme in International Relations and European Studies of the University of East Anglia, Norwich, UK.

Fabienne Greffet is Lecturer in Political Science at the University Nancy 2, France. Her research interests are based around the themes of the impacts of new technologies on politics, particularly on political parties, local, national and European elections and political elites in which she has published widely. She is the co-editor of a collection on French political parties: Andolfatto, D., Greffet F., and Olivier, L. (eds), *Les partis politiques: quelles perspectives? (Perspectives on French Political Parties)*.

Vassiliki N. Koutrakou obtained a PhD from the University of Kent, Canterbury, researching European, EU, US, and Japanese Information Technology government policies, and is currently Lecturer in European Studies and Director of the Centre for Research in European Studies (CREST) at the University of East Anglia, Norwich. Recent publications include the monograph *Technological Collaboration for Europe's Survival* (1995) and the edited collections *European Union and Britain: Debating the challenges abroad*, (co-ed) (2000) and *Contemporary Issues and Debates in EU Policy* (2004). She is currently working on a monograph on *International Organisations and Conflict Response*.

Tiago Lapa is an affiliate researcher at CIES/ISCTE (Centre for Research and Studies in Sociology), Lisbon, Portugal. He is conducing research on cross-national surveys such as the European Social Survey (ESS), Eurobarometer and European Quality of Life Survey (EQLS). His recent and present research projects and publications concern: Media and e-government in Europe, Family Change in Europe, Gendered Value Differences, Time Use Over the Life-Course, and Cross-National Analysis of Quantitative Data.

Miriam Lips is a Research Fellow at the Oxford Internet Institute, University of Oxford, and an Associate Professor at the Tilburg Institute for Law, Technology, and Society, Tilburg University. Her research concentrates more generally on the introduction of ICTs in citizen–government relationships and their implications, with a current focus on topics like identity management, personalisation, digital citizenship, e-governance and Internet Governance. Her most recent book publication (together with Simone van der Hof, Corien Prins and Ton Schudelaro) is *Issues of Online Personalisation in Commercial and Public Service Delivery* (2005).

Mike Margolis is Professor of Political Science at the University of Cincinnati. He was co-author (with the late David Resnick) of *Politics as Usual: the cyberspace 'revolution'*. His scholarly and popular publications include books chapters and articles on political parties, elections, public opinion, mass media and democratic theory. He has held visiting appointments in Scotland, at the Universities of Strathclyde and Glasgow, and in Korea at Hankuk University of Foreign Studies Seoul.

Paul G. Nixon is Senior Lecturer in Political Science at The Hague University of Professional Education, the Netherlands. He is a research fellow within the European Public Management Research Group. He has contributed chapters to many edited collections on the use of ICTs particularly in the fields of political parties, electronic democracy and social welfare. He has co-edited two previous collections for Routledge, *Political Parties and the Internet* (2003) and *Cyberprotest* (2004).

Nicholas Pleace is a Senior Research Fellow in the Department of Social Policy and Social Work at the University of York. He has been conducting policy related research on the use of ICTs in social, housing, and employment policy in the UK for the past five years. He has also conducted ESRC funded research on computer mediated social support using the Internet and was co-author of *Key Concepts in Cyberculture* (2004).

Darren Purcell teaches at the University of Oklahoma Department of Geography. His research interests focus on new communication technologies as a tool for geopolitics and governance, representations of places, and the facilitation of new forms of economic regulation. His most recent publications include 'The Military in the Noosphere: NCT Adoption and Website Development in the Slovenian Ministry of Defense', *Information, Communication and Society* (May/June 2005), 'Information Technologies, Representational Spaces, and the Marginal State: Redrawing the Balkan image of Slovenia', *Information, Communications and Society*. 4(3), 1–29 with Kodras, J., and *The Slovenian State on the Internet*. Open Society Institute (Ljubljana, Slovenia) Mediawatch monograph series (1999).

Rajash Rawal is Lecturer in European politics at HEBO, Haagse Hogeschool, The Hague University, the Netherlands. He is a visiting lecturer at the Fachochschule, Eisenstadt, Austria and the Department of European Studies, Budapest Business School. He is a research fellow within the European Public Management Research Group. He specializes in the impact of media on political agents in the modern era and has written a number of papers around this theme.

Tina Siegfried now works at Alcatel SEL Foundation in Berlin after having served as a researcher at the German Institute of Urban Affairs of the University of Oldenburg, Germany, between 1998–2004, as a researcher and consultant in e-government, dealing with the potentials of ICT as a key for modernizing the public sector through organizational and cultural changes within administrations. Her main fields of research are electronic government and electronic commerce, the modernisation of the public sector through ICT and the potentials of ICT for regional development. Publications include 'The experience of German local communities with e-government – results of the MEDIA@Komm project', in Lenk, K. and Traunmüller, R. (eds) *Electronic Government* (2002).

Katalin Szalóki is an economist, specializing in EU Affairs. She is working at the Hungarian National Assembly's EU Department, dealing with EU related issues mainly in the inter-parliamentary dimension. Among other publications, she is a co-author of a weekly newsletter on the EU. Her research interests are focussed around development of electronic information exchange in the EU and the better communication of the EU for the public sphere.

Martin van Rossum is Senior Lecturer in public management, human competence management and business administration at The Hague University of Professional Education, the Netherlands. He is a specialist on e-governance, regional innovation, e-inclusion, broadband policies, e-learning, research management, knowledge transfer, human competence management, He has been involved in projects including Interregional transfer of e-government best practise, representing ICT Center Friesland in Interreg. Recent publications include co-authoring 'BRAINCHILD, building a constituency for future research in Knowledge Management for local Administrations', in Traunmüller, R. and Lenk, K. (eds) *Electronic Government* (2002), and 'Roadmap for European Research in Learning and Knowledge Creation in eGovernment' for the Scandinavian eGov Workshop of February 2005.

Kim Viborg Andersen is Head of the Centre for Research on Information Technology in Policy Settings (CIPS) at the Copenhagen Business School Department of Informatics, Denmark. His publications include numerous journal contributions and examples of his work include *EDI and Data Networking in the Public Sector* (1998); *The Past and Future of Information Systems* (2004) and *Public Sector Process Rebuilding Using Information Systems* (2004). He is the founder of the AIS SIG on e-government and is an editorial board member for various journals.

Helle Zinne Henriksen is an Assistant Professor at the Department of Informatics, Copenhagen Business School, Denmark and is affiliated with the Center for Research on IT in Policy Organizations, at Copenhagen Business School. She is an expert in the field of Management of Information Systems with particular interest in the implications of institutional intervention with respect to inter-organizational adoption. Her research interests include: the adoption and diffusion of IT in the private and the public sector in particular. Her most recent work is focused on e-government and regulation of e-government.

Acknowledgements

The editors would like to first thank everyone at Routledge without whose commitment, skills, and faith in our book, this project would simply never have come to fruition.

Second, we wish to express our gratitude to the contributors of chapters who shared our vision, offered generously their insights and expertise, and made this book the substantial contribution to the field that we hope it will be.

This book project was galvanized at the 6th CREST Conference which was organized at the Centre for Research in European Studies (CREST), at the University of East Anglia (UEA), Norwich, UK, on the 25th November 2005. Aside from the financial sponsors of the conference, the University of The Hague and CREST at UEA who certainly merit special thanks, we also owe our appreciation to the numerous nameless attendees who, with their thoughts, comments, and contributions to the conference debates helped crystallize our focus and plans for the ensuing book.

Finally, among many special people who, in various ways, encouraged us and helped in this book becoming a reality, we would like to mention particularly Deanna Bender, Frans Dijkstra, Ben Hoetjes, Brian Loader, Berry Minkman, Ingrid Mol, Femke van Moorsel, Andres Rawal Bulnes and Sigrid Segeren.

Introduction

Paul G. Nixon and Vassiliki N. Koutrakou

As the long-accepted borders between traditionally delineated policy domains and between differing strata of governance are appearing to become ever more blurred and indistinct by technical networks, facilitating and, some might argue, stimulating the emergence of many differing modes of new social and political networks around the issues and concerns which typify our late-modern society, we have an opportunity to examine and question the ways in which e-government concepts are facilitating a re-drafting of the contexts in which citizens and governments interact. Information and Communication Technologies (ICTs) are increasingly being used as tools to facilitate this interaction.

This trend is taking place in an evolving world with e-government being viewed as an integral component of public sector reform.[1] The European Union (EU) is not immune from such change. New and revamped public services will need to be developed to meet the challenges that the EU will face in terms of demographic change, cultural and religious diversity and changing norms[2] which will in turn necessitate a rethinking of the way in which e-government services are used both in terms of service delivery and in the wider terms of state legitimization through a strengthening of democracy.

Increasingly citizens and governments use ICTs to interact regularly, for example obtaining a new driver's licence by dispatching data; or in the transfer of monies in terms of the paying of taxes and/or charges or via the receipt of social benefit payments. We see more and more improvements being made to utilise new technologies to increase efficiency, ease of use, and to make the system of government–citizen interactions more comprehensive. In order to achieve this we can observe the creation of single points of contact, 'one stop shops' or portals which are designed to allow citizen to government access 24/7. Thus, in many cases making the services available when the individual wishes to utilise them and not restricted, at least in the initial phases, by office opening hours. This contact may be available via various technologies such as a personal computer, mobile phone, digital TVs or even via future developments of existing or new technologies. As Dahlgren[3] argues new uses of ICTs are shaping, and will, presumably, continue to shape in the foreseeable future, new perceptions of government and sovereignty in the European Union member states and in the applicant states. However there is scepticism over the willingness of politicians and officials to engage with *all* of its citizens.[4]

As this book will consistently show, e-government isn't just about value-neutral technological advances in service delivery and communication. E-government is about people and how their democratic governments act in their name. People live both on-and off-line[5] and it is the mix of these two elements that represents the reality of lived experiences. As with most democratic debate there will be digression and disagreement between the contributors to this book in how they interpret what is occurring in each of their countries. This should not necessarily be viewed as a weakness; indeed the editors feel that this is one of the strengths of books such as this, in that they reflect the diversity of opinion and the overarching contested nature of the subject matter.

In recent years the introduction of e-government has been firmly placed on the policy agenda by governments across the world. The successful implementation of e-government is seen as prerequisite for modernising public administrations and providing new forms of electronic service delivery and for stimulating inclusive participation in a new information society. At first glance it would appear that the moves to e-government, the creation of the infrastructure necessary for services to be online, the elimination of digital divides, often to specific timetables laid down in strategy documents, cannot be argued against. However, on closer examination, whilst the policy may at first appear to be benevolent the reality of its implementation and the subsequent consequences for governance within democratic societies may be somewhat different. Whilst accepting e-government as almost a fait accompli, are we in effect accepting a policy or set of policies which cloak the weakening of our democracy and a benign commercialisation of our political institutions?

Definition

A useful if somewhat basic definition of e-government is given by the World Bank which refers to e-government as

> '... [T]he use by government agencies of information technologies (such as Wide Area Networks, the Internet, and mobile computing) that have the ability to transform relations with citizens, businesses, and other arms of government. These technologies can serve a variety of different ends: better delivery of government services to citizens, improved interactions with business and industry, citizen empowerment through access to information, or more efficient government management ... [A]nalogous to e-commerce, which allows businesses to transact with each other more efficiently (B2B) and brings customers closer to businesses (B2C), e-government aims to make the interaction between government and citizens (G2C), government and business enterprises (G2B), and inter-agency relationships (G2G) more friendly, convenient, transparent, and inexpensive.'[6]

There are of course different interpretations of even apparently straightforward definitions such as the one above. What is not contested is that whilst there are benefits to be derived from e-government implementation there is also potentially a downside to e-government particularly in terms of reducing human contact between citizens and the state at a time when confidence and trust in politicians and the state is waning. Finger and Pécoud note that each state faces challenges on three levels:

- challenges of legitimation;
- challenges of competition from other states; and
- challenges of a financial nature.[7]

The pressure to meet financial targets and reduce taxation is an imperative driving many ICT based projects, although of course not the only imperative as this book will demonstrate. Whichever imperative is driving policy there remain a significant number of barriers to successful implementation of e-government. Let us examine, briefly, the benefits of and barriers to effective e-government.

Benefits of e-government

The benefits associated with e-government can generally be characterised as falling under one of two headings, which are not of themselves mutually exclusive; improving the machinery of governance and increased participation. Below are some more explicit examples of the perceived benefits:[8]

- improved co-ordination of EU policies and legislation with the potential to provide joined up government;
- more efficient and effective use of resources at a time when there is increased pressure on governments to limit their spending and to reduce the tax burden upon citizens and businesses;
- the facilitation of easier access to information generated by, the various organisations and agencies of the EU the dissemination of which allows consultation and individual and collective participation;
- it has the potential to enable citizens to undertake more efficient, transparent, quantitative and qualitative auditing of government;
- e-government can assist in the ongoing challenge of inclusion and assist in bringing equality of treatment to each citizen (although this would need to be underpinned by an EU wide freedom of information act);
- it has the ability to allow for a reconfiguration of interfaces between citizen and the EU and the potential to build a more direct participatory digital democracy.

Barriers to e-government

There are also a number of barriers to effective e-government. Listed below are just some of the major political and practical barriers to e-government in the EU. The list is not an exhaustive one and is not presented in order of importance. One must also remember that it is possible for the importance attached to issues or barriers to fluctuate contingent upon the political situation at any given time. The importance of issues/barriers can also vary from country to country as can be seen from the case study chapters in this volume.

- As Webster[9] notes, any definition of an information society (and the part that e-government plays within it) is a contested one. There are differing views on the purposes, values and goals underpinning e-government. It is not a value-free area as some would have us believe.
- EU member states seem on the whole to be loath to surrender power to the EU. This of course varies from state to state and indeed in any given state over a period of time. Circumstances can change and there is hope for progress in this specific policy area.
- The EU needs to facilitate as near as possible full public and private participation in the information society.

As electronic service delivery starts to replace offline service provision in some areas there is a danger of certain groups being excluded. As we can see in Chapter 2 the EU has increasingly given this more and more priority in its strategies as access levels are still low in some EU member states and far from universal in most. Of course it is not only issues of physical access that need to be addressed. Language barriers can also be an issue.[10] Given the levels of migration within the EU this is an issue that may rise in importance, particularly when the temporary restrictions on movement for the purposes of employment by citizens of the newest member states are removed by all member states. Education is also an issue, with citizens with lower educational attainment less likely to be online. It is also possible to suggest that a further linguistic barrier may well be active given the predominantly anglo-centric nature of the Internet[11] which can act as a disincentive to access for non English speakers at present although there is some evidence that this may be changing albeit slowly.

In order to create total equality the logic would suggest that there be some form of standardisation across the EU. This would be fiercely resisted by member states jealously guarding their individual sovereignty, although as Rawal shows in Chapter 4 of this volume, states are more and more willing to collaborate in joint ventures when they feel it aids their state security. There may well be a need for some form of standardised systems of data collection and analysis across the member states. The effects of this could homogenise government and thus remove or limit the intrinsic national characteristics of each member state government.[12] This would imply a new form of governance in the EU which would need to become more 'soft' in its structure. Many more of the services traditionally delivered by government apparatus may be delivered not only via the Internet in one's home but also via other outside agencies such as banks, post offices, supermarkets, interactive broadcasting companies and others.[13] As citizens increasingly access services or information using some form of 'one stop shop' system, this could have the negative effect of dehumanising the interface and thus further loosen the already weakening ties between individuals and government. Often it can be easier to outsource in order to avoid the potential political difficulties of internal governmental integration of back office functions or cross-agency functions. Outsourcing can also facilitate change whilst integrating ICT and associated procedures without necessarily having to experience a period of organisational turbulence and the process of education and cultural change within the organisation. Further, in terms of access via one stop shops any provision of public access terminals must address the disadvantage of rural dwellers.[14] It is important to be inclusive in all areas. In order for all of these agencies to function in a joined-up way a system of digital identification, perhaps a multi-functional ID smartcard system containing encrypted digital signatures, would be needed.

When we examine the recent historical past of the moves to e-government we can see that '[t]he rhetoric of technological shifts are not always translated into successful implementation. Technology is a tool that can aid us in improving society but it does not, of itself, provide solutions to questions such as inequality, power, democracy and justice'.[15] Schuler observes that any notion that the Internet is somehow inherently democratic of itself is oversimplistic.[16] Any proposed ICT facilitated advances within e-government need to be evaluated against the general sense of public good, and it should not automatically be assumed that they are always an improvement without that being explicitly demonstrable.

Whilst technological advancements may solve some of the problems of governance, they cannot solve every problem and tend to work best where processes can be standardised and where individual discretion is limited. E-government can contribute to the creation or identification of new problems within governance such as issues surrounding privacy or lack of freedom of information.[17]

A further specific barrier to an information age EU would be that at present, its citizens owe allegiance to, and identify themselves as citizens of, the member states.[18] If the EU is to deepen its relationship with its citizens, which is often said to be vital to progress the overall 'EU project',[19] then it needs to engender some notion of European Citizenship, some idea of commonality, which can be held in collaboration with existing national identities that all its citizens can identify with.

The structure and contents of this volume

This book seeks to address questions such as:

- What are the experiences and views on e-government where it has already been implemented and what lessons are being learned from the initial experiences?
- How far are case countries meeting the broad aims set out in the e-government strategy?
- Given the propensity towards uniformity inherent in the notions listed above of exchange of best practice, benchmarking and co-ordination, what scope for national or even sub-national diversity is there?

- How does this level of difference reflect the differing political, cultural and social differences underlying the development of the style of government in the member states?
- Is there a risk for governments that, in utilising ICTs, they may add to the general disaffection with government, politics and political representatives by citizens in many countries? This disaffection can be identified via indicators such as low electoral turnout, falling political party membership and distrust of politicians by the public.
- Whilst there may be economic or efficiency gains to be made from adopting certain forms of electronic service delivery what will be the price in terms of cohesion that governments may have to pay?

In broad terms the structure and contents are split into two main thematic areas. These are firstly a number of thematic chapters analysing some of the concepts underpinning the notion of e-government, and secondly a number of case study presentations of the progress of e-government in European Union Member-states. The case studies, whilst all being different in their emphasis, in line with the political cultures of the case country, will all follow similar formats and contain comparable elements to allow for ease of use by readers seeking to draw comparisons between one or more states. This will be reinforced when broad comparisons will be made in the concluding chapter in order to give an overall picture of how government in general is changing as a result of these measures. The concluding chapter rounds off the arguments advanced in the earlier chapters presented in this book. Below is a brief synopsis of the contributions:

In Chapter 1, *E-government and democratic politics* by Michael Margolis, the reader can see an outline of the development of the notion of e-government. It focuses on the theoretical underpinnings of e-government, its potential for improving the quality of democratic governance, and an assessment of the extent to which this potential has been realised thus far. It looks at the contestation of that development charting the historical imperatives that led us to where we are today. Margolis also seeks to posit e-government not as a distinct and separate administrative reworking of governmental activity but as a coherent part of the democratic process in the modern age.

In Chapter 2, *Ctrl, Alt, Delete: rebooting the state via e-government in the EU*, Paul G. Nixon sets out the development of e-government policy within the EU up to the present day. Examining moves to foster the creation of an information society and more specifically upon the ideas which underpin EU strategies and programmes, the chapter critically analyses the eEurope action plan and examines the rationale underpinning it. It notes the dual role of the EU as both a provider of e-government through its own internal activities and also as a facilitator or aggregator in the way it seeks to engender change in member states across the EU. The chapter relates the way in which decisions on the issue of e-government in each country are the prerogative of the member states themselves, although noting some degree of policy creep as other, at first seemingly unconnected, areas of policy over which the EU does have jurisdiction impact upon the wider sphere of e-government. The chapter questions the top down nature of the eEurope approach and examines how that policy may need to be refined in order to make it more inclusive, as the EU has identified e-inclusion as one of its key policy goals.

Chapter 3, *E-government under construction: challenging traditional conceptions of citizenship* by Miriam Lips, seeks to examine attempts to re-draft the conception of citizenship in a modern age and to reflect on how new forms of technology affect the relationships between citizens and government. She notes that commentators are now observing attempts to 'turn around the telescope' to give a more citizen-focused perspective on government. She describes four major trends in how the citizen has been addressed by governments in the development of their e-government strategies and comments on the effects that these changes have had and may have in the future.

Chapter 4, *Danger mouse? The growing threat of cyberterrorism* by Rajash Rawal, shows the flip side to the coin of the arguments of how much ICT use can help governments in that it examines the ways in which ICTS can be used against governments. It examines both cyberterrorism and the use of the Internet by terrorists and explains how both can be used to pressure governments and to thwart or attempt to thwart government intentions. It also poses the question of how free we want the Internet to be? Will our cyber-freedoms be challenged by the war on terror? The very same war which is being fought, we are told, to protect our freedoms and our way of life?

Chapter 5 on the United Kingdom by Nicholas Pleace begins the second part of the book and is the first of our case studies. It examines the way in which e-government has been used as a vehicle for a threefold transformation of government in the United Kingdom with aspirations for change in the areas of e-democracy, improved public services through electronic service delivery and social inclusion in the information society. He notes how, particularly in the field of electronic service delivery there is a case to be made that the primary focus has been on cost cutting and redistributing the administrative burden from state to citizen. He also notes the 'stubbornness' of the digital divide and that despite prophecies of near universal take-up not all the UK's citizens are entranced by the lure of the web. It is not inconceivable that governments might want to discourage such resistance by effectively compelling citizens to engage online whether they wish to or not. One can already see such action in the switch to digital TV in the UK, where people will have no choice but to embrace the new technology when their analogue tv signal is switched off in the not too distant future.

In Chapter 6, *The digital republic: renewing the French state via e-government*, Fabienne Greffet notes the dominance of the anglo-saxon speaking world on the Internet and reports France's somewhat cautious response to engaging in the medium on France's own terms. She compares this remodelling of the French state to the transition between the Fourth and Fifth republics, with the adherents of e-government claiming it as a blueprint for a new digitised republic based on the same old and revered values of liberty, equality and fraternity. She notes the serious levels of division that exist within French society and how this is also replicated in a digital divide within French society. There are also regional disparities that have an impact too. The chapter shows that it is a consumerist and professional conception of e-government that is being promoted in France, following an economic rationalist model, where citizens are, above all, seen as consumers.

Chapter 7, *E-government in Germany* by Tina Siegfried, illustrates the added difficulties of implementing a system of e-government in a federal state. She notes that with some exceptions most of the uses of ICT in Germany are to mirror the 'offline' state. She posits Germany as being somewhat behind other European e-government pioneers such as the UK, Estonia and Denmark. She illustrates, also, that a move towards e-government also generates demands on other areas of government activity, for example you need to educate or train staff differently for new administrative posts. Thus we see the image of a country being constrained in the speed of adapting to change by the very social systems that only 20 years ago were being hailed as modern and progressive.

Chapter 8, *Reorganising government using IT: the Danish model*, by Kim Viborg Andersen, Helle Zinner Henriksen and Eva Born Rasmussen, investigates the adoption and exploitation of IT in the Danish government. The Danish case is particularly captivating due to the fact that over 60 per cent of Denmark's gross domestic product is re-allocated via the state. The authors describe the specific characteristics of the historical background of small size, decentralised use of IT, on-going structural changes, central state IT initiatives, and cross-agency dependencies which has made the e-government initiatives in Denmark unique. They go on to present four cases of successful e-government implementation (taxation, the health sector, case handling, and procurement), and the chapter examines the governmental policies through the lenses of normative actions, economic incentives, knowledge transfer, and management practice. The chapter identifies a shift from using primarily knowledge transfer mechanisms towards direct normative policies.

Chapter 9, *E-government in the Netherlands: from strategy to impact – the pursuit of high-volume high-impact citizen e-services in the Netherlands*, by Martin van Rossum and Desirée Dreessen, illustrates the ways in which a small EU member state can outperform the bigger states in terms of e-government adoption. They also illustrate the way in which successful implementation of e-government can raise the expectation levels of the public and lead to dissatisfaction with services that are not constantly re-engineered. Van Rossum and Dreessen also note the innovative ways in which the Dutch government have sought to engender an information society through tax breaks and so on. They also note the top-down nature of many of the moves which stem from central government that have led to the creation of a single e-government strategy backed by an e-citizens charter.

Chapter 10, *The reform and modernisation of Greek public administration via e-government* by Vassiliki N. Koutrakou, provides an interesting case study of how one of the poorer nations of the EU is attempting to overhaul and reinvent itself so as to keep up with the leaders in Europe through e-government. This chapter shows that there are signs that e-government is taking hold in Greece despite, and at the same time because of, the longstanding problems bedevilling the Greek public sector in terms of bureaucracy, citizen-unfriendly administrative processes and procedures and a heavily centralised state. Noting vital EU assistance and the increasing alacrity with which Greeks are embracing change, the chapter details a number of projects, charting Greece's progress towards revitalising government in the home of democracy and also gives examples of attempts to utilise the technology to reinvigorate the democratic traditions of Greece.

Gustavo Cardoso and Tiago Lapa in Chapter 11, *'Alt-Tab': from ICTs to organisational innovation in Portugal*, give us another example of how a country that qualifies for assistance under the EU's Cohesion policy copes with the added burden of modernisation via e-government. They note the rigid structure of Portuguese administration, with fragmented agencies working as 'archipelagos of isolated islands' even inside the same ministry, and the lack of standardisation of vocabulary, policies and rules between departments which inhibit co-operative working. They argue that we must change the focus of our attention from technology to organisational innovation in order to fully understand the changes that ICTs might bring to the State. They seek to show the scope of the e-governance initiatives in Portugal, identifying the limitations and opportunities of Portuguese society in the global context of network societies and the difficulties of the State in a society in transition, such as Portugal. They identify the ways in which organisational forms can be *de facto* altered by using ICT in public administration, but how little planned organisational change has been identified despite the recent political discourse around the notion of e-government. They seek to identify new ICT-supported forms of interaction between citizens and the Portuguese government.

Chapter 12, *Estonia: the short road to e-government and e-democracy* by Marc Ernsdorff and Adriana Berbec, provides a retrospective on Estonian public administration reform, examining the factors that contributed to the development of ICT in the public sector. They show how forward thinking and strategic planning by the Estonian state has placed Estonia at the forefront of developments of e-government within the EU 25, outstripping the performance of many other seemingly better equipped and resourced EU member states. The chapter demonstrates citizens' opportunities for involvement in the political decision-making process via ICT enabled participatory platforms such as TOM or Themis and whilst welcoming such initiatives casts a critical eye over some of the developments.

In Chapter 13, *This revolution will be digitised! E-government in Hungary*, Katalin Szalóki and Paul G. Nixon show how Hungary's experience has been different to that of Estonia although more consistent with other former soviet satellite states in central and eastern Europe. Hungary's recent accession to the EU has meant that its administrative structures, procedures and processes have undergone changes in order to meet the EU requirements. The chapter charts the progress that Hungary has made and the structural changes it has endured in order to facilitate the moves towards an information society in line with other EU states. In common with many of the new member states, Hungary has a high level of spatial inequality and limited levels of PC ownership in certain areas. It is this low level of Internet penetration that is compelling many of the new member states to examine the possibilities of using the more widely spread mobile communications towards a m-government to drive forward new relationships between citizens and government. The chapter notes the long and difficult struggles that Hungary has undergone and is relatively optimistic that once more a particularly Hungarian solution can be found to the new challenges of e-government.

Chapter 14, *E-government and Slovenia's multiple transitions* by Darren Purcell, notes the symbolic value of Slovenia's moves to e-government. Like Hungary and Estonia in the preceding chapters, it seeks to throw off the legacy of former communist rule and present itself to the EU and the rest of the world as a modern transitory state. The chapter investigates the benefits generated by e-government implementation, and how useful this is to the Slovenian people. Purcell goes on to examine the current state of e-government in Slovenia and comment upon the trends in e-government as part of the wider effort to cement Slovenia's place within the European Union.

The concluding chapter, by the editors, Paul Nixon and Vassiliki Koutrakou, explores, on the basis of the empirical chapters presented in this book, whether an affinity can be discerned between global political and social restructuring and the shaping and diffusion of the new media. It thereby reflects on the broader techno-cultural context within which the utilisation of ICTs by governments can be more clearly analysed and understood. It also seeks to draw together the experiences outlined in the case studies in order to be able to come to some judgement about the progress to date and the future prospects for e-government in the European Union.

In its diverse form this new context may give rise to a new political culture. The chapter reflects on the nature of the technologies that have been discussed in earlier chapters and examines what evidence there might be for new forms, characteristics and 'institutions' of electronic government.

Notes

1 Cenvernment in the European Union'. *Electronic Journal of E-government* 3(2): 59–66. Available at www.ejeg.com
2 Centeno, C., van Bvel, R. and Burgelman, J.C. (2005) 'A Prospective View of E-government in the European Union'.
3 Dahlgren, P. (2001) 'The Transformation of Democracy', in Axford, B. and Huggins, R. (eds), *New Media And Politics*. London: Sage.
4 Neunreither, K. (1995) 'Citizens and the Exercise of Power in the European Union: Towards a New Social Contract?', in Rosas, A. and Antola, E. (eds), *A Citizens, Europe: In Search of a New Order*. London: Sage.
5 Etzioni, A. (2003) 'Are Virtual and Democratic Communities Feasible?' in Jenkins, H. and Thorburn, D. (eds), *Democracy and New Media*. Cambridge, MA: MIT Press.
6 World Bank website. Available at web.worldbank.org/WBSITE/EXTERNAL/TOPICS/EXTINFORMATIONANDCOMMUNICATIONANDTECHNOLOGIES/EXTEGOVERNMENT/0,contentMDK:20507153~menuPK:702592~pagePK:148956~piPK:216618~theSitePK:702586,00.html
7 Finger, M. and Pécoud, G. 'From E-government to E-governance? Towards a Model of E-governance'. *Electronic Journal of E-government* 1(1). Available at www.ejeg.com/volume-1/volume-1-issue1/issue1-art1.htm

8. Nixon, P.G. and Rawal, R. (2005) 'Enabling Democracy? E-government, Inclusion and Citizenship'. Proceedings of the International Conference on E-government. Ottawa, Canada: ACL.
9. Webster, F. (1995) *Theories of the Information Society*. London: Routledge.
10. Nixon, P.G. and Rawal, R. (2005) 'Enabling Democracy?'.
11. Chen, W. and Wellman, B. (2004) 'Charting Digital Divides Within and Between Countries' in Dutton, W., Kahin, B., O'Callaghan, R. and Wyckoff, A. (eds), *Transforming Enterprise*. Cambridge, MA: MIT.
12. Nixon, P.G. and Rawal, R. (2005) 'From E-gov to "we"-gov – Social Inclusion, Government and ICT's'. Proceedings of the 5th European Conference on E-government. Antwerpen, Belgium: ACL.
13. Nixon, P.G. and Rawal R. (2005) 'From E-gov to "we"-gov'.
14. Allen, J.C. and Dillman, D.A. (1994) *Against All Odds: Rural Community in the Information Age*. Boulder, CO: Westview Press; Helve, H. (1998) 'A Comparative Study of Living Conditions and Participation of Rural Young People' in *Changing Europe*. (RYPE). Report on-line.
15. Nixon, P.G. (2000) 'Joined Up Government: Whitehall On-Line' in Gibson, R. and Ward, S.J. (eds), *Re-Invigorating Democracy: British Politics and the Internet*. Aldershot: Ashgate.
16. Schuler, D. (2003) 'The Relationship between Democracy and the Internet', in Jenkins, H. and Thorburn, D. (eds), *Democracy and New Media*. Cambridge, MA: MIT Press.
17. Nixon, P.G. (2004) 'Young People, Politics and New Media in the European Union', in Koutrakou, V. (ed.), *Contemporary Issues and Debates in EU Policy 2004*. Manchester, UK: Manchester University Press.
18. Nixon, P.G. and Rawal, R. (2005) 'Enabling Democracy?'.
19. Beetham D. and Lord C. (1998) *Legitimacy and the European Union*. Harlow: Addison Wesley Longman; Lord, C. (1998) *Democracy in the European Union*. Sheffield: Sheffield Academic Press.

1 E-government and democratic politics

Michael Margolis

'Using information technology to network government [is] relatively simple. The more complex and difficult challenges are to address issues of accountability, equity, and democratic process'

Jane Fountain (2005)

Introduction

As graphical browsers and the World Wide Web (WWW) popularised the Internet during the mid-1990s, political visionaries joined their economic counterparts in predicting radical changes for governance as well as for commerce. Just as the Internet would provide new opportunities for 'dot.com' entrepreneurs to restructure accepted business models, so it would provide new openings for political entrepreneurs to reshape the established political order. Interaction among citizens in cyberspace would enrich public opinion and increase participation in democratic politics. In contrast to the established mass media, computer-mediated information and communication technologies (ICT) would afford ordinary citizens the power to research and disseminate their own ideas about public affairs. Moreover, political activists – 'netizens', so to speak – could use e-mail, newsgroups, and websites to form new political groups and build new coalitions. Cyber-democrats like Howard Rheingold, Rhonda and Michael Hauben, and John Perry Barlow heralded the Internet's promise for realising formerly impossible dreams of informed engagement in political and civic affairs.[1] They anticipated that once citizens discovered this potential, the Internet would foster greater individual freedom as well as viable new parties and interest groups that would challenge the dominant political groups.

It hasn't happened. Established parties, together with their candidates and officeholders, dominate political activity not only offline, but also on the Internet.[2] Cyberspace is replete with familiar political and commercial interests, whose broadly linked and much advertised websites reflect their dominance of political and economic affairs of civil societies in the real world. This dominance is buttressed by a coterie of political and commercial consultants, who specialise in marketing their ideological concepts, candidates, groups, and interests online, much as traditional consultants specialise in marketing concepts and products in the real world. In sum, contrary to cyber-democrats' predictions that the Internet would broaden democracy through citizens' increased involvement in and influence over public affairs, we have witnessed a normalisation of the politics of cyberspace, the emergence of a political and economic order that largely replicates that found in the physical world.[3]

When democratically-inclined social scientists began studying the political impact of the Internet in the early 1990s, they hoped to discover many popular new political groups online whose members exercised intelligent civic and political participation that affected public policy in western democracies. Their research showed that they had been overly optimistic, however, particularly with regard to policy inputs, the process of translating citizens' preferences into laws and regulations. Instead of revolutionising policy formulation in the real world, netizens' political activities tended to reflect and reinforce the familiar patterns of behaviour they had brought from that world.[4] Nevertheless, the Internet did present new possibilities for enlightened democratic participation, especially with regard to the policy outputs of government.

Tax-paying citizens are not merely the government's financiers; they are also its customers. As such they expect – even demand – that government implement public policies efficiently and effectively, particularly when those policies affect them personally. Indeed, the burgeoning numbers of governmental services and agencies online can be seen as efforts to realise the efficiency and goodwill that stem from doing business via the Internet. Whether or not governments intend it, providing services online increases the opportunities for democratic political participation.[5]

Pundits have argued that nations must deploy ICT via the Internet in order to benefit from the global economy. If the argument holds, it follows that regardless of their ability to control (or avoid) elections, nations that aspire to prominence in world affairs must permit their citizens to access millions of externally-generated databases in order for citizens to gather the information necessary to achieve their regimes' immediate policy goals. It seems likely, therefore, that even authoritarian governments will loosen their restrictions on citizens' accessing information from external sources, even though citizens could also utilise such information to develop economic and political resources that lie beyond the governments' customary spheres of control. Preliminary evidence suggests that this argument is plausible. Even though institutional change lags behind technological innovation, governments with advanced technological sectors but few democratic traditions, such as Singapore, China, Malaysia and several Eastern European nations of the former Soviet bloc, seem to be tolerating more openness in domestic affairs as they seek more significant roles in the global economy.[6]

The next section contains a discussion of the proximate intellectual roots of cyber-democracy: the 'New Left' and the 'Counterculture' movements of the 1960s and early 1970s. The discussion suggests that cyber-democrats saw the Internet as the means to finally break the cycle of soaring promise and failed fulfillment that each new medium had engendered since the Industrial Revolution. The third section examines the difficulties of implementing direct participatory democracy despite the increased powers the Internet affords each citizen. It also questions the advantages of citizens' direct participation in policy making in comparison to citizens' judging the results of those policies. The final section discusses the advantages and dangers of democratic participation that emphasises the output side of politics. The discussion reviews how institutional arrangements, e-government and citizens' habitual behaviours affect various desiderata, such as privacy, individual liberty, civic values, national security, and domestic and global economic progress. It argues that political uses of the Internet must take these arrangements and behaviours into account, and it concludes that encouraging citizens to react to governmental policies that affect them seems more promising for achieving positive democratic outcomes than does encouraging them to participate directly in formulating those policies. In the end, the evidence and the argument hark back to a necessary (and familiar) condition for democracy. Neither ICT nor any particular institutional arrangement can substitute for a democratically-inclined citizenry that can hold its freely-chosen governmental officials to account. The critical question may be whether or not ordinary citizens, their representatives and traditional democratic institutions still have sufficient capacity to oversee the largely unelected technological élites who control modern ICT.

The roots of e-government and cyber-democracy

The 1960s in the USA saw the growth of two distinct but interrelated radical movements, the New Left and the Counterculture. They shared a number of fundamental values, but had separate political agendas. Both were anti-elitist and egalitarian; they valued openness, sharing, community, and cooperation rather than competition. They opposed the manipulation of wants and desires that characterises a commercial economy. Many who participated in them shared similar musical tastes, clothing styles and recreational drug habits, but the two movements differed in political strategy.

The New Left viewed participatory democracy as a means for citizens to reestablish control of their lives. Citizens would realise that their private problems had public causes and political solutions, and they would transform the bureaucratic, impersonal society that had pacified them. Participatory democracy would wrest power and control from the corporate and governmental elite.[7] Adherents of the Counterculture also rejected corporate America, but unlike the political activists of the New Left, they did so by dropping out rather than engaging in political struggle. They created alternative communities in which they could live as they pleased, unconstrained by the values, assumptions, material possessions and laws that governed the rest of society. While the New Left saw itself as struggling to transform American society through organised political activity, the Counterculture saw itself as subverting that society by creating freer and more attractive alternatives.

The radicalism of the 1960s had roots in previous radical movements. Many of the early leaders of the New Left were so called 'red diaper' babies, children of radicals who had been members of left wing parties and active in the trade union movement.[8] The Counterculture was also connected with earlier forms of protest. Its rejection of established cultural values owed much to the revolt against the moral, sexual, and artistic conventions of bourgeois society exemplified by a variety of nineteenth and early twentieth century European avant-garde movements. To the extent that it tried to establish alternative societies, the Counterculture also borrowed ideas from the anarchists and the Utopian Socialists.[9]

Both movements fell short of their goals. The New Left's leaders were mainly campus intellectuals who aimed to organise students and poor people to struggle for self-determination and participatory democracy. Unfortunately, they picked difficult target groups. Students and poor people had been among the least likely groups to engage in sustained political activity during the post-World War II period.[10] The New Left's efforts failed to bring about fundamental changes in the American political and economic orders, and the Counterculture failed to popularise their alternative ways of living.

Yet both movements helped to democratise the American polity and, by dint of the American mass media, to inspire political and cultural protests abroad.[11] Even though we cannot ascertain how much credit the New Left and the Counterculture deserve in comparison to other social, political and demographic pressures, the United States has become more open and inclusive *de jure* than it was in the early 1960s, as have Japan, Australia, New Zealand, Mexico, and most Eastern and Western European nations where the political and cultural unrest of the late 1960s also took place.[12]

Elsewhere, David Resnick and I distinguished three categories of Internet politics: politics *within the Net* (intra-Net politics), political *uses of the Net*, and *politics that affect the Net*.[13] Politics within the Net encompasses the political life of virtual communities and other identifiable online groups that regulate their own affairs, settle their own disputes and develop their own online lifestyles. Political uses of the Net refers to the ways in which the Net can be used by ordinary citizens, political activists, organised interests, political parties and governments to achieve their real world political goals, which often have little to do with the Internet per se. Politics that affect the Net refers to policies and actions that governments and other powerful institutions take to regulate the Internet as a new form of mass communication and as a vehicle for commercial activity. The first two types of Internet politics are relevant for sorting out the cyber-democrats' claims for the democratising potential of political activity on the Internet. The last type is most relevant for explaining why so much of that potential remains unrealised.

Prior to the advent of user-friendly browsers and the expansion of the World-Wide Web, cyberspace looked like a reincarnation of the counterculture. Online communities of the technologically savvy flourished, each with its own intra-Net politics. Freedom could be achieved in a virtual state of nature. Netizens formed their own communities independent of the values, traditions and legal constraints of the ordinary world. Communities exercised authority over their own domains, based on a set of implicitly derived rules, or 'Netiquette', without interference from outsiders. Enthusiasts proclaimed that terrestrial governments should not attempt to extend their jurisdiction into cyberspace. Indeed, some argued that the very structure of the Internet itself made the attempt to impose outside regulation futile:

> Governments derive their just powers from the consent of the governed. You have neither solicited nor received ours. ... Cyberspace does not lie within your borders. Do not think that you can build it, as though it were a construction project. You cannot. It is an act of nature and it grows itself through our collective action.[14]

What the Counterculture promised, cyberspace could deliver. Intra-Net politics was humanistic, egalitarian and voluntary in contrast to the corrupt politics of organised special interests of the real world. Cyberspace created possibilities for liberation that even the most radical counter-cultural theorists never imagined. In cyberspace people could transcend their own bodies and the cultural baggage that they carried. Abandoning the familiar trio of race, class, and gender, they could create a new identity, indeed, a multiplicity of identities. Recall the famous *New Yorker* cartoon of a canine at a monitor proclaiming, 'On the Internet, no one knows you're a dog'.[15] Others saw the possibility of cyberspace deepening and strengthening identities that were denigrated in the real world.

Hopes for change did not rely solely on the expectation that powerful identities could be forged in cyberspace. Activists saw political uses of the Internet as dynamic means for consciousness raising and political organising in the real world. By generating a public space for a true deliberative democracy the Internet would enable citizens to fulfill their democratic potentials. Citizens no longer needed to accept the corporate dominated mass media's interpretations of reality. The Internet could furnish alternative sources of information. Because they could access information on their own, citizens could make up their own minds without so-called experts to guide them. An informed citizenry could engage in political debate armed with all the information and opinions they could possibly use. Governmental officials could not hide their mistakes, nor could they claim that issues were too complex for ordinary citizens to grasp. Information, full and free, would empower an invigorated democratic citizenry.[16]

Political uses of the Net were just beginning. Grassroots politics would flourish. Citizens would access information with speed and ease, and they would use electronic networks to communicate and exchange ideas with each other or with their elected representatives and governmental officials. Open sources of information would deepen democratic discussions and debates. The Internet presented the possibility of virtual communities actualising the dreams of participatory democracy and political liberation. The independence of the Internet communities, coupled with the Internet's egalitarian architecture, would render politics that affect the Net impotent.

E-government and cyber-democracy collide with the real world

Cyber-democrats tended to give short shrift to how real world politics affect the Internet. They concentrated instead on how politics within the Net could bring about political liberation, and how political uses of the Net could influence public opinion and the conduct of real world politics. They cited virtual communities whose members carried on active civic lives even though they may never have met one another in the flesh. If democratic policymaking consisted of resolving differences among competing interests, building coalitions for cooperative action, or some combination of the two, the Internet's capacity to share equal access to vast stores of information and equal powers to send and receive that information provided the means for realising it. Political participation in cyberspace, therefore, could approximate an ideal type of communitarian democracy that emphasised mutuality.

Civic life, however, extends beyond formal issues of public policy. People interact over a variety of matters, and a sense of community often grows among those who share mutual interests. Thousands of virtual interest groups run Usenet newsgroups, listserv mailing lists, web-based chat rooms, blogs, and the like. Some virtual communities, such as The WELL, act as cooperative societies in which dues-paying members participate in conferences without the expectation of a quid pro quo for any particular information or service they provide.[17] Others, such as Wikipedia, have fostered a freely-accessible international encyclopedia 'written collaboratively by people from all around the world.'[18] Moreover, real communities throughout the world have established their own Freenets or community networks designed to enrich their civic life.[19]

Nevertheless, nothing compels virtual communities to function as mutually-beneficial societies. Traditional democratic politics attempts to work out acceptable solutions through complex exchanges that involve pressuring and bargaining. In cyberspace, however, like-minded netizens can form online communities that insulate members from exchanges with those who may hold different opinions. While hate groups like Stormfront and Aryan Nations are notorious for countenancing only those who espouse their groups' particular views, researchers have uncovered many other virtual communities that exist largely to promote their own interests, whether political or non-political, and to reinforce their own like-mindedness. These communities also make those who disagree unwelcome to join and uncomfortable if they choose to participate.[20]

Like today's cyber-democrats, political philosophers and pundits who favoured active citizen participation in policymaking in the past, viewed each new mass medium that emerged as the means to create an active, informed, enlightened and sophisticated body politic. They expected cheap newsprint, film, sound recording, radio and television would provide the populace with information on domestic affairs, expose them to foreign cultures, and introduce them to the great scientific and artistic achievements of humankind. From the popular press to community access cable television, each medium has had some impact on political and civic life, but none has fostered the enlightened democratic participation that its boosters prophesised. For better or for worse, most people generally have neither the time nor the inclination to scrutinise the day-to-day affairs of governmental policymaking, let alone the cultural achievements of civilisation. Aside from voting in periodic elections, most people become actively involved in public policymaking only when they perceive that a proposed policy will significantly affect their personal interests or the interests of friends, relatives or associates whom they hold dear. Ordinarily, their involvement with governmental policy concerns routine interactions or outputs, such as paying taxes, obtaining permits, licenses, benefits or services, or registering praise or complaints about the quality of those interactions or outputs.

E-government responds more to citizens' routine desires to receive policy outputs than to their episodic desires to devise policy inputs. Executive controlled websites generally outshine those of the legislature and judiciary. Focusing on the citizen as 'customer', they provide information, services and benefits, they frequently allow citizens to conduct transactions in part or full, and much like businesses, they increasingly provide areas for citizen (customer) feedback. Andrew Chadwick has observed that public bureaucracies are usurping 'Functions of representation and deliberation that are supposed to be the preserve of legislative bodies.' If the trend continues, he predicts: 'legislatures will find themselves increasingly marginalized.'[21]

Publicly subsidised mass media like the UK's BBC or the USA's Corporation for Public Broadcasting can afford to devote proportionately more resources to programs and materials that aim to educate as well as entertain citizens than can commercial mass media, whose high production costs favour content that attracts a large audience to whom investors, advertisers, or sponsors can be sold access. Commercial media assemble this audience chiefly by responding to popular tastes, not by attempting to raise civic, cultural and educational standards.

News media on the Web have not escaped this fate. Unorthodox Web news providers may have arrived first, but the established news media now predominate. Major newspapers, magazines, radio and television networks have the expertise and resources to gather, organise, and display relevant information more attractively and expeditiously than their upstart rivals. They also can pay more to advertise online and offline to direct traffic to their sites. Finally, they have better name recognition and more goodwill to draw upon than do their challengers. Most people, who are largely indifferent to public affairs to begin with, will turn to familiar names for the breaking news they occasionally desire.

Let us suppose, however, that most citizens really wanted to utilise the Internet's potential to increase their role in democratic governance. We still must deal with the proverbial 'elephant in the room', the ever-present digital divide. If the Internet – or any advancement of digitally based ICT – is to democratise politics, it must be easily accessible to the vast majority of adult citizens. Notwithstanding the increasing numbers of users for whom new technologies have provided Internet access, two major dimensions of the divide persist: divisions between nations and divisions within nations. Simply put, citizens of wealthy nations comprise a disproportionately large number of Internet users and, within each nation, the wealthier citizens similarly comprise a disproportionately large number of the users.

8 *E-government in Europe*

Even though rapidly expanding numbers of users combined with new technologies for access make it difficult to measure individuals' specific use of the Internet for political purposes, our imperfect measures can still reveal relationships that persist over time. Tables 1.1 and 1.2 provide a snapshot of the two major dimensions of the digital divide as of December 2005.

Table 1.1 indicates that those living in wealthy regions comprise disproportionately large numbers of Internet users. Denizens of Europe, North America and Australia number less than 20 per cent of the world's population, but they comprise the majority of the world's Internet users. In contrast, those of Asia and Africa, who number more than 70 per cent of the world's population, comprise less than 38 per cent of Internet users. The populations of African and Middle Eastern nations are most egregiously underrepresented. The contrasts regarding proportions with Internet access are even sharper: fewer than one in ten residents of Asia, Africa and the Middle East have access in comparison to over one-third of Europeans, a majority of Australians, and two-thirds of North Americans. Moreover, the distribution of access within regions is hardly uniform. In low access regions, countries with relatively higher median incomes, such as Israel, Kuwait, The United Arab Emirates (Middle East), Egypt, South Africa (Africa), Japan, South Korea, Taiwan and Singapore (Asia), denizens have access rates that are from two to eight times as great as the regional average.[22] Similarly, nations of the European Union have an Internet access rate of 49.8 per cent – nearly treble that of non-member nations. Even if the five-year trend of higher growth rates of Internet usage among poorer nations were to continue, it would take more than a decade for their levels of access to approach those of their wealthier counterparts.

Table 1.1 Internet access and usage by region, December 2005

Region	Population est. 2005 (millions)	% World population	Internet users (millions)	% Usage growth 2000–2005	% Internet penetration	% World users
Africa	915.2	14.1	22.7	404	2.5	2.2
Asia	3,667.7	56.4	364.3	218	9.9	35.7
Europe	807.3	12.4	290.1	176	35.2	29.4
Middle East	190.1	2.9	18.2	454	9.6	1.8
N. America	331.5	5.1	225.8	109	68.1	22.2
C. & S. America (incl. Mexico)	553.8	8.5	79.0	337	14.3	7.8
Australia/ Oceania	33.9	0.5	17.7	132	52.9	1.8
World Total	6,499.7	100.0	1,018.0	167	15.0	100.0

Sources: demographic (population) numbers are based on data contained in the world-gazetteer website; Internet usage information comes from data published by, Nielsen//NetRatings, by the International Telecommunications Union, by local NICs, and by other reliable sources. For definitions, disclaimer, and navigation help, see the Site Surfing Guide Information from this site may be cited, giving due credit. (Updated 12/31/05). www.internetworldstats.com/stats.htm

Using Internet access rates to measure the digital divide across nations, however, does not tell the whole story. Greater proportions of the populations of wealthier nations can afford access to high-quality broadband capacity than can the populations of poorer nations. Moreover, the Internet itself has a decidedly Anglo-American tilt. Internet World Stats estimated that at the end of 2005, 30.6 per cent of Internet users spoke English, nearly double the estimated 17.3 per cent who spoke the language worldwide. In contrast, Chinese, the most widely spoken language – 20.6 per cent worldwide – accounted for only 13.0 per cent of users. The OECD reported that 89.5 per cent of links to secure commercial servers went to pages in English in 2000; CIA estimates indicated that in December 2003, 8,731 of the world's 12,773 ISPs were in the USA, UK, Canada or Australia (7,000 of them in the USA); and as late as May 2005 the ten entities with the largest numbers of unique visitors to their various domains or URLs were all headquartered in the USA: nine private companies and the U.S. government.[23] While these percentages will decrease as global (especially American-based) corporations go multi-lingual, the dominant languages are likely to remain those of the wealthier nations: that is English, French, German, Spanish, Italian, Portuguese, Chinese, Japanese, Korean and Russian.

Table 1.2 displays parallel aspects of the digital divide within economically advanced nations of the Organization for Economic Cooperation and Development (OECD). For every country listed, greater proportions of those with high incomes have access to the Internet than do those with low incomes. Once again, the lower income groups generally show faster acceleration in expanding their access, but they still lag years behind. The data for PC ownership (not shown) for these countries reflected the same relationships. Along with income, OECD found that other indicators of affluence, such as higher education (especially among adults under 50), urban residence, owning a PC and having children in the household, belonging to economically advantaged ethnic groups and being able to afford higher access charges were also positively associated with more time spent online. Rafts of academic research and popular reports have uncovered similar patterns.[24]

New schemes are underway to manufacture and distribute to poverty-stricken nations durable handheld and laptop computers that cost less $100 (US) so that children and educators can access the Internet.[25] As long as the Internet remains primarily a commercially oriented vehicle, however, it seems doubtful that wealthy nations will support the massive subsidies necessary to pay for these computers, let alone to provide new users with sufficient broadband access to take full advantage of them. At present, the Internet tilts toward providing people access as customers rather than as citizens.[26] Lastly, we must remind ourselves that access is a necessary but not a sufficient condition for political uses of the Internet. Most people use the Internet for activities other than politics. And among those who do use it for politics E. E. Schattschneider's well-known observation still applies: 'The flaw in the pluralist heaven is that the heavenly choir sings with a strong upper-class [male] accent.'[27]

This is not to deny that notable new political and civic groups have used the Internet to constitute themselves and to organise and activate their members and

10 *E-government in Europe*

Table 1.2 Digital divide indicators within selected OECD nations

Nation	Internet penetration, 2000		Internet penetration, 2000	
	Lowest Income (%)	% Increase 1998–2000	Highest Income (%)	% Increase 1998–2000
Australia	20	217	50	85
Canada	8	55	45	20
France	3	70	50	60
Japan	5	NA	45	NA
Netherlands	7	48	67	67
United Kingdom	3	200	50	53
United States	11	80	77	32

Source: OECD 2001, 17.
1 Australia: lowest income: less than AUD 50,000; highest income: more than AUD 50,000.
2 Canada: lowest: second decile; highest: tenth decile. 1999 level. 1998–99 growth.
3 France: lowest: less than FRF 80,000; highest: more than FRF 450,000. 1999–2000 growth for Internet.
4 Japan: lowest: less than JPY 3 million; highest: more than JPY 12 million. For Internet 2000 only; no growth available.
5 Netherlands: lowest: first quartile of income; highest: fourth income quartile. 1998–99 growth.
6 United Kingdom: lowest: second decile; highest: tenth decile. 1998–99 and 1999–2000 respectively instead of 1998 and 2000.
7 United States. lowest: less than USD 15,000; highest: more than USD 75,000.

supporters. These have ranged from candidate organisations and protest groups to cause groups working to increase educational benefits or environmental protection. Established interest groups have also moved significant portions of their operations online.[28] Nevertheless, online groups' activation efforts generally attempt to reach narrower segments of the populace than do those of mass political parties, daily newspapers, news magazines or broadcast news. Cyberculture tends to fragment rather than build the 'social capital' of the communities in which people actually live.[29]

Meetup.com is a major exception: an online organisation devoted to fostering Putnam's idea of social capital throughout the developed world. Meetup.com helps 'people [to] find others who share their interest or cause, and form lasting, influential, local community groups that regularly meet face-to-face' regardless of their particular views.[30] Established in 2002, its civic and political groups enjoyed phenomenal growth in the run-up to the November 2004 American presidential election, and the organisation prospered from fees paid by commercial venues where 'Meetups' took place, as well as from 'unobtrusive text ads' on affiliated groups' websites and from optional group members' fees for 'Meetup Plus' services. After the election, however, when political interest waned (as usual) and memberships declined, Meetup.com announced that beginning May 2005 affiliated groups would have to pay nominal fees for its services.[31] On 9 May, 2005, Townhall, a politically conservative – and largely Republican – group, severed its relationship with Meetup.com substituting a 'custom solution [called 'TownSquare'] to better cater to the needs of our local groups.' In September 2005 Democracy for America, the legacy group of Howard Dean's presidential organisation, also set up its own customised tool, 'DFA-Link', to organise its local group meetings independently of Meetup.[32]

That political uses of the Net have not produced a significant restructuring of democratic politics should not surprise us. Political scientists have found time and again that most voters don't know very much about particular policy issues and that, except when cataclysmic events like war, social upheaval or economic depression impinge on their daily lives, most people's participation in policymaking is limited to casting ballots in elections. Researchers have noted the difficulty of mobilising citizens to challenge the domination of the major parties and the interest groups that support them, especially when they perceive social and economic conditions as relatively benign. Why should we expect access to the Internet to change these habits?[33]

We should not confuse the flowering of e-mail lists, websites and blogs touting all sorts of worthy causes, movements, and interests with a redistribution of power in the real world. We should remember that the high water mark of post World War II democratic activism in Europe and America occurred in the late 1960s and early 1970s, years before the Internet took root.

Using the Internet to supplement traditional methods of political participation seems more appropriate than using it to move toward direct – or even deliberative – democracy. Electronic voting, for instance, seems like a viable option, provided problems of the security and privacy of ballots and the inequalities of the digital divide can be overcome.[34] Those who extol citizens using the Internet to participate more fully in formulating public policy seem to forget that representative institutions are not second-best solutions to the problem of self-rule created in the technological dark ages before simultaneous communication among citizens became feasible. Do we have any reason to believe that participatory democracy would actually work the way its advocates hope? Where is the sign that citizens of large, pluralistic, advanced industrial or post-industrial societies care to take on the burdens of crafting public policy? While we have placed increased reliance on public opinion polls of late, do we really believe that government by public opinion polls would be good for democracy? Legislatures, executives and judiciaries, chosen according to constitutionally agreed upon rules, may not produce the wisest policies, but do we really think that it would be preferable to rely upon millions of cyber-citizens to formulate such policies over the Internet?[35]

As suggested above, using e-government to make the output side of policy more responsive to citizens looks like a better strategy for encouraging responsible democratic participation. Citizens can judge from personal experience how well governmental officials have implemented the Internet's capabilities to ease access to information, to deliver services and benefits or to conduct routine transactions, such as obtaining permits or licenses, bidding on contracts, paying taxes and so forth. They know how easily they can contact the appropriate public officials and how easily they can transact their business through e-government accurately and efficiently.[36]

Advantages and dangers of e-government

Throughout history many politicians, political philosophers and scholars have argued that direct democracy tended toward tyranny of the majority, mobocracy or worse. They have contended that evidence – systematic or anecdotal – demonstrates that citizens are better at judging the effects of governmental policies retrospectively than they are at predicting them. From the Enlightenment forward democratic theorists have advocated representative institutions that take account of diverse interests in society, elected representatives who accommodate the wishes of the majority to those of various minorities, and a citizenry that uses its reason to judge their representatives' (or their parties') performance more upon the results of their recent policies than upon their promises for the future.[37] In line with these arguments, this chapter has suggested that we look to the potential of e-government's for improving citizens' retrospective judgments of the consequences of governmental policies rather than stress its potential for encouraging citizens' direct participation in formulating those policies. Let us examine how political uses of the Internet can be structured to accomplish this.

Modern technology has outdistanced the capabilities of eighteenth century-based democratic political institutions, especially elected legislatures, to deal with it. As a result, bureaucratic elites, both public and private, play increasingly influential roles in formulating and implementing governmental policies that deal with technologically complex problems that affect the distribution of wealth, the natural environment, the military, public health, public safety, medical care, the movement of capital and the like. Moreover, legislatures have been notoriously slow in adopting ICT necessary for them to effectively engage with the executive in formulating these policies. In contrast, President George W. Bush's electronic spying on American citizens without the Foreign Intelligence Surveillance Act (FISA) Court's authorisation illustrates that executive-controlled bureaucracies not only have embraced these technologies but also have used them to shield information from legislative oversight. Paradoxically, e-government has contributed to the trend toward the weakening of the people's elected representatives and the strengthening of executive centred government.[38]

This shift toward executive government – buttressed by ICT – raises new threats to democracy. Just as the Internet can provide citizens with information about public policy, it can provide governments and other powerful interests with information about citizens' private lives. Just as it can provide citizens with the means to communicate their reactions to public policies, so too it can provide the means for governmental officials and other established groups to distort, manipulate or otherwise control accessible information. Realising this dark potential could produce a totalitarian nightmare like Orwell's *1984* where citizens fear or revere an all-seeing Big Brother, or a seemingly benign hedonistic society like Huxley's *Brave New World*, where a conditioned citizenry happily accepts the existing social order. In short, the institutional arrangements for managing the Net greatly affect the extent to which citizens can use it to exercise democratic control.[39]

Until the early 1990s governments – especially agencies of the United States – and non-profit organisations, such as educational institutions and foundations, largely underwrote the Internet. Users were disproportionately young, male, affluent, college-educated, politically active and libertarian. Self-selected groups made and enforced rules of intra-Net politics (sometimes capriciously) in accordance with their interpretations of Netiquette. Commercial usage and spam were largely excluded. By the late 1990s, however, cyberspace began to resemble ordinary space. Governments sold off or otherwise turned over most of the Internet to private hands. As simplified protocols associated with the WWW drew millions of novices to cyberspace, commercial enterprises, governmental agencies and other established social and political organisations jumped online, lest they lose touch with customers and clientele or lose out on new markets for goods and services. The 'dotcoms', which multiplied most quickly, sought to safeguard their investments by developing rules and regulations that resembled those with which their customers were already familiar. Together with real world allies – governmental and non-governmental – they soon rendered Netiquette as obsolete as Emily Post for controlling transactions via the Internet.[40]

Consumer-oriented business models have become the norm. Websites offer visitors – customers, if you will – information, goods, or services for a price. That price may involve a direct monetary exchange like an ordinary purchase in the real world or an exposure to a particular set of messages analogous to a series of commercials on radio or television. But the Internet's powers allow advertisers to extract more information about potential customers than was possible with any previous mass medium. Websites can record the pages each visitor views, the length of time spent on each page, the visitor's IP address, the advertisements shown, and whether or not the visitor responded to any particular advertisement. 'Cookies' can be implanted on visitors' computers so that subsequent visits will trigger advertisements or suggestions that cater to the interests inferred from their behavior during previous visits. (Users may be denied service if they do not set their browsers to accept the site's cookies.) Moreover, if visitors can be enticed to leave their e-mail (or postal) addresses and demographics, advertisers and other interested parties can be sold access to pre-screened potential customers or supporters without the seller necessarily revealing specific information about any particular individual on the list.[41]

Executive agencies control nearly all the most frequently-visited governmental websites. As these sites emulate the customer service features of commercial websites, citizens can conduct personal transactions interactively, frequently on a '24/7' basis. And just as commercial sites can extract information about their visitors, so too governments can use the Internet's monitoring capacities to extract information about theirs. The service is convenient, but the danger is obvious: it is no trick for executive agencies to assemble and to 'mine' data on how each citizen uses the Internet. As the epigram at the head of this chapter implies, unless the people's representatives – elected legislators, ombudsmen or their designates – demand unfettered access to nearly all the executive branch's digitised information, there is little to stop the executive from using the data its agencies gather to exploit the Internet's dark potential. Formal legislation or regulations that require accountability are not self-enforcing. The burden of demonstrating the necessity of restricting information accords with criteria set down by general legislation or through exclusions granted by special legislation; otherwise, the executive can deny citizens and their representatives the means to fairly assess policy outcomes.

To rectify this imbalance, legislators need to exert more control and better oversight over e-government and to reinforce that control by assuring citizens' easy access to digitised information about how public policies are implemented. They must also provide effective means for citizens to communicate to their representatives and other governmental officials regarding how those policies are affecting them.

No solution is perfect, however. Even though these initiatives would enhance the power of the people's elected representatives relative to the largely unelected executive branch and its technologically adept bureaucracy, they would also increase the danger of demagogic legislators – and their financial backers – acquiring new powers which they could then utilise for selfish or nefarious purposes. Some unscrupulous legislators would undoubtedly exploit their privileged access to information for private advantage, as they have done in the past. But consider the alternatives. Should unelected bureaucrats and technological elites control the information? What assurances do we have that they will act in the public interest more often than will the legislators? At least legislators must answer directly to the citizenry through periodic elections; the others need not.

Nonetheless, to argue that strengthening the legislature's control over e-government's information will promote democracy requires two leaps of faith. First, that the great majority of the people's representatives will use their unfettered access to the digitised information to expose to public scrutiny the false claims and deleterious consequences of their colleagues' actions as well as those of the executive. And secondly, that citizens will use their own experience to evaluate the information and will vote to oust the unscrupulous and return responsible representatives in their place.

That citizens or their representatives use the Internet to acquire the information required to make intelligent judgments about the consequences of public policies is necessary – but not sufficient – for actualising the retrospective type of cyber-democracy this chapter has discussed. Information must be organised and presented in a manner that people can understand, citizens and representatives must be encouraged to pay attention to one another's communications, and institutional arrangements must prevent powerful moneyed interests (national and international) from controlling information necessary for legislators to determine the likely consequences of their laws and policies or, worse still, from buying those laws and policies outright. Many such arrangements, albeit more with regard to policy inputs than to retrospective judgments of policy outputs, have been discussed elsewhere at length. These include education vouchers as awards for community service volunteers, protection for knowledgeable whistleblowers, facilitators or moderators for listservs, blogs and discussion groups, methods of accounting that include environmental costs and other externalities, public interest representatives appointed to serve on corporate boards, and various reforms of campaign finance and of methods for casting and counting ballots.[42]

In the last analysis, however, no set of institutional arrangements can guarantee that citizens make effective political uses of the Net. As in the real world, a viable democracy requires that its citizens pay attention to the quality of e-government and the consequences of public policies for the polity, not merely to how easily they personally receive governmental services and how public policies affect their personal interests. John Stuart Mill said it very well in 1861, when western nations contemplated massive expansions of their electorates:

> Thus, a people may prefer a free government, but if, from indolence, or carelessness, or cowardice, or want of public spirit, they are unequal to the exertions necessary to preserve it; if they will not fight for it when it is directly attacked; if they can be deluded by the artifices used to cheat them out of it; if by momentary discouragement, or temporary panic, or a fit of enthusiasm for an individual, they can be induced to lay their liberties at the feet even of a great man or trust him with powers that enable him to subvert their institutions; in all these cases they are more or less unfit for liberty; and though it may be for their good to have had it, even for a short time, they are unlikely long to enjoy it.[43]

In this regard, the advent of e-government changes nothing.

Notes

The author thanks Russell Dalton, Hans-Dieter Klingemann and Eric Rademacher for their comments and suggestions on earlier drafts of this chapter.

1 Rheingold, H. (1993) *The Virtual Community: Homesteading on the Electronic Frontier*. Reading, MA, New York: HarperPerrenial; Hauben M. and Hauben R. (1997) *Netizens: On the History and Impact of Usenet and the Internet*. Los Alamitos, CA: IEEE Computer Society Press; Shapiro, A. L. (1999) *The Control Revolution: How the Internet is Putting Individuals in Charge and Changing the World We Know*. New York: PublicAffairs, HarperPerrenial; Barlow, J.P. (1996) 'A Declaration of Independence of Cyberspace', homes.eff.org/~barlow/Declaration-Final.html (accessed 9/1/05).
2 Margolis, M., Resnick, D. and Levy, J. (2003) 'Major Parties Dominate, Minor Parties Struggle: US Elections and the Internet' in *Net Gain? Political Parties and the Impact of New Information Communication Technologies*. London: Routledge; pp. 53–69; Margolis, M., Resnick, D. and Wolfe, J. (1999) 'Party Competition on the Internet: Minor Versus Major Parties in the UK and the USA' *Harvard International Journal of Press/Politics* 4(3):24–47.
3 Gibson, R., Nixon, P. and Ward S. (eds) (2003) *Net Gain? Political Parties and the Impact of New Information Communication Technologies*. London: Routledge; Howard, P.N. (2005) *New Media Campaigns and the Managed Citizen*. Cambridge: Cambridge University Press, pp. 43–54.
4 Fisher, B., Margolis, M, and Resnick D. (1996) 'Surveying the Internet: Democratic Theory and Civic Life in Cyberspace', *Southeastern Political Review*, 24: 399–429; Margolis, M. and Resnick, D. (2000) *Politics as Usual: The Cyberspace "Revolution"*. Thousand Oaks, CA: Sage Publications, Inc.
5 See chapter 3 (Lips) in this volume.

6 West, D. (2005) *Digital Government: Technology and the Public Sector*. Princeton, NJ: Princeton University Press.
7 Thayer, F.C. (1973) *An End to Hierarchy! An End to Competition! Organizing the Politics and Economics of Survival*. New York: New Viewpoints; Hauben, M. 'Participatory Democracy from the 1960s and SDS into the Future On-line', www.columbia.edu/~hauben/CS/netdemocracy-60s.txt (accessed December 9, 2005).
8 Davis, S. (ed) (1996) *American Political Thought: Four Hundred Years of Ideas and Ideologies*. Englewood Cliffs, NJ: Prentice Hall. Even though they opposed McCarthyism and other excesses of the Cold War, the New Left's leaders also rejected Soviet style communism. They embraced the critiques of postwar radicals like C. Wright Mills and Herbert Marcuse. The former had intellectual ties to American Progressivism; the latter had ties to the Frankfurt School.
9 Reich, C.A. (1971) *The Greening of America*. New York: Bantam; Roszak, T. (1969) *The Making of a Counter Culture: Reflections on the Technocratic Society and Its Youthful Opposition*. New York: Doubleday.
10 Campbell, A. et al. (1960). *The American Voter*. New York: Wiley; Verba, S. and Nie, N.H. (1972) *Participation in America: Political Democracy and Social Inequality*. New York: Harper & Row.
11 Tunstall, J. (1977) *The Media are American*. New York: Columbia University Press.
12 Wikipedia entry on the 1960s. en.wikipedia.org/wiki/1960s (accessed 11/1/05).
13 Margolis, M. and Resnick, D. (2000) *Politics as Usual: The Cyberspace "Revolution"*. Thousand Oaks, CA: Sage Publications, Inc.
14 Barlow, J.P. (1996) '*A Declaration of Independence of Cyberspace*'. homes.eff.org/~barlow/Declaration-Final.html (accessed 9/1/05).
15 Steiner. P. (1993) *New Yorker*, July 5, p. 61.
16 Margolis, M. (1979) *Viable Democracy*. New York: St. Martins Press; Barber, B.R. (1984) *Strong Democracy: Participatory Politics for a New Age*. Berkeley, CA; University of California Press; Barber, B.R. (1998) *A Place for Us: How to Make Society Civil and Democracy Strong*. New York: Hill and Wang; Davis, R. (2005); *Politics Online: Blogs, Chatrooms, and Discussion Groups in American Democracy*. New York: Routledge; Chadwick, A. (2006) *Internet Politics: States, Citizens and the New Communication Technologies*. Oxford: Oxford University Press.
17 The WELL. www.well.com/ (accessed 9/1/05).
18 As of December 2005 the collaboration involved over '13,000 active contributors working on over 1,800,000 articles in more than 100 languages.' (Wikipedia entry on About Wikipedia: www.wikipedia.org).
19 Chadwick, A. (2006) *Internet Politics: States, Citizens and the New Communication Technologies*. Oxford: Oxford University Press; pp. 90–96. For lists, see Freenets & Community Networks: www.lights.com/freenet/ (accessed 2/27/06).
20 Aryan Nations. www.aryan-nations.org/ (accessed 2/27/06); Bimber, B. (1998) 'The Internet and Political Transformation: Populism, Community, and Accelerated Pluralism', *Polity* XXXI #1: 133–60; Hill, K.A. and Hughes, J. E. (1998) *Cyberpolitics: Citizen Activism in the Age of the Internet*. Lanham, MD: Rowman and Littlefield; pp. 71–75; Galston, W. (2002) 'The Impact of the Internet on Civic Life: An Early Assessment', in Kamarck, E. C. and Nye, J.S. (eds) *Governance.com: Democracy in the Information Age*. Washington DC: Brookings Institution Press; pp. 40–58; Putnam, R. D. (2000) *Bowling Alone: The Collapse and Revival of American Community*. New York: Simon & Schuster; Stormfront. www.stormfront.org/forum (accessed 2/27/06); Wikipedia entry on Aryan Nations. en.wikipedia.org/wiki/Aryan_Nations (accessed 2/27/06); Wikipedia entry on Stormfront. en.wikipedia.org/wiki/Stormfront_%28website%29 (accessed 2/27/06).
21 Chadwick, A. (2006) *Internet Politics: States, Citizens and the New Communication Technologies*. Oxford: Oxford University Press; p.203; see also Curtin G.G., Sommer, M. and Vis Sommer, V. eds. (2003) *The World of E-government*, New York: Haworth Press; West, D. (2005) *Digital Government: Technology and the Public Sector*. Princeton, NJ: Princeton

E-government and democratic politics   17

   University Press; pp.107–13; Gibson, R., Nixon, P. and Ward S. (eds) (2003) *Net Gain? Political Parties and the Impact of New Information Communication Technologies*. London: Routledge; chapters 2; Chapter 3 (Lips), in this present volume.
22 As of December 2005 the access rate for Iraq was about one-tenth of one per cent (0.1%). See links on Internet World Stats for details.
23 NationMaster. http//www.nationmaster.com (accessed 3/1/06); Internet World Stats. www.internetworldstats.com/stats.htm (accessed 2/28/06); OECD. (2001) *Understanding the Digital Divide*. Paris: OECD Publications; p. 23. This predominance of English and developed nations' languages holds for articles written for Wikipedia and for the directors of and the websites associated with ICANN, the International Corporation for the Assignment of Names and Numbers. See: Wikipedia entry on About Wikipedia. en.wikipedia.org/wiki/Wikipedia:About (accessed 12/7/05). See also: ICANN (Internet Corporation for Assigned Names and Numbers). www.icann.org/index.html (accessed 12/8/07).
24 Norris, P. (2001) *Digital Divide: Civic Engagement, Information Poverty, and the Internet Worldwide*. Cambridge: Cambridge University Press; chapters 3–6; West, D. (2005) *Digital Government: Technology and the Public Sector*. Princeton, NJ: Princeton University Press; chapters 7–10; Chadwick, A. (2006) *Internet Politics: States, Citizens and the New Communication Technologies*. Oxford: Oxford University Press; chapter 4. See also numerous reports released by the Pew Internet and American Life Project (www.pewinternet.org/reports.asp).
25 Media Lab (2005) laptop.media.mit.edu/ (accessed 11/19/05); BBC News (2005) 'Sub-$100 laptop design unveiled'. September 29: news.bbc.co.uk/1/hi/technology/4292854.stm (accessed 11/19/05).
26 Coleman, N. (2005) 'Beware a "Digital Munich"'. *Wall Street Journal*, November 7; Redling, V. (2005) 'Icann? We All Can'. *Wall Street Journal*, November 11.
27 Schattschneider, E.E. (1960) *The Semisovereign People; A Realist's View of Democracy in America*. New York: Holt, Rinehart and Winston; p. 35.
28 Bimber, B. (2003) *Information and American Democracy: Technology in the Evolution of Political Power*. Cambridge: Cambridge University Press; Chadwick, A. (2006) *Internet Politics: States, Citizens and the New Communication Technologies*. Oxford: Oxford University Press.
29 Norris, P. (2001) *Digital Divide: Civic Engagement, Information Poverty, and the Internet Worldwide*. Cambridge: Cambridge University Press; Schier, S.E. (2000) *By Invitation Only: The Rise of Exclusive Politics in the United States*. Pittsburgh: University of Pittsburgh Press; Putnam, R.D. (2000) *Bowling Alone: The Collapse and Revival of American Community*. New York.
30 Meetup. www.meetup.com/about (accessed 9/1/05 and 3/2/06); Putnam, R.D. (2000) *Bowling Alone*.
31 Wikipedia entry on Meetup. en.wikipedia.org/wiki/Meetup (accessed 9/8/05 and 3/2/06).
32 Townhall. www.townhall.com/meetup/ (accessed 8/22/05); DFA-Link. tools.democracyforamerica.com/link/ (accessed 9/8/05). While the imposition of monthly fees, which range from $12 to $19 (US) motivated these changes, Townhall nonetheless boasted that the added 'improvements' would include 'Conservatives only! No Deaniacs, no liberals.'
33 Gibson, R.K., Römmele, A. and Ward, S.J. (eds) (2004) *Electronic Democracy: Mobilisation, Organisation and Participation via new ICTs*. London: Routledge.
34 Alvarez, R.M. and Hall, T.E. (2004) *Point, Click & Vote: The Future of Internet Voting*. Washington, DC: Brookings.
35 Mill, J. S. (1962) [1861] *Considerations on Representative Government*. Chicago: Regnery; Lippmann, W. (1993) *The Phantom Public*. New Brunswick, NJ: Transaction Publishers; Alvarez, R.M. and Hall, T.E. (2004) *Point, Click & Vote: The Future of Internet Voting*.

Washington, DC: Brookings; Bishop, G.F. (2005) *The Illusion of Public Opinion: Fact and Artifact in American Public Opinion Polls*. Lanham, MD: Rowman & Littlefield.
36 Curtin G.G., Sommer, M. and Vis Sommer, V. (eds) (2003) *The World of E-government*, New York: Haworth Press; Curtin is also editor of the *Journal of E-government*, which completed its first year of publication in Fall 2005. See also: Lam, W. (2004) 'Integration Challenges Toward Increasing E-government Maturity'. *Journal of E-government*, I(#2): 45–58.
37 Burke, E. (1774) *Speech to the Electors of Bristol* (November 3); Hamilton, A., Jay, J., Madison, J. (orig. 1787–88.) *The Federalist Papers*, Nos. 10, 14, 39 and 52; Eulau, H. et al. (1958) 'The Role of the Representative', *American Political Science Review*, LIII: 742–56; Chapman, J.W. and Pennock, J.R., (eds) (1968) *Representation*. New York: Atherton Press; Pitkin, H. (1967) *The Concept of Representation*. Berkeley, CA: University of California Press; Budge, I. et al. (1972) *Political Stratification and Democracy*. London, Macmillan; Fiorina, M.P. (1981) *Retrospective Voting in American National Elections*. New Haven, CT: Yale University Press.
38 West, D. (2005) *Digital Government: Technology and the Public Sector*. Princeton, NJ: Princeton University Press; Margolis, M. and Resnick, D. (2000) *Politics as Usual: The Cyberspace "Revolution"*. Thousand Oaks, CA: Sage Publications, Inc.; Davis, R. (1999) *The Web of Politics: The Internet's Impact on the American Political System*. New York: Oxford University Press; Chadwick, A. (2006) *Internet Politics: States, Citizens and the New Communication Technologies*. Oxford: Oxford University Press.
39 Gibson, R.K., Römmele, A. and Ward, S.J. (eds) (2004) *Electronic Democracy: Mobilisation, Organisation and Participation via new ICTs*. London: Routledge; Fountain, J.E. (2001) *Building the Virtual State: Informational Technology and Institutional Change*. Washington, DC: Brookings Institution Press.
40 Fisher, B., Margolis, M, and Resnick D. (1996) 'Surveying the Internet: Democratic Theory and Civic Life in Cyberspace', *Southeastern Political Review*, 24: 399–429; Margolis, M. and Resnick, D. (2000) *Politics as Usual: The Cyberspace 'Revolution'*. Thousand Oaks, CA: Sage Publications, Inc..
41 For example, an informational website might invite users to register for chances to win a big ticket item in exchange for permission to allow the website to forward them information from sellers who would offer products about which they had inquired during recent visits. Alternatively, an e-mail service like Yahoo's might sell political parties, candidates or interest groups access to users who live in particular locales or have expressed interest in particular social or political issues of causes.
42 Margolis, M. (1979) *Viable Democracy*. New York: St. Martins Press; Budge, I. (1996) *The New Challenge of Direct Democracy*. Cambridge, MA: Polity Press; Barber, B. R. (1998) *A Place for Us: How to Make Society Civil and Democracy Strong*. New York: Hill and Wang; Davis, R. (1999) *The Web of Politics: The Internet's Impact on the American Political System*. New York: Oxford University Pres; Schier, S. E. (2000) *By Invitation Only: The Rise of Exclusive Politics in the United States*. Pittsburgh: University of Pittsburgh Press.
43 Mill, J. S. (1962) [1861] *Considerations on Representative Government*, pp. 14–15.

Further reading

Fountain, J. E. (2005) 'The Virtual State is Not a Virtual Corporation' in *Taubman Center Annual Report*. Cambridge, MA: Kennedy School of Government, p. 27. www.umass.edu/digitalcenter/ (accessed 2/27/06).

Pew Internet and American Life Project. *Reports*. www.pewinternet.org/reports.asp (accessed November 19, 2005).

2 Ctrl, Alt, Delete

Re-booting the European Union via e-government

Paul G. Nixon

Introduction

The European Union (EU), in all its varying previous guises, has been part of the political landscape of Europe for nigh-on 60 years. Though still not representing all nation states to be found on the whole of the European continent, through its developments and expansions – which are still ongoing – it has grown to become a strategic political and administrative entity incorporating 25 independent nation states in levels of co-operation and partnerships almost unthinkable at the time of its inception. Whilst a common perception of the EU is that its operations are bound by the various treaties that punctuate its history and indeed set out the major span of its activities, it could be argued that that this is not necessarily the case. The EU treaties prescribe the scope and range of powers that are assigned to the EU with other powers remaining the prerogative of individual member states' national governments. Whilst one can see that in the specific case of e-government, the Treaty on the European Union and the Treaty establishing the European Community confer no such specific responsibility upon the EU, it would be wrong to think that this issue was therefore not part of the action plans of the EU. Whilst the primary initiator of e-government implementation policies has remained the individual member states' national governments, one can clearly view in the EU other policy areas for which it has been granted powers of action being used to build upon national efforts. This policy synergy has developed as a consequence of actions taken in a number of, sometimes overlapping, policy domains such as Industrial Policy, Trans European Networks, Research and Technological Development, Internal Market, Competition Policy and Regional Development Policies.[1]

With regards to the EU treaties, responsibility or competence for e-government issues is placed quite categorically in the realm of national competence, with each government being responsible for any e-government measures. New uses of ICTs are shaping, and may continue to shape, changing perceptions of government and sovereignty[2] in the modern European Union member states. The member state governments also retain control and competencies over the development of ICT use by sub-national government. This is an important area for consideration when discussing the EU, as 70 per cent of all EU wide legislation is actually implemented by sub-national levels of governance. Thus one could argue that local or regional government offices or electronic presence are the front line in the EU/citizen interface.[3] Of course, the system of sub-national governance differs from member state to member-state. However as we shall see later in this chapter there are voluntary agreements between the member states' representatives to try to achieve broadly similar advances in the utilisation of ICTs within government.

We can see from the Ministerial conference, held under the auspices of the UK's EU Presidency in Manchester in November 2005, that there is a clear commitment from all 25 member states to continue to develop their existing strategies to modernise public administration using e-government services and to widen the availability and access to those services from a number of different platforms, including via mobile telephony. There is also a quest among member states to create e-government services that are transforming and citizen-centric. Such services should improve quality of life for the user at the same time as rebuilding relationships between the governed and those who govern. It is hoped that the development of such services will go some way to contribute to addressing the issue of declining trust in governments. A notion of partnership through inclusion was one of the key themes of the recent conference: 'the focus for e-government should be on the use of ICTs in order to achieve better and more inclusive government.'[4]

Having noted that the responsibility for e-government initiatives rests with the EU member states' national governments, it can also be seen that there is an EU-wide element to this process as well. We can see this shown in many ways. Below are just two examples. Firstly, and perhaps most obviously, the EU, itself, is a form of public administration and therefore needs to embrace the benefits and be well aware of the barriers to successful implementation of e-government services within the realm of its competencies. Those competencies are mostly but not exclusively manifested in the activities of the EU Commission. One can also see this shown in the rhetoric of the Commission. If one examines the then EU President Romano Prodi's outline of the strategic objectives for his 2000 to 2005 Commission, one can see that 'Promoting new forms of European governance' is given as its first objective. This led to a succession of discussion documents and white papers on Reforming the Commission and European Governance, including the Sapir Report (2003) which argued that in order to meet the goals of successfully expanding the EU and becoming the world's most dynamic, competitive economy it needed to 'adapt the EU's governing instruments to the new situation' and give '… an in-depth reconsideration of the distribution of responsibilities among the member states, the European institutions and any autonomous organisations that may be created to perform specific tasks.'[5]

In November 2005 the Commission agreed to adopt a specific strategy 'e-Commission 2006–2010' which set out a framework for the development of e-services. Within this strategy there are four levels of e-government deployment:

- Level 1: Having a website presence.
- Level 2: Offering online services.
- Level 3: Providing integrated services.

- Level 4: Fully transformed and paperless services which are focused on the user and not the provider.

At present the Commission views itself as having reached the second level of e-government, and intends to meet the objectives stated in the i2010 initiative (discussed below) in order to achieve Level 3 status by 2010. The Commission is also increasingly using ICTs as a medium for soliciting interaction, views and comments from its citizens through a variety of means including a recently-launched Internet based discussion forum on the future of Europe which is available in 20 different languages.[6]

Secondly, the policies of the EU can also be impacted by the moves to e-government. This is most evident when one thinks of the completion of the single market which ensures equal and fair competition for businesses, particularly SMEs and citizens throughout the EU. The use of e-procurement (defined in EU Directive 2004/18/EC, and which put simply is the Internet tendering for the supply of goods or services to governments and public administrations within the member states) means that the systems used to facilitate such processes must be ensured to be open and flexible. They also need to incorporate basic tools such as electronic registration of companies, interoperability (particularly in terms of the use of electronic signatures) and to deal with issues related to translation. Whilst, to date, over 50 per cent of all procurement is being published electronically,[7] the submission stage is only employed electronically in 9 per cent of all tenders although this is expected to rise sharply within the next few years.[8]

However it is important to bear in mind that the use of ICT by governments of all levels to carry out the tasks of public administration is not a new phenomenon. The history of computerisation of public administration dates from the 1960s although the introduction of the capacity to utilise the Internet for routine administrative tasks, ICT development and diffusion of the technologies have rapidly increased the pace of adoption. Although, it must be said, that such modernisation has not always met with unqualified success.

The early years

There can be little doubt that there is some difficulty in unpicking the drivers behind the moves to e-government. Is it simply a matter of technological harmonisation facilitating greater integration of administrative practices across member states? Is that harmonisation compelled by the logic of enlargement? Have the varying enlargements of the EU led to an inevitability of reform? Has the EU's wish to be closer to the people provided a boost to the process of reliance on ICT driven solutions to governmental and administrative challenges in the recent years?

In order to understand the evolution of e-government, it is important to know the pre-history that has contributed to and informed its evolution. The present notion of e-government has developed from a range of initiatives in other policy areas, which can give interesting insights into the problems and potential obstacles faced by those wishing to move further along the e-government scale.

The First Framework Programme (FP) of the early 1980s, which attempted to redress Europe's dependency on high technology imports and knowledge from Japan and the USA, was the first real EU-wide attempt to marry the concepts of integration and innovation.[9] It was felt that Member States could only challenge the domination of others in the fields of Research and Technological Development (RTD) by coming together and co-ordinating research efforts under targeted programmes. Indeed, the member states are now obliged, under the Amsterdam Treaty, to undertake European research policies and programmes. Each FP has its own specific detailed objectives and actions. This process has carried on through overlapping five-year programmes to the present 6th Framework Programme, which is due to finish at the end of 2006.

An example of a project funded under FP6 would be the Paganini Project on Participatory Governance and Institutional Reform, which '… investigates the ways in which participatory practices contribute to problem solving in a number of highly contentious fields of EU governance. PAGANINI looks at a particular dynamic cluster of policy areas concerned with what we call the "politics of life": medicine, health, food, energy and environment.'[10] The researchers on the project hope to find ways in which governance within the EU can be re-shaped in order to build trust through a participatory framework.

FP6 will soon be followed by the 7th Framework Programme, with a projected budget of over €73 billion over its programme life that has now been extended to seven years. One of the prime objectives of FP6 and FP7 is the creation of the European Research Area (ERA) which is a form of knowledge-based equivalent to the common market of goods and services and is meant '… to co-ordinate these national research policies in the direction of shared objectives, expertise and resources.'[11]

However, as the recent Aho report shows there is still a greater need for action. It argues that there is a gap between the political rhetoric about the knowledge society and the reality of budgetary and other priorities that have shown little shift in engaging with it. They would also like to see the monies set aside in the Structural Funds trebled in order to give all regions a stake in the knowledge economy.[12]

EU Community Support Frameworks (CSF) were aimed at the integration of diverse and often uncoordinated actions into discrete, focussed operational programmes in a number of sectors including Public Administration and Telecommunications. CSFs marked the beginning of the production of a plethora of initiatives designed to make the European Union an information society. Initiatives such as the European Strategic Programme for Research in Information Technology (ESPRIT) Research and Development in Advanced Communication Technologies in Europe (RACE) sought to combat the hitherto dilution of research resources and effort by creating a collaborative framework between researchers, particularly between academics and practitioners. In effect these are the early forerunners of the European Research Area.

The year 1994 saw the publication of the Bangemann report,[13] which focused on the development of an information society within the EU. The Bangemann Report somewhat neglected the potential of public administration to play a leading role in the developments necessary to set the EU on the road towards achieving an information society. The report's focus was too heavily skewed in favour of business and private investment being the driving force that would achieve the creation of an information society. Of course, one of the major inferences of a business-focussed strategy is that it ignores the fundamental differences of ethos and culture between the public and private sectors. In the private sector it is the innovators who are normally rewarded, but Kamark in 2004 notes that in the public sector any rewards normally accrue to the State and not to the innovator, leaving public administrators little reason to indulge in entrepreneurial innovation.[14]

Certainly one can see the ideological arguments underpinning the Bangemann report being jettisoned in later initiatives, described below, whereby the role of the public sector was seen as increasingly vital to success. Of course this has to be placed in a context whereby nation states were also forming their own national plans to develop information societies and to create conditions where radical structural change could occur. Actors within nation states, and the differing sub national levels of government, could see that they were to play an increasingly dualistic role in the future information society. Firstly, that they would be the bodies who would facilitate the development of that information society by encouraging other organisations to adopt ICT solutions, and secondly, as prime users of ICT in their own sphere of influence and day to day activities.

At the same time there were similar efforts to restructure the fragmented nature of the European economy and in the process to ensure a level playing field of competition by removing state subsidies, protectionism and beginning to open up areas of public procurement. TESTA, an initiative set up in 1996, sought to engender an inter-administrative network which would include all the then 15 EU member states, those countries seeking accession to the EU and EFTA (European Free Trade Area) countries and EU accession-stage countries to incorporate each country's national efforts, and to establish administrative networks, via a 'Euro-Domain' to attempt to foster independence and inter-operability of local domains within the EU's scope of policy activities.

The focus was on producing an interlinked set of EU policies that would ensure cross-border cooperation, halt the 'brain drain' from academia, and encourage innovation and entrepreneurialism within a revitalised EU society.

The move to an information age was seen as heralding new horizons for the EU and its citizens, with contemporary social scientists arguing that 'the accelerating pace of technological change in the late 1990s make it a more important determinant of the way in which economies, polities and societies are organised than ever before'.[15] This of course contrasts with the fragmented nature of European society and therefore led to a welter of measures to try to harness the potential of e-government described below. The problem, as noted elsewhere in this chapter, was that the EU did not have responsibility for this specific policy domain and could only advise and facilitate joint initiatives between member state governments whilst using its other policy areas such as telecommunications, regional policy and so on to lever change in attitudes and behaviour.

'eEurope 2002'

Following a series of Ministerial meetings in 2000, the EU agreed to adopt a set of initiatives which became known as 'eEurope 2002' or a part of the Lisbon Strategy. As Dinan points out, the Lisbon Strategy marked a clear departure in EU rhetoric and was '… a tacit acknowledgement that the EU had to adopt a more aggressive American style approach …'[16] The major aim of eEurope 2002 was to stimulate cheaper, faster, secure Internet focussed on connectivity. It also set out to engender 'all encompassing' strategies recognising the interlinking nature of e-government. It benchmarked 20 basic services which were to be offered online in order to exploit the efficiency gains of ICT use. By the end of eEurope 2002 most of those services were available in the member states, but it must be said to varying degrees of sophistication. A potential problem identified by Lowe in 2003 in terms of public perception of e-government issues is that the public are often being asked to use services that are half built or 'under construction'.[17] Whilst this may be no different to the process of incremental developments in 'traditionally' delivered government services, online, such a scenario is more apparent and perhaps can add to the reluctance of citizens to trust e-government service delivery modes.

eEurope 2002 demonstrated one of the side issues of re-engineering of government through the use of ICTs in that there was a recognition that many of the issues that the Lisbon Strategy was to deal with did not fit neatly into the organisational architecture of the EU Commission with proposed activities relating to more than one Commission portfolio. One could make the argument that one of the unstated outcomes of e-government within the EU may have profound effects upon calls for reform of the structure of the EU's institutional architecture.

There can be no doubt that the proposals were ambitious, perhaps overly so, and the deadlines that it set were hard for member states to meet in their entirety.[18] However, eEurope 2002 was seen as having achieved the following:

- increased the number of citizens and businesses connected to the Internet;
- reshaped the regulatory environment for communications networks and services for e-commerce;
- facilitated new generations of mobile and multimedia services;
- helped the workforce to acquire the skills needed in a knowledge-driven economy;
- brought computers and the Internet into schools;
- brought governments online; and
- focussed on the need to ensure a safer online world through increased security measures.[19]

'eEurope 2005'

Following on from the Lisbon agreements to provide modern online public services and a dynamic e-business environment enabled by widely available broadband access at competitive prices operating within a secure information infrastructure, eEurope2005 aimed to offer everyone the opportunity to participate in the global information society. eEurope 2005 sought to secure this through four linked strategies:

- policy measures;
- exchange of good practice;
- benchmarking; and
- greater overall co-ordination of existing policies.

The goal of the plan was to develop '... secure services and applications and content based on a widely available broadband infrastructure'.[20] The availability of broadband was a crucial enabling infrastructure for the plans to modernise public services throughout the EU with an emphasis upon e-government, e-learning, e-health and e-business.

The notion of an exchange of good practice is taking shape with many organisations pooling their knowledge in order to improve compatibility, interoperability and enhanced efficiency, particularly through the EU Commission supported Good Practice Framework.[21] The present Austrian Presidency of the EU has proposed the setting up of a new E-government Resources Network to further this aim.

The European Union is at the forefront of the drive towards rolling out the changes needed in all member states in order to further facilitate the adoption of e-government. Broadly speaking one can separate the EU's activity into three major areas of activity. Firstly, regulation: mirroring the broader communications policy in which rapid development is followed by a second stage of controls based upon public interest grounds.[22] The EU is producing a series of regulations which seek to control the information environment, for example those which seek to combat the spread of 'harmful' material via ICTs, or as Rawal notes later in this volume the EU's attempts to force Internet service providers and mobile phone operators to retain call records and Internet logs for up to two years to aid law enforcement. Secondly, by use of stimulation: by promoting infrastructure development and encouraging service delivery via ICTs. Thirdly, through the exploitation of benefits whilst, at the same time, ensuring security and privacy.

The European Union's policy towards the use of ICTs and the creation of an e-society sets a clear outline for the introduction of such services throughout the Union. The EU set out five major areas for progress:

- Knowledge management and organisational innovation
- Interoperability and pan-European services
- Secure e-government and identity management

- User interaction and mobile services
- E-democracy

'i2010'

The most recent initiative to facilitate an information society in the EU is that of 'i2010'. The EU seeks to promote a system of joined-up, integrated policy initiatives via i2010 that attempt to place the EU at the forefront of moves towards establishing a true information society. The EU contends that only an overarching, all embracing strategy can effectively harness the benefits that ICTs can bring to its population in many areas including that of enhancing e-government services.

It seeks to achieve its goals through three major areas as noted in COM (2005a) 229 EU Commission 2005. Of course these are often overlapping areas so that, for example, the creation of a single European space feeds into the quest for strengthening innovation and investment as well as facilitating the potential of an inclusive information society within the EU. It seeks to achieve its goals in partnership with the member states' governments. The three areas are:

1. The completion of a *Single European Information Space* governed by a consistent system of rules which promotes an open and competitive internal market for information society and media. This is needed in order to achieve digital convergence and to address four main challenges. First is the need for a framework of faster broadband connectivity which will help to deliver hi-level content. At the time of writing the EU25 had 48.4 million subscribers to broadband, or approximately 10 per cent of the population – although this is not evenly spread throughout the European Union.[23] It should be noted that the take-up rates for broadband are increasing rapidly as it becomes cheaper and more attractive to subscribers. Second, it is to facilitate the creation of such 'rich content', in order to encourage new service and content provision. Third is the development of enhanced security requirements in order to secure information and also perhaps more importantly to increase the trust users have in the systems. Fourth is the creation of interoperability, so that systems can work together and it can be ensured that services are portable from one platform to another.

The differing forms and tiers of government at the national, regional and local levels in the EU present a challenge to the adoption of e-government. In order to function effectively, all these organisations need to be able to exchange information not just vertically or horizontally but also diagonally on a matrix basis, thus, allowing for interoperability between organisations, across organisational levels which may or may not be operational in different member states.

In its recent communication, the Commission[24] calls for renewed efforts to attain interoperability at three different levels. Firstly, *organisational interoperability*: which allows for information flows relating to what the EU term as 'life-time events' for citizens such as birth, marriage, claims for social security and so on, or 'business-events' participating in procurement activities or establishing a company and so on. Secondly, *semantic interoperability*: which allows comparability between documents, produced by governments at all levels in member states, which, whilst they may share the same purpose, are often vastly different. This may be due to those documents being presented in differing languages or displaying similar information in quite different ways perhaps by adopting differing lay outs. An example of these differences could be the differing types of birth certificates issued by the EU member states. An example of a more unified approach can be seen in the adoption of a standard format for driving licenses throughout the EU. Thirdly, *technical interoperability:* encouraging the adoption of a standardisation of software and hardware that allows the differing systems to communicate and thus share information. For example, as van Rossum and Dreessen show later in this book, in 2007 the Dutch government will introduce a system of collecting data on individuals from birth in an Electronic Child File which can be continually updated. But how useful will this data be without similar capabilities to utilise the information in other member states should individuals exercise their rights to freedom of movement under the Treaties?

The Commission is thus seeking to aid the Member States in order to set priorities, publish policy documents/guidelines and technical recommendations and to encourage standardisation. Whilst the responsibility for interoperability rests with Member States there can be no doubt that EU wide interoperability is a pre-requisite in order to implement common EU policies and it is for this reason that i2010 includes interoperability as essential for ICT-enabled public services.

2   Strengthening *Innovation and Investment* in ICT research to promote growth and more and better jobs. As Table 2.1 shows, the level of investment in ICT research in the then EU 15 falls behind that of our competitors. To this end the Commission has put forward proposals such as the 7th Research Framework Programme and the Competitiveness and Innovation Programme to attempt to pump prime more research and development into ICTs. The 7th Framework Programme will run from 2007 until 2013.

3   Achieving an *Inclusive European Information Society* that promotes growth and jobs in a manner that is consistent with sustainable development and that prioritises better public services and quality of life. We can already see, as shown by a plethora of initiatives mentioned in the later case-study related

Table 2.1 Investment in ICT research (2002)

ICT R&D	EU-15	US	Japan
Private sector investments	€b 23	€b 83	€b 40
Public sector investment	€b 8	€b 20	€b 11
Inhabitants	€383 m	€296 m	€127 m
Investments / inhabitant	€80	€350	€400
ICT R&D as % Total R&D	18%	34%	35%

Source: IDATE (for EU-15); OECD in COM (2005a) 229 EU Commission 2005.

chapters of this book, how ICTs are helping to improve services in general; for example, via better health care opportunities and in particular for caring for ageing people by addressing technologies which can contribute to better health and independent living through adaptive technologies. In terms of e-government, improvement is sought specifically in terms of the way in which e-government services are being adopted and, to a large extent, accepted by the public. Online tax returns are now the norm in the Netherlands, for example. If one looks at recent reports one can see that in the EU member states approximately 40 per cent of public services are now available online (Cap Gemini Report). One can also see that the difference in the interactions and use of online services show marked differences between the usage by enterprises and individuals.[25] The use of online services of course saves on time and indeed also has the potential to save other resources and therefore is a more pressing need for cost-conscious enterprises. Although perhaps some of the disparity between the two groups may be attributable to the focus of member states' information policies. The Commission is committed to introducing a European Initiative on e-Inclusion in 2008[26] which will seek to address inequalities of access in terms of opportunities, skills and regional disparities. As well as operating in a spirit of partnership with member states' governments', it is envisaged that more attention should be focussed on the latter via utilisation of existing EU financial instruments such as the Structural Funds.

Perhaps one potential problem may be found in the reasons as to why governments transfer services to the Internet. Often such measures are seen as cost-cutting exercises and ways to save money and other resources. Though it should be noted that the capital costs of such schemes can be extremely high and although operating website-based services is often cheaper than staffing traditionally functioning offices, there are considerable ongoing costs particularly in terms of training. It is tempting to see this as a win-win situation where the reduction in costs is of benefit to all. However, tasks previously paid for collectively via various government mechanisms, and undertaken by government officials, are being redesigned – with some of the associated costs thus being transferred directly to individuals. It has been argued that the costs of online engagement with government, particularly where it is the only means of initial engagement, amount to a regressive taxation for a person on a low/no income.[27] This situation may be more intense in areas of deprivation and uneven economic development; as one can see from Reis,[28] there are severe differentials between the rates of use in differing member states. This is re-enforced by e-Inclusion Revisited,[29] which suggests that the recent enlargement has increased the task faced in narrowing such gaps between rich and poor – a situation that is vital to achieve if we are truly to create an equal information society for all.

Conclusions

The history of ICT development in relation to e-government is one that needs to be evaluated carefully. Without doubt there are great savings (in all senses of the word) to be made from implementing e-government systems. But the question must be posed: at what cost? Whilst ICT use may solve some problems, it may also create new problems or demands around issues such as privacy or lack of freedom of information.[30] There is quite a gap between stated intentions, wishes, goals and aspirations and the actual outcome of the delivery of e-government projects. 'The rhetoric of technological shifts is not always translated into successful implementation.'[31] A range of studies show that the number of e-government projects that can be considered as total or partial failures ranges, depending on the survey used, from 60 to 85 per cent of all projects.[32] It could be suggested that the experiences of the moves towards creating viable e-government provision are still in their infancy and may be said to resemble a type of 'virtual klondike', with some early adopters never recouping their investment whilst others strike it rich first time. Perhaps it also suggests that some projects may be introduced without the necessary forethought as to what will happen and what the potential pitfalls may be. Nevertheless, it must be noted that all government is, in part, a set of experiential learning circumstances and it is only by trying and trying again with a refined plan that success is achieved. Should we expect any more of governance simply because modern technology is involved? Perhaps we should be more tolerant of the time it takes to refine e-government initiatives, to modify them in order to fit in with our modern and diverse societies. As Torres et al. note, e-government is not likely to remodel governance in the short term, because e-democracy initiatives are not on the present agenda of most EU countries.[33] The increasing emphasis upon competitiveness and ICTs as an instrument of growth in the EU economy is of course vital and necessary for the development of a true information society within the 25 member states. However, there is a tendency for the notion of e-democracy to be only a secondary consideration and not an integral part of the mix.[34] The rhetoric of statements on i2010 and its predecessors seem to stress the more market driven, 'new Europe' Anglo Saxon inspired model of economic development over the older, previously dominant social model as championed by France and Germany.

We can see that there is a dual role for the EU within the field of e-government. Firstly, as a unifying facilitator creating the conditions whereby member states can share experiences and pool expertise in order to create flexible, interoperable service provision that are citizen-centred and fulfil the aspirations of a free and open society. Secondly, the EU has a role as an example to the member states of how government can be re-booted through the adoption of modern technologies which transform the way in which we think about governance.

There can be no doubt that e-government will become increasingly important and, as we noted earlier in this chapter, not just for the member states' national governments but also for the workings of the European Union, as shown by the moves towards an e-Commission. Once more though, this raises the problem of control over the Commission. Is it not time that the public at large in the EU had more direct democratic control over the things, purportively, done in their name? Perhaps the very technologies that are supporting the move to an e-Commission could be utilised to provide greater citizen input to a large public administration organisation that many see as unresponsive and undemocratic. The aforementioned online debate on the future of Europe (europa.eu.int/debateeurope/) points the way and demonstrates the potential of ICTs to stimulate a successful EU, but perhaps a greater and deeper collaboration is needed between the EU and its citizens. If the EU were to redirect more of its efforts and attempt to strengthen the relationship with its citizens, this may help to address the criticisms of a democratic deficit within the EU.[35] There is evidence that the Commission is moving in this direction. Perhaps in future years, the EU itself may lead by example in the use of ICT-enabled governance. An efficient, effective and inclusive EU is achievable. Technology can aid its creation, but such a future won't be built by using technology alone; courage, entrepreneurship and a pioneering spirit are all required if the EU is to transform itself into a citizen-centric organisation as noted by Lips later in this volume. E-government could be a part of a revitalised and, implicitly, more democratic EU. Could e-government be a conduit to help rebuild that relationship between the EU and its citizens?

Notes

1 Alabau, A. (2004) *The European Union and its eGovernment Development Policy: Following the Lisbon Strategy Objectives*. Madrid, Spain: Fundación Vodafone; p. 18.
2 Dahlgren, P. (2001) 'The Transformation of Democracy' in Axford, B. and Huggins, R. (eds) *New Media And Politics*. London: Sage.
3 European Commission (2003a) *The Role of eGovernment for Europe's Future*. COM (2003), p. 567; Information Society Commission (2003) *eGovernment*. Dublin: Information Society Commission, Department of the Taoiseach.
4 www.egov2005conference.gov.uk/
5 Cited in Alabau, A. (2004) *The European Union* pp. 26–7.
6 europa.eu.int/debateeurope/
7 www.egov2005conference.gov.uk/
8 www.egov2005conference.gov.uk/
9 Koutrakou, V.N. and Nixon, P.G. (2000) 'Integration, Communication and Transparency in Europe: Innovating Integration or Integrating Innovation' in Koutrakou, V.N. and Emerson, L.A. (eds) *The European Union and Britain: Debating the Challenges Ahead*. Basingstoke, UK: Macmillan.
10 www.paganini-project.net/
11 European Commission (2004a) *The European Research Area*. Brussels: EU Commission.
12 europa.eu.int/invest-in-research/pdf/download_en/aho_report.pdf
13 European Commission (1994) 'Europe and the Global Information Society'. Bangemann Report, available online at europa.eu.int/ISPO/docs/basics/docs/bangemann.pdf
14 Kamarck, E. (2004) '*Government innovation around the world*', Harvard University, Cambridge, MA: John F. Kennedy School of Management, Faculty Research Working Paper Series.
15 Peterson, J. and Sharp, M. (1998) *Technology Policy in the European Union*. Basingstoke, UK: Macmillan; p. 1.
16 Dinan, D. (2005) *Ever Closer Union*. Basingstoke, UK: Palgrave Macmillan; p. 387.

17 Lowe, C. (2003) 'Ten Steps to Massive Take-Up of EGovernment in Europe' *International Journal of Communications Law and Policy*, Issue 8, winter 2003/2004:5.
18 European Commission (2003b) *eEurope 2002 Final Report*. COM (2003); p. 66.
19 www.eu.int/information_society/eeurope/2002/news_library/documents/eeurope2005/execsum_en.pdf
20 European Commission (2002) *eEurope 2005: An Information Society for all*. COM (2002); p. 263.
21 www.egov-goodpractice.org/
22 Van Cuilenburg, J. and McQuail, D. (2003) 'Media Policy Paradigm Shifts: Towards a New Communications Policy Paradigm', *European Journal of Communication* 18(2): 181–207.
23 European Commission (2005b) Information Society Benchmarking Report. Available online at www.eu.int/information_society/eeurope/i2010/index_en.htm
24 European Commission (2006) *Interoperability for Pan-European E-government Services*. COM (2006); p. 45 final.
25 Reis, F. (2005) *E-government: Internet based interaction with the European businesses and citizens*. Eurostat 9/2005.
26 COM (2005) 229 EU. See: European Commission (2005b) Information Society Benchmarking Report. See also: European Commission (2005c) *e-Inclusion revisited: The Local Dimension of the Information Society*.
27 Nixon, P.G. and Rawal, R. (2005) 'Enabling Democracy? E-government, Inclusion and Citizenship' in Remenyi, D. (ed.) *Proceedings of the International Conference on E-government*. Ottawa.
28 Reis, F. (2005) *E-government*.
29 European Commission (2005c) *e-Inclusion revisited*.
30 Nixon, P.G. (2004) 'Young People, Politics and New Media in the European Union' in Koutrakou, V. (ed.) *Contemporary Issues and Debates in EU Policy* (2004). Manchester, UK: Manchester University Press.
31 Nixon, P.G. (2000) 'Joined Up Government: Whitehall On-Line' in Gibson, R. and Ward, S.J. (eds), *Re-Invigorating Democracy: British Politics and the Internet*. Aldershot, UK: Ashgate.
32 Heeks, R. (2006) *Implementing and Managing eGovernment*. London: Sage; p. 3.
33 Torres, L., Pina, V. and Royo, S. (2005) 'E-government and the transformation of public administrations in EU countries: Beyond NPM or just a second wave of reforms?' *Online Information Review* 29(5): 531–53.
34 Olsen, J.P. (2003) 'What is a Legitimate Role for Euro-Citizens?' *Comparative European Politics*. Basingstoke, UK: Palgrave MacMillan; Vol. 1, pp. 91–110; Pech, L. (2003) 'La Solution au "Déficit Démocratique": Une Nouvelle Gouvernance Pour L'UnionEuropéenne.' *European Integration*, Vol. 2, June 25: 131–50.
35 Lynch, P. Neuwahl, N. and Rees, W. (2000) *Reforming the European Union*. Harlow, UK: Pearson; Pech, L. (2003) 'La Solution au "Déficit Démocratique".

Further reading

European Commission (2000) *Strategic Objectives 2000–2005. Shaping the New Europe*. COM (2000); p. 154.

European Commission (2004b) *eEurope 2005 Mid-term Review*. COM (2004); p. 108.

European Commission (2005a) 'i2010 – A European Information Society for growth and employment', COM (2005); p. 229.

European Commission website: www.eu.int/information_society/eeurope/2002/news_library/documents/eeurope2005/execsum_en.pdf

Sapir Report (2003) *An Agenda for a Growing Europe*. Available online at www.euractiv.com/ndbtext/innovation/sapirreport.pdf

www.emeraldinsight.com/Insight/ViewContentServlet?Filename=Published/EmeraldFullTextArticle/Articles/2640290507.html

3 E-government under construction

Challenging traditional conceptions of citizenship

Miriam Lips

Introduction

Since e-government has been put on policy agendas around the world, it has been strongly related with a citizen-centric approach in government reform efforts. Through time these reform efforts have become more ambitious, in the sense that where e-government used to be treated as a tool for modernising government it has gradually been recognised as a strategic approach to transform government from a citizen point of view. These reform efforts are all the more remarkable when recognising the producer-centricity by which the organisation of public services have hitherto been dominated.[1]

Recent e-government publications point at scepticism with regard to governments' achievements on improved citizen-centricity as a result of their reform efforts. Nonetheless, the policy aim itself is still recognised as a fundamental change to improve e-government or even government itself. For example, a recent OECD publication focused on how to achieve better e-government advises the following: 'A key challenge is to somehow "turn the telescope around" – to view the government from the user's perspective, rather than from that of government. This is not easy; in many cases government will find itself sailing in uncharted waters. Becoming more user-focused will be counter-cultural, and it will often fit poorly with "local" interests. But without this fundamental change, user-focused government will remain out of reach.'[2]

In the EU Ministerial eGovernment Declaration presented at the EU Ministerial eGovernment Conference in Manchester, November 2005, good e-government services are acknowledged to be transformed, citizen-centric public services. These services will improve citizens' quality of life, reduce administrative burdens on citizens and contribute towards citizens' trust in government and democracy. However, the Ministerial agreements reached at this conference also recognised that there is still a lot to do to deliver good e-government services and have them used by the citizen. For example, EU Ministerial agreements were decided upon to deliver high-impact services designed around customers' needs and to offer widely available, trusted access to public services across the EU, facilitated through the use of secure and trusted means of electronic identification and authentication. Moreover it was decided that no citizen should be left behind in the development of e-government, and that citizen inclusion should take place by design: 'the focus for e-government should be on the use of ICTs in order to achieve better and more inclusive government. This could include improved services and policies with outcomes such as increased transparency, inclusion, accessibility and accountability or greater participation in decision-making, all built into their design from the outset.'[3]

After more than a decade of implementing e-government projects, strategies, and conditions with a strong focus on the citizen these public statements raise the fundamental question as to what implications e-government actually has had, and will have, for the citizen. Does e-government indeed lead to a situation in which the citizen has an improved, central position in their service relationships with government? In what way and to what extent does the citizen encounter changes in their roles and relationships with government by moving from a paper-based service environment to a digital service environment? And what effect might this emerging electronic public service environment have on the application of administrative principles founded upon traditional notions of citizenship, such as universal service and equality for the law?

Although a clear definition is lacking of what e-government is or should be in the future,[4] awareness is gradually rising that the emergence of e-government may coincide with an unprecedented challenge to the institutions, procedures and concepts through which public governance is delivered.[5] One of these concepts is citizenship, and the related principles and procedures through which citizen–government relationships have been shaped. It is the exploration of the impact of e-government developments on this institution that this chapter will cover.

To be able to do so we first need to know more about the conceptions of citizenship which have been shaping citizen–government relationships in the offline world, and how, based on those conceptions, public service provision to the citizen has traditionally been organised. We then apply a citizen-centric perspective ourselves to explore what is actually known about the e-citizen and changes in citizen–government relationships after more than a decade of e-government reform efforts. Unfortunately, we need to conclude that there is not much useful empirical data available at present. Therefore we are forced to turn the telescope around and explore in what ways governments have been trying to relate to their citizens in their e-government efforts. In the final section we will analyse to what extent traditional conceptions of citizenship underpinning public service provision in the offline world are still applicable for the emerging digital public service environment after more than a decade of e-government evolution.

Serving the citizen in a paper-based world

Notions of 'citizenship' underpin the way in which relationships between citizens and governments have been shaped. Consequently, they will determine the way in which public service delivery to the citizen has been organised. History, however, shows us that these notions have been changing over time. For example, in our modern liberal-democratic world, the concept of citizenship has a special relationship with history, fraternity and nationality.[6]

From an historical point of view, a citizen has an awareness of his relationship to his 'state' and to his fellow citizens. As this relationship changes over time it needs to be understood in its historical context. Smith & Smythe[7] point out that since the French Revolution the concept of citizenship has been *defined and given meaning by nation states*. Further history provides us with examples of similar roles for the city-state, church, and market-institutions like serfdom. Fraternity expresses the fact that a citizen belongs to a group with a common morality, a common sense of purpose, and engaged in common activities.[8] Citizenship identity provides a person belonging to that group with an *egalitarian* membership status. In relation to nationality a citizen has both a legal status and a cultural bond related to a certain geographical territory. Formal nationality therefore entails certain *universal* entitlements to a citizen: rights that every citizen is entitled to exercise and which, in the post-war liberal-democratic welfare state, can have a civil, political, or social nature. Each of these entitlements emerged sequentially in the modern era.[9] Civil citizenship embodies rights that secure individual freedoms, such as liberty, freedom of speech, the right to ownership, and the right to justice. Political citizenship is composed of the democratic rights of participation, such as voting, the right to exercise political power, and demonstration. Finally, social citizenship refers to the rights to a minimum standard of welfare and income facilitated by, for example, employment, education and housing.

These conceptions of citizenship are at the basis of public service provision to citizens in a traditional 'offline' world. Especially due to the emergence of the welfare state in western democratic countries after the Second World War and therefore based on the notion of social citizenship, public service provision to citizens has expanded enormously, resulting in a silo-structured government with different public counters for individual government service domains towards the citizen.

Traditionally, the process of public service provision to the citizen has been mainly paper-based and often supported by face-to-face contact. A citizen usually gets authorised access to public services on the basis of manual form-filling, the writing of letters and/or the submission of official documents, such as a passport, driving licence or birth certificate. As these records are proofs of entitlement to a certain public service they are often stored in personal files, turning public service providing organisations into vast repositories of stored paper records. Derived from the administrative principle of 'equality under the law', the collection and filing of these records, however, guarantees different forms of administrative equity to citizens: equity in terms of content (equal service outcome for similar cases) and procedure (equal treatment during the service process). Furthermore, the service accessed by citizens is 'universal', that is, within any particular governmental jurisdiction (national, regional, local, functional), rights to the same service level are afforded to all citizens, often based on the egalitarian principle of 'service by waiting list'.[10]

Moreover, in the paper-based public service world personal identification of the citizen and the verification of that identity through authentication processes reside at the heart of government service provision. Throughout history, authentication processes related to the use of paper-based authentication systems, such as the passport, have been largely constant. The passport holder shows his or her passport to the person officially recognised to check and verify that the document carrier is the person shown and referred to in the information, including photograph, included in the document. Set within a traditional environment of trust, these authentication processes have often been supplemented by a face-to-face assessment of the citizen by the official, based upon the citizen's appearance of honesty or upon the official's knowledge of the citizen within the local community.

What about the e-citizen?

In the emerging digital era, governments are looking for ways to reorganise their public service provision to citizens, making use of the possibilities offered by new information and communication technologies (ICTs). Besides paper-based public service delivery, governments are developing electronic public service provision in ways that they might be better able to serve the citizen. That is, even more than under the paper-based public service system, they want to take the desires and needs of citizens into account and fit the design of the new digitally-based public service system better to the citizen's perspective of government.

In these efforts to set up and develop e-government, we may recognise several general phases through time. In their first attempts to put information online, governments added more interactive features to their websites and started to communicate with citizens (for example by email). After these 'information' and 'communication' phases, we may now observe a phase in which governments are setting up online transaction facilities in their relationships with citizens, and are trying to develop neccessary digital alternatives for the traditional paper-based identification and authentication means.

Analogously, we may observe that governments have been through several developmental stages of e-government. Usually, these development stages range from an online presence of government towards a stage at which transformation of public service provision is taking place. Recent studies show that most governments can be situated at these first levels of e-government development.[11] To be able to reach higher development levels governments need to be willing to reorganise their entire organisation – that is, to not merely have an electronic public counter or 'front-office'. To do so, they are required to approach e-government not exclusively from a technological point of view but to treat it as a strategic issue for the organisation, with many different administrative aspects attached to it as well.

Currently, from a citizen's point of view, e-government is present at many ICT-mediated locations and in many forms. This is not surprising as many public organisations are implementing e-government: government departments and agencies at different administrative levels (local, regional, national, and supranational), but also police organisations, hospitals, schools, public libraries, and many other types of public organisations. In addition, Internet portals have been set up where the citizen can have access to the same public information and services as through the websites of individual organisations, presented, however, in an integrated way. This situation actually implies that in recent times, especially due to public organisations applying a multi-channel approach, the citizen has been confronted with more public counters than ever before. The silo structure of the public domain seems to have been translated to the digital environment and further networked into different points of public service access for the citizen.

In general, looking at the policy aim to improve citizen-centricity in e-government applications, it is very interesting to observe that the citizen so far has hardly played any role in reform processes related to e-government implementation. Although it is often proclaimed that the citizens' needs are the starting point for e-government development, the reality is that citizens themselves have scarcely been consulted.[12] E-government can therefore be acknowledged as a supply-driven concept: the technology offers governments new opportunities to reorganise their service provision to their citizens.[13]

Moreover, it is remarkable to note that there is hardly any empirical data available on the use of electronic public services by citizens.[14] Consequently, we so far seem to know very little about the e-citizen and his or her evolving relationships to (e-)government. What we do know is primarily based on quantitative data about whether the citizen is consuming online public services, how much, and with what degree of satisfaction. In general, the available survey results show that the take-up of e-government services remains rather limited and in some countries has even declined.[15]

Survey results from the USA, for example, show that 77 per cent of Internet users were e-government service consumers in 2003. This consumption, however, could imply the full range of e-government service provision, from visiting government websites to emailing government officials. Compared to 2002 this figure represented an increase of 50 per cent. However, citizens who contacted government said they would be more likely to turn to traditional means – either by telephone or in-person visits – rather than the Internet to deal with government.[16]

Comparably, a recent survey in ten selected EU member states points out that although a large part of the European population is online at present, a relatively small proportion of Internet users are users of e-government services (11 per cent). Interestingly, a much larger percentage of online users use government services 'offline'.[17] In general, in European countries, the media channel used by citizens when contacting government is still overwhelmingly face-to-face. In some countries, such as the UK and Ireland, the use of the postal service (70 per cent in the UK; 68 per cent in IE) and the telephone (74 per cent in the UK; 67 per cent in IE) has overtaken face-to-face contacts (50 per cent in the UK; 64 per cent in IE) and is much higher than online contacts (23 per cent in the UK and IE).[18]

Unfortunately, the scarcity of empirical data prevents us from gaining deeper and more qualitative understanding about what is happening to citizen–government relationships as a result of e-government implementations. As what we currently see in e-government is what we measure, the more fundamental question here is whether we are using the right perspective to make judgements about potential changes going on in citizen–government relationships, and the citizen-centricity achieved by e-government. E-government projects are, by definition, information intensive; they often involve large-scale sharing of data, much of it personal data about the citizen, and increasingly these projects involve the personal identification and authentication of individual citizens as they consume electronic public services. First observations of the changes in information relationships between citizen and government due to shifting from a paper-based public service system to a digital public service system indicate that there may be more to this than the available statistical data reveals. The creation, collection, exchange, use and holding of information involved in e-government projects are of paramount significance to our full understanding of citizen–government relationships, yet is little discussed in the gathering literature on e-government.[19] Now that ICTs are being applied more and more extensively in citizen–government relationships and new information resources about the citizen are being developed, deeper questions about the implications for citizens and citizenship need to get our full attention as e-government scholars so we are truly able to design future e-government in a citizen-centric way.

Unfortunately, as we have seen above, we are lacking the required empirical data to be able to address these questions properly at present. This would require a profound empirical study of the nature of change in relationships between government and citizen as a result of e-government implementation.[20] Consequently, at this stage we will make use of available data on general trends in citizen-centred e-government development, while putting these trends into an historical context – as the vast literature on citizenship development has taught us. In doing so, we would like to explore in what way governments have been trying to relate to their citizens in e-government relationships and, with that, to what extent the traditional notions of citizenship underpinning the paper-based public service system can be recognised in the emerging digital public service arena after more than a decade of e-government evolution.

A decade of e-government policy strategies and putting citizens first

In the evolution of e-government policy design we may observe that the e-government domain has gradually been broadened in several ways. Firstly, from an exclusive focus on public service provision, governments have widened their perspective on e-government to include all primary processes of government (agenda setting, policy development, policy evaluation, and so on). Secondly, governments have been including different citizen roles in their e-government designs after an exclusive focus on the customer role of the citizen. Thirdly, governments have gradually been recognising the value of (new) information sources deriving from the citizen to improve e-government design and better meet e-government policy ambitions. In the following sections we will take a more detailed look at how citizen-centred e-government evolved over time. Broadly, we can distinguish four major trends where in each case the citizen has been differently addressed.

Treat government as a business: the citizen as a customer

'Today, information technology can create the government of the future, the electronic government. Electronic government overcomes the barriers of time and distance to perform the business of government and give people public information and services when and where they want them.'[21] One of the first visions on what electronic government might be can be found in a 1993 US Federal Government policy document called 'Re-engineering Through Information Technology'. At that time, then US Vice President Al Gore instigated the National Performance Review, an extensive review of the US federal government's functions and performance that resulted in an agenda to create a more effective and efficient government. ICTs were acknowledged as important tools for changing the structure and functioning of government more towards the needs and desires of citizens.[22] Moreover, this early perspective on e-government reveals the e-commerce analogy of e-government in that period.[23] Similar to online commercial services, public service customers could have 24/7 online access to public services provided by a seamless government instead of a range of stove-pipe organisations, which obviously would contribute to the citizen's 'customer experience' of government.

This early e-government thinking matches the ideology of the influential New Public Management (NPM) reform movement in public administration of the 1980s and 1990s. According to NPM ideologists, government needed to be reshaped in order to function better in modern times. An important change in perspective for governments has been the introduction of a service orientation: government needed to better connect with its citizens and become more responsive to societal developments by improving access and use of public services.[24] For example, a major trend in early e-government was aimed at creating improved access to public services for the citizen. In many cases single points of access to electronic public services were created. These so-called 'one-stop shops' offered governments the possibility to present themselves in an integrated way to the citizen, overcoming the dominant silo-structure of government and therefore better fitting the acknowledged citizen's perception of government. A further improvement of access to public service provision was offered by governments with the introduction of integrated online service provision organised around 'life events' of the citizen, in essence a rearrangement of public services into categories of situations that citizens would need at various points in their lives.[25] Other alternatives to improve access to public services from a user-centred perspective were to offer public services through a variety of service 'channels': offering the customer a choice in doing business with government, and to offer public services directly to the citizen in an automatic way, that is to say without any 'offline' interaction between government and the citizen – also called 'no-stop shopping'.[26]

Balancing e-government: the citizen as a democratic participant

During the development of e-government projects around the world several authors concluded that in many cases a narrow definition of e-government was used, limiting the meaning of the concept to the provision of electronic public services.[27] More and more, a wider understanding of the concept of e-government has become broadly accepted. For example, in 2002, the German Bertelsmann Foundation published a report on what they called 'balanced e-government', a combination of electronic information-based services for citizens with the reinforcement of participatory elements.[28] In 2003, in a communication on the role of e-government for Europe's future, the European Commission emphasised that the introduction of ICTs in public service provision to the citizen would not automatically lead to e-government. From the point of view of the European Commission, e-government could improve user-centric public service provision, democratic participation and transparency, and policy making, if ICT-implementation was met by a vision of organisational change and new skills.[29]

In addition, others have pointed at the need to use a wider perspective on e-government that would be more in keeping with a citizen's perspective of the full range of government's tasks and activities – not restricted to public service provision but including democratic participatory tasks and activities.[30] Opportunities for citizen-centred e-government were perceived in situations where governments and citizens were not opposite each other, 'us-versus-them', but where partnerships would be built between government and citizens.[31] The later emergence of a wider perspective on e-government can be further explained by the fact that initially, governments made an explicit distinction between policy in the field of public service provision ('e-government') and policy to stimulate online democratic participation of citizens ('e-democracy'). Moreover, the narrow focus on public service provision in the early days of e-government could be further explained by the fact that political attention, money and efforts were mainly available for the realisation of electronic public service delivery to citizens and businesses.[32]

More productive e-government: the citizen as a democratic supervisor of the state

Efficiency gains and the business case for e-government have increasingly received close attention from politicians and policy makers (see for example the UK Efficiency Review).[33] Service and process integration among government agencies not only warrant seamless public service provision, but also substantial cost reductions for both government and the citizen. For government, e-government could achieve economies of scale and reduce duplication of services or processes.[34] And for the citizen too, e-government could decrease duplication of processes (for example form filling, supplying personal data). As an example, a recently adopted e-government policy strategy is to look for possibilities to achieve a reduction of the administrative burden upon a citizen by means of citizen-centred e-government (for example, EU

Ministerial eGovernment Declaration, 2005). Increased standards for the effectiveness of electronic public service provision to the citizen and for the internal efficiency of the public organisation concerned have become important renewed policy ambitions of e-government programmes around the world. Consequently, governments use ICTs for automation, collaboration and integration of both their internal and external operations to be able to create value for money for the taxpayer. As an example, back-office integration, faster turnaround of public service delivery, and more recently the introduction of shared services can be mentioned in this respect, but also the development towards more online 'self-service' counters for the citizen.[35] Increasingly, the impact of e-government projects is being evaluated and monitored, both from a government and a user-perspective.

Moreover, online public service integration may contribute to increased transparency for the citizen (for example, EU Ministerial eGovernment Declaration, 2005). As a result of their NPM reform ambitions, governments have sought to focus on output and outcomes to improve their ability to deliver what they promise.[36] Online availability of comparable outputs of a specific government service (for example primary education, health) can offer citizens better insight in the performance of government. This situation makes it easier for citizens to 'vote with their feet' and therefore be better able to hold government accountable for its performance. Governments themselves may actively seek to improve transparency and accountability to the citizen through their e-government policies,[37] or citizens may actively look for public information available online to be able to make comparisons and assessments on government's performance in a simple way (for example rankings of public schools, waiting lists in health care).

Next generation e-government: the citizen becoming a unique customer

E-government definitely seems to have reached a new development stage as the November 2005 EU Ministerial e-government declaration may show us: 'as our e-government services become more transactional, the need for secure electronic means of identification for use by people accessing public services is essential for citizen trust and in ensuring the effectiveness and efficiency of our public administrations.'[38] Governments around the world are introducing, managing and using digitised personal identification and authentication systems in addition to, and increasingly in replacement of, traditional paper-based forms of personal identification and authentication. Authentication, or the assurance that a person is who [s]he says [s]he is, is generally acknowledged as an essential requirement for the provision of many government services to citizens. Digitised personal identification and authentication systems thereby become the essential condition of successful e-government.[39] Emerging within the digital era are three main ways of identifying a person operating within an electronic environment: accepting a self-declared statement of identity that draws upon details known by that person about who they are (for example a username, registration number, address details, password, PIN); accepting an item of identity the person physically possesses (for example a smartcard, electronic tag, mobile phone); and scrutinising aspects of the physiological identity of the person (for example fingerprint, iris, face, DNA). Moreover these means of identification can be used in combination, as an affirmation of identity and as a step towards authentication of that identity (for example showing a credit card and supporting it with a PIN).

With the increasing use of these new forms of personal identification and authentication we can observe new types of 'personal data' being involved in citizen–government service relationships. In abstract, these new types of personal data can be perceived in concentric circles at varying distances from the individual's core identity.[40] The outermost circle is that of individual information which includes any data that can be linked to a person, for example a licence plate, email-address or click behaviour on the Internet; the inner-most circle represents the individual's core identity based on biological ancestry and family relations. Inbetween are concentric circles of private, intimate and sensitive information, followed by unique identification. Moreover, in the emerging electronic public service environment we recognise the multiple relationships that the citizen is developing with government agencies, each supported by an assembled form of a citizen's personal data.[41] For example, the citizen has an Inland Revenue taxpayers identity, a Health Service patient identity, a Social Security identity as a contributor and claimant within the system, a driver's identity, and a resident identity within a public housing scheme. Traditionally, a separate citizen's identity profile was constructed, managed and used for each of these relationships. In the current digital environment it has become much easier in principle to create and manage an integrated identity profile on the citizen, for example through the use of a unique number (such as a social security number), or for the citizen to make use of a singular personal identification and authentication system to access a variety of government services.

Combinations of different types of personal data are at the basis of new forms of e-government service provision. Examples of these new forms are personalised public service provision and Customer Relationship Management (CRM). Within these new forms of public service provision we may observe new and more complex ways of categorising, segmenting and grouping citizens that enable different modes, levels and paces of service provision to be implemented. For example, both CRM and personalisation have been introduced into business settings in ways that lead to the segmentation and classification of consumer groups so as to allow for the building of models designed to predict consumer behaviour.[42] These models enable the profiling of individual consumers, the aggregation of those consumers into designated 'consumer types' and their targeting for the marketing of goods and services. Moreover, CRM focuses upon the achievement of a longer-term relationship between businesses and consumers, leading to a situation where information captured on actual or potential customers may have value over a considerable period of time.

Where CRM is now being extensively incorporated into e-government practices in the UK, personalisation has still only been introduced in a few cases of e-government service provision around the world. Political leaders in the UK, however, have come to see personalisation as a strong citizen-supportive organisation model for public service provision, providing citizens with 'more power, more information, more choice and more convenience' as well as being a 'route to addressing the disadvantages' of some social categories.[43] For Gordon Brown, Chancellor of the Exchequer, personalisation can correct 'information asymmetries' between service producer and consumer.[44] Political leaders are thus offering a vision that is inspired by the success of well-known 'dotcom' businesses such as Amazon.com, Yahoo!, and eBay. These companies have clearly demonstrated that they are able to deliver online customer-centric services through their ability to accumulate information on customers' browsing and buying habits and their tastes and preferences. The overt capture of transaction data, together with more or less covert data delivered by 'cookies' and click behaviour, for example, enables these companies to build customer profiles, both at aggregate and personal levels, and to apply new methods of 'collaborative' and 'content filtering' to determine personalised services for each individual customer.[45]

Changing conceptions of citizenship in developing e-government

Looking at these e-government developments and comparing them with the traditional paper-based public service system and its underlying citizenship conceptions, several important changes may be perceived.

For example, in this e-government evolution we can recognise a gradual shift from 'universalism' to what may be called 'particularism' as an underlying conception of citizenship in an e-government service environment. This development particularly manifests itself when the citizen is becoming a unique customer of government. An individual citizen who, due to good behaviour in using public services, receives loyalty points on his smart card for spending on public service cost reductions, or a citizen paying for an online public service transaction whereas under the paper-based public service system this transaction would have been free, are practical examples of an increasingly particularistic understanding of citizenship, moving away from, for example, universal access rights or democratic participation rights to more individually-based public service arrangements between a citizen and government. Interestingly, at the same time we can observe a gradual assimilation of different types of citizenship, or universal citizen entitlements, under the flag of e-government. Starting from the narrow perception of social citizenship at the basis of early e-government design, namely the introduction of a universal, customer approach of the citizen in electronic public service provision, the conception of citizenship progressively has evolved back in the direction of its traditional meaning by including political citizenship as a basic notion for e-government design.

Another important change we may observe is the shift from an egalitarian membership status as a citizen to citizen segmentation. Again, this development becomes apparent when looking at the latest e-government policy strategies but can also be recognised in strategies focused at achieving a more productive and transparent e-government. Unique treatment on the basis of a citizen's individual preferences or online behaviour and administrative sorting into 'trust profiles' of citizens for establishing conditional online access to public services are two practical examples of a more differentiating conception of citizenship compared to the traditional administrative equity principle. Remarkable in this respect is that the digital equivalent of citizens' filed records, which have been used under the paper-based service system to guarantee this administrative principle of 'equality under the law', are used more and more to deliver differentiated, tailor-made public services to individual citizens.

A citizenship conception that has not changed much so far, after a decade of e-government development, is that nation states are still those government organisations which define the concept of citizenship. Looking at the evolution of e-government so far, it becomes more and more questionable whether this situation can be maintained in the future. For example, civil citizenship entitlements defined for the offline world, and applicable within clear national geographical boundaries, will be difficult to preserve in the borderless virtual territory of many e-government projects. Similarly, political and social citizenship may not be tied in with nationality, and the legal status derived from that, in future e-government relationships between citizens and governments. Where traditional citizenship attribution in the offline world is usually based on geographical territory, *ius soli* ('law of the soil'), or blood ties, *ius sanguinis* ('law of the blood'), citizenship attribution in the online world appears to be taking place on the basis of an evolving 'law of informational identity', *ius informationis*.[46] Borders for access to e-government services will then be set between, for example, customers and non-customers of government organisations; identified or non-identified democratic participants; authenticated citizens or non-authenticated citizens. Moreover, analogous to the former Prussian Kingdom where intermediaries such as landowners, innkeepers and cart-drivers supported the government in the checking and validation of a person's identity, new trusted third parties, such as banks, ICT companies or credit reference agencies, are emerging in the e-government domain to help government to check people on their trustworthiness first before getting access to government services.

History has shown us that conceptions of citizenship are dynamic, and that usually these dynamics are initiated by major societal 'crises', such as wars or the revolution. The emergence of e-government may not be a natural evolution of existing public sector structures and processes as well.[47] Recent societal crises, such as the September 11th attacks on the US, may shake the institutional settings of citizen–government relationships in a way that new conceptions of citizenship emerge. We may, for example, observe that government is becoming freer in its use of information on the citizen as it seeks to respond both to the demands imposed by CRM and the demands for enhanced citizen safety and state security.[48] It again proves the importance of profound empirical studies to the nature of change in relationships between citizens and government, with and without the prefix 'e', and the ways in which conceptions of citizenship evolve.

Notes

1 Taylor, J.A. (2006) 'Citizen-centric E-government: a contradiction in terms?' in Halpin, E., Griffin, D. and Trevorrow, P. (eds) *The E-government Reader: The Impact of Electronic Public Administration; Theory and Practice.* Palgrave: Basingstoke, UK.
2 OECD (2005) *E-government for Better Government.* OECD E-government Studies, OECD: Paris; p. 42.
3 EU Ministerial Declaration on E-government 2005. Manchester, Ministerial eGovernment Conference, 24 November 2005, Transforming Public Services; p. 2. Available at www.egov2005conference.gov.uk/documents/proceedings/pdf/051124declaration.pdf
4 See for example: Bekkers, V.J.J.M., van Duivenboden, H.P.M. and Lips, A.M.B. (2005) 'Van e-government naar e-governance' in: Lips, A.M.B., Bekkers, V.J.J.M. and Zuurmond, A. (eds) *ICT en openbaar bestuur. Implicaties en uitdagingen van technologische toepassingen voor de overheid.* Uitgeverij Lemma: Utrecht; pp. 419–440. See also: Prins, J.E.J. (ed) (2001) *Designing E-government. On the Crossroads of Technological Innovation and Institutional Change.* Kluwer Law International: The Hague.
5 Leitner, C. (2003) *eGovernment in Europe: The State of Affairs.* EIPA: The Netherlands.
6 Heather, D. (2004) *Citizenship. The civic ideal in world history, politics and education.* Manchester University Press: Manchester, UK.
7 Smith, P.J., and Smythe, E. (2000) *Globalization, Citizenship and Technology: The MAI Meets the Internet.* Working paper presented at the International Studies Association 41st Annual Convention, Los Angeles, CA, March 14–18 2000. Available at www.ciaonet.org/isa/smp01/
8 Heather, D. (2004) *Citizenship.*
9 Marshall, T.H. (1964) *Citizenship and Social Class. Class, Citizenship and Social Development.* Doubleday: New York. See also: Bovens, M.A.P. (2005) 'De digitale rechtsstaat' in Lips, A.M.B., Bekkers, V.J.J.M. and Zuurmond, A. (eds) *ICT en openbaar bestuur. Implicaties en uitdagingen van technologische toepassingen voor de overheid,* Uitgeverij Lemma: Utrecht; pp. 583–602.
10 Taylor, J.A., Lips, A.M.B. and Organ, J. (2006) 'Freedom with Information: Electronic Government, Information Intensity and Challenges to Citizenship' in Chapman, R.A. and Hunt, R. (eds.) *Freedom of Information: perspectives on open government in a theoretical and practical context.* Ashgate, in press.
11 See for example: OECD (2003) *The E-government Imperative: Main Findings,* OECD Policy Brief, OECD: Paris. See also: Accenture (2003) *E-government Leadership: Engaging the Customer,* Accenture.
12 Lips, A.M.B., Nouwt, J., Gosh, R. and Glott, R. (2002) *Roadmap for Socio-Cultural and Economic Research in Privacy and Identity Management,* European FP5-project Roadmap for Advanced Research in Privacy and Identity Management (RAPID), European Commission. See also: van Duivenboden, H.P.M. and Lips, A.M.B. (2003) 'Taking Citizens Seriously. Applying Hirschman's Model to Various Practices of Customer-Oriented E-governance' in A. Salminen (ed) *Governing Networks,* EGPA Yearbook, IOS Press: Amsterdam; pp. 209–226.
13 Bongers, F.J., Holland, C.A. and Bilderbeek, R.H. (2002) 'E-government: de vraagkant aan bod' in *Openbaar Bestuur,* No. 3; 25–31.
14 See for example: eEurope, *Top of the Web. User Satisfaction and Usage Survey of eGovernment Services* (2004) European Commission: Brussels. Available at: europa.eu.int/information_society/activities/egovernment_research/doc/top_of_the_web_report_2004.pdf
15 eEurope, *Top of the Web.* (2004) . See also: eUser Population Survey (2005) available at: www.euser-eu.org/eUSER_PopulationSurveyStatistics.asp?KeyWordsID=1&MenuID= 78. Also: Dutton, W.H., di Gennaro, C. and Millwood Hargrave, A. (2005)*The Internet in*

Britain: *The Oxford Internet Survey (OxIS)*, Oxford Internet Institute, University of Oxford: Oxford, UK.
16 Horrigan, J. (2004) *How Americans get in touch with government*, May 2004. Pew Internet & American Life Project. Available at www.pewInternet.org/pdfs/PIP_e-Gov_Report_0504.pdf
17 eUser Population Survey (2005).
18 eUser Population Survey (2005).
19 Taylor, J.A., Lips, A.M.B. and Organ, J. (2006) 'Freedom with Information'.
20 An empirical study in this area is presently being conducted at the Oxford Internet Institute, University of Oxford: ESRC e-Society Project: Personal Identification and Identity Management in New Modes of E-government. Ref.: RES-341-25-0028
21 US Federal Government (1993) *Reengineering Through Information Technology*, National Performance Review; p. 4.
22 Lips, A.M.B. and Frissen, P.H.A. (1997) *Wiring Government. Integrated Public Service Delivery through ICT in the UK and the USA*, NWO/ITeR-series, volume 8, Samsom Bedrijfs-Informatie bv: Alphen aan den Rijn/Diegem; pp. 67–164.
23 See for example: Hagen, M. and Kubicek, H. (eds) (2000) *One-Stop-Government in Europe. Results from 11 National Surveys*, University of Bremen: Bremen, Germany.
24 Bellamy, C. and Taylor, J.A. (1998), *Governing in the Information Age*, Open University Press.
25 See for example: Bhatnagar, S. (2004) *E-government. From Vision to Implementation. A practical guide with case studies*, Sage Publications: London.
26 Bekkers, V.J.J.M. (2001) 'De strategische positionering van e-government', in van Duivenboden, H.P.M. and Lips, A.B.M. (eds) *Klantgericht werken in de publieke sector. Inrichting van de elektronische overheid*. Lemma: Utrecht, the Netherlands.
27 See for example: Office of the e-Envoy (2001) *Benchmarking Electronic Service Delivery*, London. See also: European Commission (2003) *The Role of eGovernment for Europe's Future*, 26 September 2003. Communication from the Commission to the Council, the European Parliament, the European Economic and Social Committee and the Committee of the Regions, COM (2003) 567 final: Brussels. Also: Leitner, C. (2003) *eGovernment in Europe*.
28 Bertelsmann Foundation (2002) *Balanced E-government – Connecting Efficient Administration and Responsive Democracy*. The Bertelsmann Foundation: Gütersloh; p. 4.
29 European Commission (2003) *The Role of eGovernment for Europe's Future*.
30 See for example: Leitner, C. (2003) *eGovernment in Europe*. OECD (2005) E-government for Better Government. Grönlund, A. (2003) 'Emerging Electronic Infrastructures. Exploring Democratic Components' in *Social Science Computer Review*, Vol. 21, No. 1, Spring 2003: 55–72.
31 Silcock, R. (2001) 'What is E-government?' in *Parliamentary Affairs*, Vol. 54: 88–101.
32 Perri 6 (2001) 'E-governance. Do Digital Aids Make a Difference in Policy Making?' in J.E.J. Prins (ed), *Designing E-government. On the Crossroads of Technological Innovation and Institutional Change*. Kluwer Law International: The Hague, Belgium.
33 Gershon, P. (2004) *Releasing Resources to the Front-line: Independent Review of Public Sector Efficiency*. HM Treasury: London. See also: OECD (2005) E-government for Better Government.
34 Gershon, P. (2004) *Releasing Resources to the Front-line*.
35 See for example: Grönlund, A. (2003) 'Emerging Electronic Infrastructures. Exploring Democratic Components'.
36 Kettl, D.F. (2000) *The Global Public Management Revolution. A Report on the Transformation of Governance*. Brookings Institution Press.
37 See for example: European Commission (2003) *The Role of eGovernment for Europe's Future*.
38 EU Ministerial Declaration on E-government (2005).
39 Lips, A.M.B., Taylor, J.A. and Organ, J. (2006) 'Identity Management as Public Innovation: Looking Beyond ID Cards and Authentication systems' in Bekkers, V.J.J.M.,

    van Duivenboden, H.P.M. and Thaens, M. (eds) *ICT and Public Innovation: assessing the modernisation of public administration.* IOS Press: Amsterdam.
40 Marx, G.T. (2003) *Varieties of Personal Information as Influences on Attitudes Toward Surveillance.* Paper prepared for a Conference on 'The New Politics of Surveillance and Visibility', available at web.mit.edu/gtmarx/www/vancouver.html
41 Fishenden, J. (2005) *eID: Identity Management in an On-line World.* June 2005, paper presented at the 5th European Conference on E-government, Antwerpen: Belgium.
42 Gandy, O. (2000) 'Exploring Identity and Identification in Cyberspace', *Notre Dame Journal of Law, Ethics and Public Policy*, Vol. 14, Part 2: 1085–1111.
43 Reid, J. (2004) *Providing a Faster, Better NHS.* Speech to the Labour Party Conference, Brighton, UK, 29 September.
44 Brown, G. (2004) Speech by the UK Chancellor of the Exchequer to the Social Market Foundation, 18th May 2004.
45 Lips, A.M.B., S. van der Hof, S., Prins, J.E.J. and Schudelaro, A.A.P. (2005) *Issues of On-Line Personalization in Commercial and Public Service Delivery.* Wolf Legal Publishers: Nijmegen, the Netherlands.
46 Lips, A.M.B., Taylor, J.A. and Organ, J. (2006) 'Identity Management as Public Innovation'.
47 Roy, J. (2003) 'E-government', in *Social Science Computer Review*, Vol.21, No.1, Spring 2003: 3–5.
48 Taylor, J.A., Lips, A.M.B. and Organ, J. (2006) 'Freedom with Information'.

4 Danger mouse?

The growing threat of cyberterrorism

Rajash Rawal

Introduction

The September 11th attacks were 'textbook acts of symbolic terror'.[1] They were carefully choreographed to achieve the maximum visual effect and 'total' response from their target. Following on from these attacks, the President of the United States of America declared a, so-called, 'War on Terror'. This is a war that is presented as being very different to any other war that has ever been waged before. Moreover, as noted by Matai[2] this war is 'asymmetric' – unlike traditional symmetric warfare that focuses on nation-to-nation combat. Indeed, it can further be suggested that this asymmetric war is somewhat veiled and camouflaged making it extremely difficult to ascertain as and when, or indeed if any, progress is made. This vagueness has been grasped by both governments and terrorists and used to their advantage.

One aspect which has come under increasing scrutiny is the role the Internet plays in this 'war on terror'. Longstanding criticisms of the Internet, such as its openness and the lack of a regulatory power,[3] have been vented with renewed vigour. Governments have readily highlighted that terrorists have been quick to utilise the potential that the cyberworld has to offer them to deliver their messages, communicate with each other, and retain their anonymity.[4] Scott and Street[5] further argue that the Internet has presented the opportunity for groups to plot in secret and 'bypass' nation state mechanisms. Terms first coined in the late eighties, such as 'cyberterrorism', have become fashionable, whilst governments have ensured that scaremongering tactics have helped to fuel the doubters and fill the media.

It is the intention of this chapter to examine the developments in Europe by looking at what the actual threats of cyberterrorism are, and what threats are posed by the use of the Internet by terrorists. The chapter will challenge the notion that September 11th actually *changed* anything, and examine whether contemporary developments in terrorists' use of cyberspace have continued in a similar vein to that of prior to September 11th. It will also analyse the trends in government measures to attempt to control hyperspace, question the nature of these measures, and present how these measures threaten e-democracy whilst at the same time highlighting the need for legitimate e-identity mechanisms to be created. Finally, it will endeavour to present a conclusion as to whether (or not) cyberterrorism is a real and actual threat to modern society.

Context

As suggested above, governments and media alike have been very keen to present the threat of cyberterrorism and the use of the Internet by terrorists as being very grave and real.[6] Indeed, the lack of a regulatory power for the Internet has been a topic of much discussion for sometime now.[7] Due to this lack of a regulatory power, government is on the back foot and can merely react; it is unable to act proactively.[8] The scenario of doom and gloom is only alleviated by the somewhat strange hope, given the ideas stated above, that the terrorists will be stopped. However, there are potent questions to be asked at this juncture, such as 'what evidence is there of any cyberterrorist attacks?' and 'is it really true that little can be done to limit the terrorists who use the Internet?'

These are questions which this chapter will endeavour to answer in more detail, however, it is interesting to note at this point that a strange anomaly occurs when trying to look for examples of cyberterrorist attacks. For example, Matai[9] suggests that the power outages across North East America that affected cities such as New York, Detroit and Toronto in August 2003 were caused by the MSIBlast worm which created a digital traffic jam. This in turn overloaded US power stations and led to the collapse of electric power on a scale never seen before. The UK, Sweden, Denmark, Italy and Switzerland[10] suffered power outages around this time too. The US government investigations suggested that whilst the outage was rare, no foul play was suspected. This is rather strange considering we are warned of the threats of a cyberterrorist attack, but yet when one allegedly takes place it is dismissed as an unfortunate accident. A reason for this perhaps being that such an attack taking place successfully would further undermine the notion of national security that is held so dearly by governments around the world. Moreover, it would challenge the argument to move to e-government systems as surely these large databases would be lucrative targets for the cyberterrorist.

However, there is clearly a divide between the threat cyberterrorism poses and those presented by the use of the Internet by terrorists. It is these differences which we will now examine.

'Cyberterrorism' vs. terrorist 'use' of the internet

As is the case with traditional terrorism, finding an adequate, mutually acceptable definition is a very difficult task. Cyberterrorism, a term first coined by Barry Collin in the 1980s,[11] is a wide reaching concept which has no single, universally accepted definition. Crudely put, it is considered that cyberterrorism consist of acts of terror which take place in 'cyberspace'; it is worth noting it is not the same as 'cybercrime', as it must have strong 'terrorist elements'. Terrorist attacks must seek to instil terror and fear and additionally they must have a political motivation, whereas cybercrime does not. Painter adds the notion of 'cyberactivism' to the fray which can be easily confused with cyberterrorism by the authorities. The May Day riots of 2000 and the anti-globalisation protests of 2001 were all partially organised online, with websites being created to imform activists of their 'legal' rights and to give phone numbers of sympathetic lawyers.[12]

However, Denning argues that 'Cyberterrorism exists only in theory'[13] while 'cybercrime' and 'cyberactivism' are real. The following definition can be put forward:

> Cyberterrorism is the convergence of cyberspace and terrorism. It refers to unlawful attacks and threats of attacks against computers, networks and the information stored therein when done to intimidate or coerce a government or its people in furtherance of political or social objectives. Further, to qualify as cyberterrorism, an attack should result in violence against property or persons, or at least cause enough harm to generate fear.[14]

This definition implies a very 'involved' element to the concept of cyberterrorism. Potential examples of cyberterror include spreading virus, spamming (a 23 year old was jailed in the UK for 'anarchic behaviour' after spreading abusive spam emails threatening to fire-bomb the headquarters of his county's trading standards office and petrol-bomb his local police office),[15] digital jamming and hacking (the Israelis and Palestinians engaged in a Cyber War between 2000 and 2002, where each party attacked the other's web resources).[16] Aggressive campaigns fought out on the Internet, or so called 'NGO-swarms'[17] have also been identified by the American military think-tank RAND as potential forms of cyberterrorism. Additionally, in the aftermath of the riots that swept French cities in the autumn of 2005, French authorities jailed two bloggers for inciting violence.[18] However, it is questionable as to whether the latter can be considered to be an act of cyberterror or terrorist use of the Internet, as shall be illustrated later in the chapter. The authorities will often confuse protest and terror, which will allow them to classify protest as terror to meet their own political needs. However, it can be argued that the standard definition of cyberterrorism as quoted above is not one that the wider public would adhere to. They view cyberterrorism as the use of the Internet by terrorist groups to propagate their message. This view is further endorsed by the popular media,[19] who as 'conduits for symbolism'[20] have become enmeshed in the symbolic war against terror where fear becomes the main element.

'In newspapers and magazines, in film and on television, "cyberterrorism" is the zeitgeist'.[21] Moreover, Lanzone[22] adds a special new 'war on terror' element to cyberterrorism that he phrases as 'cyberjihad'. In addition to this, Weimann[23] identifies that terrorism on the Internet is a very dynamic phenomenon. However, what exactly does this involve? What is cyberterrorism and how do terrorists use the Internet?

Why terrorists use the internet

Considering Webster's assertion that ICTs have had a 'massive and ongoing' impact on society,[24] it is natural, as Knight and Ubayasiri suggest, that terrorist groups have 'embraced the Internet'[25] and have challenged the existing balances on information flow and news coverage. This point is further emphasised by Scott and Street,[26] who suggest that the Internet has shifted 'editorial' control to activists which allows them to present news and opinion as they would like to. As a result, terrorist use of the Internet is very active; websites will appear, change format, and disappear, or simply change their addresses.[27] This is a normal progression in regard to the development of protest politics; as noted by Dahlgrenas cyberspace has become a 'vital link and meeting ground for the civically engaged and politically mobilised'.[28] Weimann further expounds the idea that terrorists are drawn to the web to target three main audience categories:

- *Supporters.* Terrorist websites will keep supporters informed of their (recent) activities. Merchandise can be sold to help raise funds, and organisations will 'localise' their site in order to provide more detailed information; often this is done in minority languages. Al Qaeda is one such group who employ this tactic.
- *Public opinion.* Even those who are not directly involved maybe affected. Most sites offer information in a number of languages in order to draw as wide an audience as possible. ETA, the Basque Separatist Group, for example, has pages in Basque, Castilian, German, French and Italian. The main premise of this is perhaps to capture international journalists' attention and hence get the organisation into the traditional media. One of the Hezbollah's websites is aimed exclusively at journalists, inviting them to email the group's press office.
- *Enemy publics.* This is one of the less obvious targets, but an equally important one. Sites will aim to promote the past activities of the terrorist group and threaten more, wider and dangerous campaigns. The idea is to try to demoralise the enemy. This in turn gathers media attention and begins debate and may weaken the governments' rule, which is the ultimate aim of most groups. An example of this is the March 11 2003 bombings in Madrid. The ruling Peoples' Party maintained through the state rule news agency EFE that ETA were behind the attacks, however, various wings of Al Qaeda began to spread news via the web that it was they who were responsible. The commercial, non-state-run, media began to publish this, and the citizenry began to doubt the government. This culminated in the ruling party being ousted in the March 13th election in favour of the Socialist Party.

Attractions of cyberspace

The Internet has been heralded as being the integrator of cultures;[29] it has also been the 'instrument of a political power shift'.[30] As one of the first many-to-many broadcasting systems as opposed to the one-to-many systems it has opened up numerous possibilities for groups of activists to freely air their views and opinions.[31] It has become a medium in which businesses, consumers and governments communicate with each other. It is, as such, unparalleled in its creation of a truly global forum that provides for the 'virtual' existence of McLuhan's much quoted 'global village'.[32] However, as positive a development as the Internet has been, utopian visions were quickly challenged by the proliferation of sites such as those that contain (child) pornography, violence, and extremist aims.[33] That said, the Internet remains an exciting proposition as it challenges existing regimes of power and presents information and opinion in a less hieracrchical way than traditional media.[34]

The attractions the Internet holds for terrorists are numerous. It is an ideal arena for activity as it offers:[35]

- easy access;
- little, or no, regulation/government control;
- the potential of huge global audiences;
- anonymity – false identities are easy to create and use;
- speed of the flow of information;
- inexpensive to develop and maintain media;
- multimedia possibilities (websites can combine text, graphics, films and sound which can be downloaded by users);
- the ability to gather attention (mass media increasingly use the Internet as source for (potential) news stories).

With this in mind, governments have had to be imaginative and creative in their approach to combat terrorist use of the Internet. An evaluation of the mechanisms introduced and their wider implications will be put forward later in this chapter.

How do terrorists use the internet?

When considering modern, or rather post-September 11 terrorism, and the obvious difficulties the Internet has presented in policing against terrorism, there is a clear lack of an answer to the above question. To begin with, one could ask how one identifies a terrorist using a computer to further their aims. However, this remains a very difficult task to perform and has been the subject of many heated debates as *identifying* the terrorist remains a perilously difficult thing to do. Therefore, a broad brush approach is often taken by authorities who categorise all members of particular ethnic or religious groups by the actions of a few. The dangers of 'risk profiling' potential terrorist suspects are highlighted by Kip Viscusi & Zechauser,[36] and illustrated by the shooting of Jean Charles de Menezes who was wrongly identified as a terrorist suspect partially due to his appearance after the July 7th bombings in London in 2005. As a consequence, the terrorist finds it is relatively easy to use the Internet as they can be easily hidden in 'normal' society.

Terrorist websites are rife and appear in all shapes and forms. Almost all major terrorist organisations have websites; many have more than one and they appear in several languages. Terrorist organisations have embraced the Internet as a vital cog in their machinery to:[37]

- transmit propaganda on their aims and objectives;
- raise money by selling articles, merchandise or asking for donations;

- attract new members; and
- communicate with existing activists.

It must be remembered however, that although the use of the Internet as a tool may be new, terrorist groups have *always* sought to spread propaganda by whatever means possible. The appeal of the Internet is that it goes beyond the means of traditional media to 'allow for completeness of storytelling'.[38] It means that the terrorists can now bypass media controls and edit their own news agendas.

One of the earliest examples of the use of the Internet by terrorists was back in March 1996 when the 'Terrorists Handbook' was placed online. The handbook contained guidelines on how to make a bomb; the same type of bomb which was later used in the Oklahoma bombings.[39]

A further example of how terrorists can use the web aside from creating websites is by registering 'weblogs'. 'Blogging', as it is commonly referred to, offers terrorists the potential to air their views and present information in an unedited way, whilst at the same time allowing others to voice their support by joining in discussions held in the forum. It would appear that all viewpoints are available and given equal space and prominence, however, the 'owner' of the weblog can decide whose viewpoints he/she wishes to publish, hence, there is a form of editorial control, albeit in the hands of the 'terrorist blogger'. The example of the French 'bloggers' arrested on suspicion of inciting violence given earlier in this chapter[40] illustrates how seriously the French authorities considered this potential threat.

It is further argued by Weimann that terrorists seek to use the Internet to maintain their 'psychological warfare'.[41] Their websites will not only re-enact past actions but will also present more general threats aimed at illustrating to the public the potential of their reach, for example disabling air traffic, destroying computer networks, and so on. A horrific example of this was the airing of the brutal murder of the American hostage Daniel Pearl in 2004 that was posted on several terrorist websites. Groups can also spread disinformation, which exaggerates the scope of their potential attacks and can generate 'cyberfear'. Al Qaeda has been particularly successful in this, continually talking of impending attacks on the United States that has kept the nation on high alert since September 11 2001. Moreover, many terrorist organisations have created their own newsgroups to counter the power of traditional journalists.[42]

Al Qaeda has proven to be an excellent example of how a terrorist group can utilise the Internet. According to Knight and Ubaysiri, the structure of this organisation is in many ways parallel to the Internet which affords limitless possibilities for it. They are listed as follows:

- it is transitional;
- it lacks a geographic centre;
- it consists of disparate nodes or activist cells; and
- it relies on software of ideas, rather than hardware of the military, such as aeroplanes as bombs.[43]

Subsequently, we can say that Al Qaeda is 'simultaneously everywhere and nowhere'.[44] National governments often complain of the lack of wherewithal to control the net due to its borderless, translucent world; the United States government has found it tough to eliminate and negate the threat Al Qaeda poses.

Government control mechanisms

This chapter has thus far only really spoken of the measures that terrorists take in using the Internet. It has also spoken of the weakness that governments feel they have in their arsenal in being able to deal adequately with the potential threats. However, the picture of a meek, mild and limited government does not really fit the reality of things. In this section we will analyse the somewhat considerable powers that government does have, and challenge the notion the Internet is a wilderness beyond control.

Internet regulation and governance

One of the greatest myths of the Internet age is that there is no control over the Internet whatsoever. As Sunstein argues 'The Internet is hardly an anarchy or regulation free';[45] mechanisms do exist to monitor and regulate. The Internet Corporation for Assigned Names and Numbers (ICANN), based in California, has long been the main body that has regulated how Internet domain names and addressing systems function, as well as managing how email and net browsers direct their traffic. Established in 1998,[46] ICANN reports to the United States government.[47]

It is this very issue, the United States relationship with ICANN, that formed the basis of heated debate during the World Summit on the Information Society (WSIS) held in Tunis in November 2005. Nations such as Brazil, China, France, Iran and South Africa wanted a more neutral body to be created under UN auspices to oversee the net,[48] whilst others, such as the Internet think tank group 'The Internet Governance Project (IGP)' wanted greater reforms of ICANN's powers and a democratisation of its structure.[49]

A concept paper prepared by IGP identified the main criticisms of ICANN to be:[50]

- the unilateralism of the United States Government in its control and supervision of ICANN,
- dissatisfaction with ICANN's Government Advisory Committee (GAC) where governments have only advisory powers,
- that ICANN does not reflect the needs and interests of developing countries in balance to those of developed countries,
- the general feeling that ICANN lacks legitimacy.

This concept paper was mooted during WSIS in an attempt to create an agreement that would see the development of an internationally, legally recognised body to replace US government supervision, with a more mulit-lateral body similar to the International Telecommunications Union founded in 1865.[51] It was further suggested that ICANN, whilst being central to Internet governance, does not meet all of the challenges that are faced and indeed lacked transparency, accountaliblity and legitimacy itself.[52] These ideas were substantiated by the Working Group on Internet Governance (WGIG), who last met in June 2005, and presented four models for Internet Governance.[53]

However, despite these pressures for reform of ICANN, the outcome of WSIS resulted in little change to the current situation. ICANN remains in the hands of the United States, although an agreement was reached to set up an Internet Governance Forum (IGF) which will convene in 2006 under the guidance of the United Nations Secretary General.[54] Kawamoto argues[55] we should seek to create a body that satisfactorily regulates the Internet and points to the role of the UN, a key international body in the past, when looking to form a global consensus. These experiences should not be lost and the UN should have a major role in his opinion. The IGF has a tough task ahead of it.

In addition to the ICANN provisions, however, there are other ways in which the Internet is regulated. The Security Intelligence Products and Systems (SIPS) framework has been in operation since 1995. It forms part of the British based 'mi2g Intelligence unit' and boasts 'the world's largest digital attack database'.[56] SIPS contains information on all major hacking groups, Internet malware attackers (saboteurs), and has relationships with virtually all global actors in order to maintain a peerless status in holding confidential information with regard to digital risk.[57]

A secondary wing of the above-mentioned intelligence unit is the Asymmetric Threats Contingency Unit (ACTA), which was initiated post-September 11th. ACTA monitors activities throughout the world focussing on terrorist and organised crime cartels.[58] ACTA draws up a thorough database of potential threats by compiling monthly reports of posting of information gathered through monitoring of terrorist groups' websites and intercepted communication of terrorist organisations.

Control of internet users

If it is considered to be important that cyberspace is regulated, then it may be suggested that it is of equal importance to monitor the users that surf the World Wide Web. A simple reason for this is highlighted by the fact that the hijackers on September 11th booked at least nine of their airline tickets online a few weeks prior to the attacks.[59] It is further suggested that the hijackers set up a number of 'largely anonymous ... temporary (email) accounts',[60] such as Hotmail, and accessed the web from public places such as libraries. Notably, these are all actions which are perfectly legal.

In order to combat this element of 'web abuse', authorities are beginning to introduce a number of new measures. One such example is in Italy, where new anti-terror laws will affect how people can access the internet in public places. Celeste[61] suggests that these new laws are part of the most extensive anti-terror packages introduced in Europe. Whilst encompassing more than Internet use, these laws now require people who wish to use the Internet in public places such as libraries or Internet cafés to submit a photocopy of their passport before being allowed to log on. Moreover, Internet cafés have to obtain public communications business licenses and install expensive tracking software, or so called 'eavesdropping technology',[62] costing up to US $1,400.[63]

Additionally the European Union has introduced a directive that will allow police authorities to access user 'traffic data'.[64] The directive, which must be introduced in every member state of the European Union before July 2007, compels every telephone company and Internet Service Provider (ISP) to save telephone call and Internet records for up to two years. The ISP data is comprehensive and includes websites visited and header information of email correspondence detailing the sender, recipient, date, time and internet address.[65] Whereas law enforcement agencies have welcomed the new legislation, privacy advocates fear for the wider implications. The prospect Gibb presents[66] of our communication tools forming part of the largest surveillance system ever created in the near future, surely causes reason to worry.

A threat to cyber freedom?

The 'War on Terror' and its ensuing implications on society have left many spectators lamenting the 'abuses' of privacy and freedoms that governments can now legitimately undertake. Indeed, as noted by 'Reporters Without Borders' in 2002 many governments have used the anti-terror drive as an excuse to curb freedoms and limit the use of the Internet by domestic opponents.[67] These initiatives, which have introduced surveillance and removed the protection of privacy, may threaten the healthy existence of democracy.[68] The benefits of e-government in making society more open and democratic may be undone by e-policing and e-control.

The dynamics at play here bring together the divergent needs of government and society. On the one hand, as mentioned earlier in the paper, the Internet has enabled society to freely express its opinions at a global level. Borders have been surpassed and in some cases rendered irrelevant. However, as positive an element for society as this may have been, it has also triggered a need for governments to adjust antiquated laws and regulations which the existence of the Internet has challenged. For example, it is illegal to own a copy of Adolf Hitler's 'Mein Kampf' in Germany. In the pre-Internet world this was a simple policy to implement and maintain; it was not available. However, in the new 'Amazon.com' age it is easily possible to order a copy of the book online without the authorities ever knowing about it. A law change was needed.

The post-September 11th world seemed to legitimise the opportunity for governments to make these changes due to the large scale public fear that was generated by the media for potential terrorist threats, although the desire to adjust laws pre-dated September 11th; indeed, the British government has been interested in the idea of data retention since 1998[69] as had the German government.[70] However, as Loundy suggested *before* September 11th 2001, the Internet must not be made into a scapegoat ahead of other methods of communications, despite concerns over its misuse being 'legitimate'.[71] However, if there are concerns that terrorists communicate using email, why are there no such concerns that they may communicate using regular mail? It is this question which guardians of Internet privacy ask in retort to the clampdown and ultra-secure era that is dawning in the cyberworld. Indeed, as noted by Loader, the Internet has presented a 'paradigmatic change in the constellation of power relations ...'[72] between governments and individuals. This is perfectly illustrated by Williams, who argues that post September 11th the Internet became an invaluable source for 'neutral' information as the traditional media was seen as the mouthpiece of the US government.[73]

However, the opportunities to harness the new cyberworld were only fully grasped by governments post September 11th. The fear of terrorism in all its forms has become heightened since September 11th, forming part of our daily political diet; it has thus become the 'raison d'être for countless examples of political excess'.[74] Cynics have argued that there has been an overemphasis of the threats faced so that the public would accept a diminishing of rights without a public outcry. Although, as Sunstein argues, free society has always known some form of regulation.[75]

Legislation passed in the United States, Britain, France, Germany, Spain, Italy, Denmark, tied in with policy from the European Union, the Council of Europe and the G8 have all limited cyber freedoms in some way.[76] The danger of many of these law changes is, not only do they challenge personal freedoms, they also risk turning ISPs and telecommunication companies into a potential arm of the police, the upshot being governments seem to be willing to exact 'a high price in terms of liberties to the high toll of terrorism'.[77]

The risk is that society has accepted changes without much debate, whereas had changes been introduced to control more traditional media and methods of communication, discussion would have been rife.[78] The need for a legitimate form of developing e-identities has never been greater. As presented by Fishenden,[79] the need for eID to monitor online government services and online commerce now encompasses online security.

Conclusions

The so called 'zeitgeist' of cyberterrorism has reached an important juncture: governments have retaliated in their policy to counteract the growing prospective threats of cyberterror, while terrorists continue to seek a safe haven in the dark corners of cyberspace to advance their campaigns based on creating fear and panic.

However, as Matai noted 'physical terrorism and digital attacks go hand in hand',[80] thus the potential of cyberterror should not be overestimated and exaggerated. Terrorists will continue to use violence to overcome their 'invisibility'.[81] However, the 'use' of the Internet by terrorists is a far more alarming prospect and one that is tougher to combat. It is here that a delicate balance needs to be addressed; on the one hand restrictions need to be tough enough to serve as an adequate deterrent, but on the other they need to maintain the existing freedoms and allow cyber society to develop along current trends. Mechanisms to monitor public Internet access points, as in Italy, can work, but they should not burden the host (for example an Internet café) such that they are impeded by the financial capital needed to meet modern regulations, as this may only lead to closure of much-needed public access points which help address the issue of the digital divide.[82]

In our fight against modern terrorism and its role in cyberspace, a few things must be noted. September 11th has not been a watershed, it has been an excuse. The threat existed before this date and nothing since this date has heightened its potential as a threat. However, events since this date have allowed governments to implement restrictive legislation which they have wanted to introduce for some time now – the examples put forward earlier from the United Kingdom and Germany highlighting this. The simple fact remains, we need to better monitor how the internet is used and limit its capacity to be abused by net-aware terrorists. However, heavy restrictions will only hand the initiative to authoritative governments who may violate privacy, curb the free flow of information and hamper freedom of expression, ironically the very core values of the society we are claiming to be trying to protect. As noted by Moore,[83] the relationship between cyberspace and democracy is indeed a complex one, it behoves us all to protect it.

Notes

1. Louw, E. (2005) *The Media and Political Process*. Sage Publications, London; p. 241.
2. Matai, D.K. (2005) *Cyberland Security: Organised Crime, Terrorism and the Internet*. Oxford Internet Institute, University of Oxford; accessed 10/2/2005.
3. Buckler, S. and Dolowitz, D. (2005) *Politcs on the Internet*. Routledge, Abingdon, UK.
4. Knight, A. and Ubayasiri, K. (2002a) 'eTerror: Journalism and the Internet', *Ejournalism* Vol. 2, No. 1. Available at www.ejournalism.au.com/ejournalist_v2n1.htm
5. Scott, A. and Street, J. (2001) 'From media politics to e-protest?' in *Culture and Politics in the Information Age*, Webster, F. (ed). Routledge, London; pp. 32–51.
6. Conway, M. (2002) 'Reality Bites: Cyberterrorism and Terrorist 'use' of the Internet', *First Monday* Vol. 7, No. 11. Available at firstmonday.org/issues/issue7_11/conway/index/html
7. Cukier, K.N. (2005) 'Who will control the Internet? Washington battles the World', *Foreign Affairs* Vol. 84, No. 6; pp. 7–13.
8. Segoviano Monterrubio, S. (2005) 'Al Qaeda en la Red', *Papeles de Cuestiones Internacionales* Numero 89, Primavera.
9. Matai, D.K. (2005) *Cyberland Security*.
10. Matai, D.K. (2005) *Cyberland Security*, p. 5.
11. Conway, M. (2002) 'Reality Bites', p. 6.
12. Painter, A. (2001) 'The Contagious Campaign (part 2)' in *Viral Politics*, Painter, A. & Wardle, B. (eds). Politicos Publishing, London; pp. 154–167.
13. Denning quoted in Conway, M. (2002) 'Reality Bites', p. 6.
14. Denning quoted in Conway, M. (2002) 'Reality Bites'.
15. BBC News online (2005) *Spammer convicted of £1.6m scam*. BBC News, London; accessed 16/11/2005. Available at news.bbc.co.uk/go/pr/fr/-/1/hi/england/cambridgeshire/4442772.stm

16 Conway, M. (2002) 'Reality Bites'; Weimann, G (2004) *www.terror.net How Modern Terrorism Uses the Internet*. United States Institute of Peace Special Report 116, March 2004; available at http//www.usip.org
17 Rosenkrands, J. (2004) 'Politicizing Homo economicus' in *Cyberprotest – New media, citizens and social movements*, van de Donk, W., Loader, B.D., Nixon, P.G., Rucht, D. (eds). Routledge, London; pp. 57–76.
18 Plunkett, J. (2005) *French bloggers held after Paris riots*. Guardian Unlimited Special, The Guardian; available at www.guardian.co.uk
19 Weimann, G. (2004) *www.terror.net*.
20 Louw, E. (2005) *The Media and Political Process*, p. 249
21 Conway, M. (2002) 'Reality Bites', p. 2.
22 Lanzone, R. (2005) *Cyberjihad*. AuthorHouse, Indiana.
23 Weimann, G. (2004) *www.terror.net*.
24 Webster, F. (2001) 'A new politics?' in *Culture and Politics in the Information Age*, Webster, F. (ed). Routledge, London; pp. 1–13.
25 Knight, A. and Ubayasiri, K. (2002a) 'eTerror'.
26 Scott, A. and Street, J. (2001) 'From media politics to e-protest?'.
27 Weimann, G. (2004) *www.terror.net*, p. 1.
28 Dahlgren, P. (2001) 'The Transformation of Democracy?' In *New Media and Politics*, Axford, B. & Huggins, R. (eds). Sage Publications, London; pp. 64–88.
29 Weimann, G. (2004) *www.terror.net*, p. 3.
30 Conway, M. (2002) 'Reality Bites', p. 3.
31 Dahlgren, P. (2001) 'The Transformation of Democracy?'.
32 McLuhan, M. (1964) *Understanding Media – the extensions of man* (reprinted version 2002). Routledge, London.
33 Weimann, G. (2004) *www.terror.net*.
34 Stevenson, N. (2001) *The future of public media cultures* in Culture and Politics in the Information Age, Webster, F. (ed). Routledge, London; pp. 63–80.
35 Weimann, G. (2004) *www.terror.net*; Knight, A. & Ubayasiri, K. (2002b) 'Reporting online: the Internet and terrorism', *ON-LINE opinion – Australia's e-journal of social and political debate*. Available at on-lineopinion.com.au/view.asp?article = 1101
36 Kip Viscusi, W. and Zechauser, R.Z. (2003) *Sacrificing Civil Liberties to Reduce Terrorism Risks*. John F. Kennedy School of Government, Harvard University, Faculty Research Working Paper RWP03–017.
37 For an elaborative review of terrorist websites and their aims and objectives please refer to Conway (2002), Knight and Ubaysiri (2002a) and Weimann (2004).
38 Kawamoto, K. (2003) *Media and Society in the Digital Age*. Allyn & Nacon, Boston, MA; p. 36.
39 Sunstein, C. (2002) *Republic.com*. Princeton University Press, Princeton.
40 Plunkett, J. (2005) *French bloggers held after Paris riots*.
41 Weimann, G. (2004) *www.terror.net*.
42 Knight, A. and Ubayasiri, K. (2002b) 'Reporting on-line'.
43 Knight, A. and Ubayasiri, K. (2002b) 'Reporting on-line'.
44 Knight, A. and Ubayasiri, K. (2002b) 'Reporting on-line', p. 2.
45 Sunstein, C. (2002) *Republic.com*, p. 135.
46 Internet Corporation For Assigned Names and Numbers (ICANN) (2004) *Fact Sheet*. Available at www.icann.org/general/fact-sheet.html
47 BBC News online (2005) *US retains hold of the Internet*. BBC News, London, accessed 16/11/2005. Available at news.bbc.co.uk/go/pr/fr/-/hi/technology/44441544.stm
48 Cukier, K.N. (2005) 'Who will control the Internet?'; BBC News online (2005) *US retains hold of the Internet*.
49 Klein, H. and Müller, M. (2005) *What to do about ICANN: A Proposal for Structural Reform*, Concept Paper by the Internet Goverance Project, April 5, 2005. Available at www.InternetGovernance.org
50 Klein, H. and Müller, M. (2005) *What to do about ICANN*.

51 Cukier, K.N. (2005) 'Who will control the Internet?'.
52 Cukier, K.N. (2005) 'Who will control the Internet?'.
53 Report of the Working Group on Internet Governance (WGIG) (2005) Château de Bossey, June 2005, Available at www.wgig.org/
54 BBC News online (2005) *US retains hold of the Internet.*; World Summit on the Information Society (WSIS) (2005) *Tunis Agenda for the Information Society* Document: WSIS-05/TUNIS/DOC/6(Rev.1)-E. Available at www.itu.int/wsis/docs2/tunis/off/6rev1.pdf
55 Kawamoto, K. (2003) *Media and Society in the Digital Age.*
56 Matai, D.K. (2005) *Cyberland Security*, p. 1.
57 Matai, D.K. (2005) *Cyberland Security.*
58 Matai, D.K. (2005) *Cyberland Security*, p. 2.
59 Conway, M. (2002) 'Reality Bites', p. 11.
60 Conway, M. (2002) 'Reality Bites'.
61 Celeste, S. (2005) 'Want to check your e-mail in Italy? Bring your passport' *The Christian Science Monitor*, October 4 edition. Available at www.csimonitor.com/2005/1004/p07s01-woeu.html
62 Gibb, J. (2005) *Who's Watching You?* Consipracy Books, Collins and Brown, London; p. 209.
63 Celeste, S. (2005) 'Want to check your e-mail in Italy?'.
64 Grossman, W.M. (2006) *Will logging your email combat terrorism in Europe?* Guardian Unlimited Technology Section. Available from technology.guardian.co.uk/weekly/story/0,16376,1683944,00.html
65 Grossman, W.M. (2006) *Will logging your email combat terrorism in Europe?*
66 Gibb, J. (2005) *Who's Watching You?*
67 Reporters Without Borders (2002) *Anti-terrorism drive threatens Internet freedoms.* www.ThinkCentre.org, 12 September. Available from www.thinkcentre.org/article.cfm?ArticleID = 1724
68 Raab, C.D. (1997) 'Privacy, Democracy, Information' in *The Governance of Cyberspace* Loader, B.D. (ed). Routledge, London; pp 155–174.
69 Grossman, W.M. (2006) *Will logging your email combat terrorism in Europe?*
70 Gibb, J. (2005) *Who's Watching You?*
71 Loundy, D. (1995) *Constitution Protects All Modes of Speech.* Chicago Daily Law Bulletin, accessed 11/05/95; p. 6. Available from www.loundy.com/CDLB/Terrorism. html
72 Loader, B.D. (1997) 'The Governance of Cyberspace' in *The Governance of Cyberspace* Loader, B.D. (ed). Routledge, London; pp. 1–19, p. 1.
73 Williams, B.A. (2003) 'The New Media Environment, Internet Chatrooms and Public Discourse after 9/11' in *War and the Media* Thussu, D.T. & Freedman, D. (eds). Sage Publications, London; pp. 176–189.
74 Gibb, J. (2005) *Who's Watching You?* p.20.
75 Sunstein, C. (2002) *Republic.com.*
76 Reporters Without Borders (2002) *Anti-terrorism drive threatens Internet freedoms.*
77 Weimann, G. (2004) *www.terror.net*, p.12.
78 Loundy, D (1995) *Constitution Protects All Modes of Speech*; Reporters Without Borders (2002) *Anti-terrorism drive threatens Internet freedoms*; Celeste, S. (2005) 'Want to check your e-mail in Italy?'.
79 Fishenden, J. (2005) 'eID: Identity Management in an On-line World' in *Proceedings of the 5th European Conference on E-government* Remenyi, D. (ed.). University of Antwerp.
80 Matai, D.K. (2005) *Cyberland Security*, p. 3.
81 Louw, E. (2005) *The Media and Political Process.*
82 Nixon, P.G. and Rawal, R. (2005) 'From E-gov to we-Gov – Social Inclusion, Government and ICTs' in *Proceedings of the 5th European Conference on E-government* Remenyi, D. (ed.). University of Antwerp.
83 Moore, R.K. (1999) 'Democracy & Cyberspace' in *Digital Democracy* Hague, B.N. and Loader, B.D. (eds). Routledge, London; pp. 39–59.

5 E-government and the United Kingdom

Nicholas Pleace

Introduction – government in the United Kingdom

The United Kingdom (UK) is composed of four nations, England (the largest), Scotland, Wales and Northern Ireland. The three smaller nations all possess various forms of devolved elected national government, which oversee most of the domestic policy for each country including health, education, justice, rural affairs and transport. England is governed by the UK central government.

The UK legislative assembly is referred to as Parliament, with members (MPs) elected from all four nations. Effective power rests with the 'lower' house, the House of Commons. The Prime Minister and Cabinet ministers emerge from the dominant political party within the Commons.

The 'upper' house of Parliament, the House of Lords, is a non-elected assembly which has limited powers, currently undergoing extensive reform. Nominally, the UK is a monarchy though in practice the monarch only has a ceremonial role.

The UK elects 78 MEPs to the European Parliament. In common with other member states, the UK has devolved certain regulatory powers to the EU, but unlike France, Germany or Italy, the UK has not yet joined the Euro. Turnout for European elections is very low.[1]

The UK has elected local authorities. Local government is responsible for local economic growth, transport, education, social services and strategic planning for housing it also has a host of minor functions such as refuse collection and running car parks. London differs from the rest of the UK in having an elected mayor with city-wide strategic powers.

During the 1980s and 1990s, a massive shift occurred from the direct provision of public services by local and central government and towards the 'contracting out' of services. Even so, two public sector agencies interact with the public on a very large scale. The first is the National Health Service (NHS) which provides free universal health care to the UK population and is Europe's single largest employer (www.nhs.uk/). The second agency is the Department for Work and Pensions (DWP) which administers welfare payments via its local 'Jobcentre Plus' offices (www.dwp.gov.uk). Although smaller than the NHS, DWP is again one of the largest bureaucracies in Europe.

The emergence of e-governance in the UK

The British State has sought greater administrative efficiency through computerisation for decades. Many early projects were large-scale attempts by agencies such as the DWP and the NHS to streamline their administration, that either met with mixed success or were highly expensive failures.[2] Successive governments were not deterred by these experiences and by the early 1990s, much of the day-to-day administration of public services had been at least partially computerised.

In the mid-1990s, government's service-related transactions with the public were undertaken by telephone, letter, face-to-face meetings in local offices and through the postal system using paper forms. Elected politicians were contacted at their offices via letter, telephone or, as is common in the UK, via weekly 'surgeries' during which elected politicians make themselves available to the public in their constituencies or wards. There had been huge changes in public administration since the 1950s, as government now used computerisation to store and manipulate the data from service transactions – yet the mechanisms by which the public could communicate with government were essentially the same. Interaction with elected politicians had not really moved on from where it had been decades before.

E-governance policy began to develop apace in the late 1990s and can be divided into three distinct areas:

- the use of ICTs to promote increased political participation;
- the use of ICTs to increase the efficiency and effectiveness of public services; and
- the use of ICTs to facilitate social and economic inclusion for people who are excluded from British society alongside the promotion of an 'information economy' in the UK.

Increasing political participation

Electronic democracy creates new mechanisms for voter participation and interaction with elected politicians. This includes politicians having email addresses, perhaps hosting the occasional online chat via one form of Computer Mediated Communication (CMC) or another, and also probably having their own website.

The local, national and central government of the UK now publishes a vast amount of material online. The UK Parliament publishes all its debates, reports and minutes on its website[3] as do the elected national assemblies for Wales and Scotland. Local government has also followed suit.

The activities of elected politicians have become much more transparent than was the case before the advent of the Web. Of course, information was available publicly prior to the advent of the Web, but it meant a trip to the assembly one wanted to know about, or access to a decent sized library at the very least, to get hold of the information one might want. For many voters their Internet connection makes it much easier to see what elected politicians are doing than used to be the case, assuming they have an inclination to look in the first instance.

UK government websites are not simply repositories of information. These same websites also allow politicians the chance to advance their ideas and arguments directly to the public without the need for journalists. The Web gives politicians direct access to the tools of the mass media, because it is in itself mass media. The website for Number 10 Downing Street,[4] the official residence of the Prime Minister, has a dual role. Firstly, it exists to inform the public about the role and functions of the Prime Minister, and secondly, it also uses mass media techniques to counteract unfavourable news reports.

While politicians can now often be emailed, the use of the Web to facilitate democratic debate *by elected politicians* is not particularly well advanced at the time of writing. It is much more common to see invitations to comment on current events on the BBC news website[5] than it is on the websites of elected politicians or legislative assemblies.

The Web is, of course, a campaigning and debating tool like no other and there is a mass of political activity by UK citizens via websites, blogs and older CMC such as Usenet. Even small UK pressure groups now have access to a mass audience. Issues such as the contentious attempt to introduce identity cards in the UK are being opposed by groups using the Web, for example the No2id campaign.[6] The possibility that groups and, indeed, individual citizens are able to put across their viewpoint, without the help of journalists, has the potential to change political debate. If a document from central government is leaked, one can quite often find the document itself online, rather than just journalists' reports of its contents. It is much easier to access direct representation of the different sides in a debate than used to be the case in the UK, as citizens need no longer rely solely on the mass media for their information. Some media even actively encourage citizens to look beyond their own reports, for example, the BBC routinely provides links to the websites of the various parties involved when reporting stories on its news website.

It is thus possible to view the Web as a new mechanism for facilitating democratic debate in UK society, by making information and opinion on issues much more accessible. It might even perhaps be argued that it is potentially a mechanism for making debate more evenly balanced, as left-wing, ecological and scientific arguments have often been badly represented in the sensationalist mass media of the UK. This may have far-reaching effects on the nature of governance. It is also worth noting that there has been no real attempt to control or censor the Web in the UK, although the online activities of some individuals and organisations are being monitored by law enforcement and security services.

Serious consideration has been given to the use of ICTs as a mechanism for voting. This includes web-based systems and the possibility of using SMS (short message service) or mobile phone 'texting' as a means by which young people might be encouraged to vote. Disengagement from mainstream politics among the young is seen as a particularly worrying trend within British society.[7] However, at the time of writing, there has yet to be an attempt to hold either a local or national election that allows people to vote online or via SMS. There are also various experiments underway in increasing local accountability, for example the Local e-Democracy National Project[8] aimed at improving accountability and interaction with local government, but they are modest in scope. As noted, much of what has been achieved in practical terms in e-democracy centres on more information about government activities being available on the Web.

Electronic service delivery

The computerisation of public *administration* and publicly funded *service delivery* is referred to as 'e-government' and 'Electronic Service Delivery' (ESD) in the UK. It is difficult to underestimate the attraction of ESD to the many large service-providing agencies in the UK that are part of the public sector, or which are funded, in whole or in part, via the public sector.

The main attraction of ESD, from the perspective of national and local governments and large providers of publicly-funded services is that the administrative staffing that is needed for the delivery of services to the public, can be either be significantly reduced or removed altogether. The attraction is quite simple, as cutting administrative staff allows increases in service levels without tax increases, or allows tax cuts while maintaining service levels. The central UK government has been greatly influenced by American ideas about administrative savings through ICTs from the early 1990s.[9] These American ideas emerged after US politicians saw what was happening within the private sector, particularly in transnational corporations, which used ICT networks to remove entire tiers of administrative staff while maintaining their customer base.

Two main ideas underpin the British interest in ESD. The first is simply that it will save money, potentially a very large amount of money, through cuts in administrative staffing. As a Cabinet Office report put it in 2000:

> Of course public services will still be delivered by teachers, social workers, doctors and nurses, fire fighters, police and other frontline staff, but much of the organization of services and initial public contact can be handled electronically. So processes which currently depend largely on the exchange of physical documents or attendance at a specific place will be very widely augmented and in many cases replaced by the application of new technology. The core processes that typify government interactions with citizens and businesses – giving and receiving money, giving and receiving information, regulation and procurement – will be able to be done electronically.[10]

The other attraction is that local and central government services will become more accessible to the public. This was one of the key arguments deployed by American advocates of ESD. The British state is a confusing array of agencies and an individual might potentially need to contact a number of different agencies if they require a range of services. The American idea of a *portal*, or one website from which all agencies could be easily contacted, was advocated as being a way to increase accessibility to citizens seeking public services:

> People should not need to understand how government is organized, or to know which department or agency does what, or whether a function is exercised by central or local government. We need a strategy that will provide this – by helping departments and agencies, central and local government, cooperate in partnerships that will offer their services in ways that make sense to the customer.[11]

This avowed aim was, indeed is, something of a smokescreen. There is, of course, an interest in making services more accessible to citizens, but the portal model is again primarily a mechanism for administrative cutbacks. If there is one, clear, simple accessible point of access, then the presence of the traditional points of access becomes superfluous, meaning they can be removed. At the time of writing, larger local authorities are adopting this strategy. Instead of five or six administrative staff answering the telephone or dealing with emails within each of five or six departments, there is instead one member of staff supporting a telephone call centre/website portal that deals with all enquiries.[12] Central UK government has itself expressed its commitment to this model through the Directgov website portal, which is designed to provide 'public services all in one place'.[13]

The interest in ESD does not stop at alterations to public services themselves. There is seen to be scope to further reduce the costs of service delivery to the public purse. Essentially, this involves the encouragement of the development of private and voluntary sector portals; the view being that the private and voluntary sectors will be interested in developing a website that provides access to both public and private sector services. Thus, portals are envisaged as being delivered through a 'mixed economy', in which government might only pay for some aspects of the portals through which publicly funded services are accessed.

> Electronic delivery of government services offers enormous new opportunities for the private and voluntary sectors. There should be a new, mixed economy in the electronic delivery of government services in which the public, private and voluntary sectors can all play a role on the basis that what matters is what works rather than who does it.[14]

Within all of this, there also is the possibility that service transactions with the public can be wholly or partly automated. Total automation represents a public administration nirvana, as most of the costs of interacting with the State are pushed onto the individual who processes their own requests aided by automated online systems, creating 'self-service' delivery.[15] An individual does all or most of the work that was previously undertaken by administrative staff for themselves, with the portal or website of the service guiding them through the process. However, even partial automation and limited 'self-service' can potentially save money, as significant staff cuts can still be made through automating part of a process.[16]

The information economy and digital inclusion

There is longstanding desire to promote the UK as a 'digital' or 'knowledge-driven' economy, in which ICTs and associated industries predominate.[17] Incentives for ICT companies, the development of broadband infrastructure and the provision of an ICT-literate workforce are all part of this broad objective.

The developments within e-governance are part of wider strategies that are designed to promote 'digital inclusion'. Essentially, this involves getting as much of the population as possible online and making them ICT literate. Over recent years this has evolved into providing ICT training and securing a reasonable amount of bandwidth for the population, as higher bandwidth facilitates both ESD and e-commerce. This objective is sometimes expressed as countering the 'digital divide' in UK society through promoting an information economy.[18]

ICTs are also seen as a mechanism by which to promote social inclusion within the UK. There is a concern that elements within the UK population are becoming characterised by a lifetime of worklessness, a situation sometimes described as 'NEET' status (for Not in Education, Employment or Training). This is held to subject the individuals concerned and UK society to a number of unacceptable risks, as individuals in this situation have poor health and are also more likely to become involved in crime. This has high costs for the State as well as for the individual.[19] ICTs are viewed as a way to address economic exclusion, by connecting excluded citizens to the information economy and the opportunities it offers, particularly in respect of excluded young people.[20]

Current objectives for social and employment policy across the UK partially reflect European ideas about 'social exclusion', particularly French concerns about the impact of a marginalised group on the social cohesion of society. However, these policy objectives are arguably more strongly influenced by US ideas about exclusion being a result of obstacles to *opportunity*. This 'communitarian' approach can be described as a 'rights and responsibilities' social and employment policy. The citizen has a right to help and support to become economically active and socially engaged, but sanctions will be employed if that citizen is able to work but 'refuses' to work.[21] Some commentators have argued that UK ESD policy reflects these wider imperatives, particularly in respect of 'communitarian' welfare policies.[22]

Parallels with strategies within and across the EU

The UK e-governance objectives are extremely close to those of the EU. This is exemplified by the *e*Europe 2005 objectives[23] and the strategies of individual nations, particularly in Western Europe.[24] The recent report of the discussions of the EU e-government subgroup,[25] reported key objectives for e-government in the EU that included:

- 'no citizen left behind';
- 'efficient and effective government'; and
- 'delivering high impact services designed around customers' needs'.

The concept of 'no citizen left behind' is very similar to the ideas found in the UK about countering the 'digital divide'. The EU strategy is centred on using ICTs to facilitate and enhance citizenship, social cohesion and economic inclusion. There is little distinction between these EU objectives and the specific national objectives of the UK in respect of the promotion of a socially inclusive information society that is positioned to compete in an ICT dominated World economy.

Similarly, the objectives for 'efficient and effective government' and designing services 'around customers' needs' mirror the concerns of the UK government in promoting ESD. Much of what is written by the EU in respect of promoting e-government and ESD could literally be cut and pasted into the strategies and policies of UK government.

The intentions of the EU to maximise accessibility to broadband, alongside a general aim to ensure a high degree of Internet usage amongst the general population, is also found in UK strategies. The UK includes mobile devices within its planning, as the UK market has one of the highest rates of mobile telephone usage in the world. Thus, the EU interest in M-government (that is to say, interaction between citizen and state via mobile phones and other wireless mobile devices) is reflected within the UK, for example in exploring the use of SMS for voting.

Current progress in the UK

During the early 2000s, many optimistic statements about the potential of e-government were being made by Number 10.[26] The UK government created a senior civil service appointment called the 'e-Envoy', who had their own specialist office and who reported directly to the Prime Minister. During 2000, the target date to have all public services 'accessible online' was *reduced* from 2008 to 2005, with the new e-Envoy spearheading the digitisation of government. Publications appeared describing how the barriers to a new ICT-led interrelationship between citizen and government could be overcome.[27]

By 2006, government statements of anticipated progress had grown less optimistic, as the reality of what could be done within the given timeframe began to sink home. The Office of the e-Envoy quietly ceased to be, replaced by a smaller unit within the Cabinet Office, and statements about the great potential of ESD started to become slightly less frequent.[28] Four issues had emerged in implementing ESD and e-government that were proving difficult to fully address.

The first issue was a slow down in the rate at which the population was taking up Internet access. This showed a similar 'plateau' effect to that which had been experienced slightly earlier in the US. Alongside this, the relative exclusion of poorer households and individuals, as well as other 'digitally excluded' groups such as older people, had proved stubbornly resistant to policy initiatives.[29] Serious barriers to some parts of the population using ESD also remained, particularly in relation to accessibility.

Secondly, there were problems in respect of engagement. Citizens had looked at what was being provided in terms of ESD and in some cases expressed a rather low opinion of it. Alongside this, there were questions about the extent to which the typical day-to-day use being made of the Web by UK citizens was furthering political engagement.

The third issue might be characterised as a kind of dawning realisation about the capacity of 'self-service' ESD to handle more complex transactions with the public. There were also still some technical barriers that had not yet been overcome.

The fourth issue was around privacy and human rights. This issue centred on the compatibility of e-government and the ESD model with citizens' privacy and their right to control the ways in which their personal information was processed by government and other agencies.

Difficulties in ending the digital divide

Internet access has risen, at the time of writing, to around 60 per cent of the UK population.[30] Within that group, 60 per cent are using broadband (although what ISPs call 'broadband' ranges from 256k to 8mb/sec connection speeds, at the time of writing), with about 36 per cent of all UK citizens having broadband access at home.

Under one third of households with an income of up to £12,500 have Internet access (27 per cent), compared to 70 per cent of those earning over £25,000, with the rate increasing to around 84 per cent for top earners.[31] Internet use also increases with the level of education of individuals. Alongside this, there are age effects, with only around one third of retired people having Internet access.[32]

At the time of writing, mobile web access is just developing; although it has theoretically been available for some years through WAP enabled mobile phones, this technology was basically too slow to be useable. Both 3G mobile phones[33] and mobile wi-fi devices are increasingly common and offer quite high bandwidth, but these devices are only affordable to those on higher incomes who generally already have other forms of Internet access. This pattern will change with time and it seems likely that many people who cannot afford landline telephone services will have the option of cheap, relatively high bandwidth, access to the Web through mobile devices, probably within a few years.

For some time, it had been assumed that almost everyone in the UK would eventually have Internet access as the costs of connection plummeted. However, there seems to be a plateau effect in the UK that mirrors what has happened in the US, in that while some people are not connecting because it is still not affordable, others are not adopting the technology because they have no interest in it.[34] At least some people who can afford Internet access are not opting for it.

This situation creates something of a problem for ESD. The potentially big savings in administrative costs are to be made in respect of the heavy users of public services, which, with the partial exception of the NHS, are poor and socio-economically marginalised people. If these individuals are not taking up Internet access or engaging with new technologies, then ESD looks less feasible. It is still the case that engagement by middle-class citizens who pay their tax or apply for their passport online does have potentially significant administrative savings, but this group simply does not engage with public services to the extent that poorer people do. Poor Internet access remains strongly associated with households with low incomes, the very people with whom e-government needs to engage. Beyond this, there is now the concern that some people may not use the Internet no matter how affordable it becomes.

There are also the concerns about people who find it difficult to engage with a text-based medium that requires someone to be able to read English and use a keyboard and mouse.[35] A recent report found that the standard of HTML on UK government websites meant that many pages were inaccessible to someone using a talking browser, a person with certain types of physical disability, or someone who is unable to read English.[36]

The implications for electronic voting are obvious. The poorer parts of the population are less likely to vote. If socio-economically marginalised groups are not engaging with these technologies, electronic voting cannot address one of the key concerns about political disengagement among the UK population.[37] Equally, there are barriers to political participation via the Web for disabled people for whom many government websites may be inaccessible.

Citizen engagement

In the early days, the assumption was that citizens would want access to all public services online and that those services could, at least to an extent, be made accessible via the Web. ESD was envisaged as offering new and convenient ways of using public services with 24 hour access, seven days a week, where citizens could access all the services they wanted from a single portal.[38]

In part, the problem with citizen engagement with ESD has been that the reality of service delivery has often fallen rather short of the initial expectation. The Directgov portal has met with a rather negative response in part, and has been criticised as merely providing a series of links to agencies and service providers that are as bureaucratic and confusing as ever.[39]

There is also the point that white, middle class, university-educated professionals conduct much of the business of government in the UK. The written material they place on government websites reflects this, raising some questions about how accessible this material is to those without a shared background.

In addition, there are the concerns about whether people will use their Internet access in 'democratic' ways. For example, 3G mobiles and broadband for home are being sold largely on their capacity to download music and video. It would be interesting to know how Parliament's website compares with the UK *iTunes* site, in terms of the number of hits (visits) it receives, as this might provide a useful short-hand about how much 'democratic' use of the Web is being undertaken by UK citizens.

The Web becomes a tool to facilitate democratic debate, raise citizen awareness and increase political participation *if* the population can be persuaded to use it that way. Clearly, some citizens do use the Web as a way of seeking information on issues and expressing their opinions, all of which adds to the democratic life of the UK. However, it does seem likely that the majority mainly use the Web for personal communication, shopping and other entertainment. Technology cannot, on its own, make UK citizens become more politically active. An over-emphasis on the supposed capacities of the Web to promote democratic life may distract attention from more fundamental questions, such as the degree of disengagement between mainstream politicians and British society.[40]

Limitations in respect of complex transactions

For large, service-providing agencies undertaking a lot of simple interactions with the public (for example a large social landlord collecting rents from thousands of tenants), the attractions of ESD are considerable.[41] Administrative tasks that can be wholly or mostly automated exist on a large scale within publicly-funded services in the UK and across government. For example, the tax returns for self-employed people and most of the process of applying for a passport have been successfully automated using Web-based systems. A significant part of the interaction between the State and citizen is being conducted online.

However, while simpler transactions are occurring in the ESD of public services at increasing levels, it has proven difficult to automate some complex transactions. Two problems have arisen here. The first is the capacity of ICTs to process relatively complex transactions and the second is the capacity of some individuals to use relatively complex 'self-service' procedures.

The administration of some public services is quite complex. In the UK, decisions about welfare services can involve determining whether or not a household is entitled to publicly-subsidised housing and, in addition, assistance with paying the rent for that housing. Often, individuals are being given access to services and benefits that amount to very significant amounts of public investment and there are obviously concerns that these services are properly allocated. The advocates of ESD had looked at the commercial sector, seen the simplicity, speed, convenience and above all the cost effectiveness of selling products online, using something like the Amazon.com model, and thought that the same model could be the basis for a revolution in publicly funded services.[42] In reality, publicly funded service transactions are unlike a commercial transaction in that they are often much more complex.[43] This meant that the task of programming these processes was more technically challenging than had perhaps been realised by the advocates of e-government.

Existing complex processes can, of course, be redesigned so they are better suited to ESD. However, a machine can only make a given level of allowance for the comprehension of an individual citizen and is far less flexible than a frontline worker can be in adapting itself to their needs. This creates the second problem, in that the limitations around the capacity of ESD to handle complexity may be more a matter of the capacity of some individuals to use quite complex automated procedures unaided, rather than whether or not creating such a system is technically feasible.

For example, the procedures needed to detect welfare fraud make the process of claiming welfare benefits complicated, as many cross-referenced questions are used to check for inconsistency and ineligibility. Government wants to prevent fraud, but it does not want a lot of vulnerable people who need financial assistance to be denied that assistance because making a claim is too complicated. This means that staff need to be on hand whenever a vulnerable person might not be able to complete the required forms or answer the required questions on their own. People have their limits; a self-service Web portal cannot demand too much of them before they start to become unwilling, or unable, to engage with it.[44]

In respect of electronic voting, the obstacles are essentially technical. Progress on electronic voting has stalled because of concerns about security.[45] There seems to be no obvious way of ensuring voting by SMS or over the Web can be secure, although digital signatures are being explored, and the issue has drifted off the agenda to some degree.

Individual rights and data sharing

Some commentators take the view that tensions have emerged between the ESD model, the right to privacy and the rights of citizens to have a say over how data about them is stored and processed.[46] The portal model and the whole idea of preventing administrative duplication through reducing 're-keying' (double and triple entry of the same data by different agencies) both depend on data sharing. Free flows of information have to exist if an ESD network is to function and deliver what is wanted. However, the UK laws protecting human rights in respect of data processing regulate data sharing, which means that personal information cannot be processed arbitrarily by government or publicly-funded services.

Again, this problem is arguably related to early advocates of e-government and ESD looking to the US and to private sector models as their guides. The idea that the citizen might have grounds for objecting to having sensitive information shunted around government departments and agencies without their consent had not, initially, been seen as an issue. The current legislative framework prevents the exchange of sensitive personal information without a free and informed consent. Inclusion of the EU directives of Human Rights into UK law added a further complication from the perspective of ESD advocates, by creating a legal right to privacy.[47] Data sharing of sensitive information can occur, but it can only occur when demonstrably free and informed consent for that sharing has been secured, which means something that is theoretically testable in court.

This threatens the vision of super-streamlined administration held by e-government advocates, as at the very least it means a bureaucracy must be in place to ensure free and informed consents are properly secured. There are also practical difficulties, in that it is difficult and perhaps sometimes not really practical, to ensure that an individual has given his/her free and informed consent.

Conclusions – UK progress in fulfilling EU e-governance objectives

British objectives in respect of e-governance are essentially very similar to those found across EU members states in Western Europe and the pan-EU strategies agreed across the EU, such as the 2005 *e*Europe objectives. There are differences between the UK and some other EU nations' terms of the detailed objectives of policy, such as the current UK focus on 'communitarian' social and employment policy,[48] but the broad goals are very similar.

ICTs are in the process of changing public services in the UK. It is clearly the case that more and more interaction, particularly in respect of simple transactions for services, will be online. However, it is only in a few cases that services will be largely, or wholly, processed via automated 'self-service' transactions. For many public services, the processes of application, fraud detection and delivery will remain complex, and some human capacity to help individuals deal with those processes will need to be in place. The need for free and informed consent for data sharing also creates a requirement for bureaucratic structures within e-government and ESD.

The Web is a platform for political debate and it may be the case that it will begin to rival and perhaps one day even eclipse other media, especially as it undergoes the process of merging its content with the video and audio of traditional broadcast media. However, it may well be the case that huge trans-national mass media companies adapt to this new environment and come to dominate it, just as they have done with newspapers and broadcasting. It is also important to bear in mind the extent to which the usage of the Web may reflect the preferences of UK citizens for shopping, downloading music and personal communications and that for many people, it may not significantly alter their political participation. Just because they are happy to shop online doesn't mean they want their government online too.

Encrypted digital signatures may mean that the security issues associated with making electronic voting practical are overcome, though this may facilitate political engagement mainly among those who are engaged in any case. Mainstream politics in the UK has far bigger problems to overcome than making it easier to vote if it is to really re-engage with the public.[49]

Notes

1. Rose, R. (2004) *Turnout for the European Parliament: A Comparative Perspective*. London: The Electoral Commission.
2. Margetts, H. (1991) 'The Computerization of Social Security: The Way Forward or a Step Backwards?' *Public Administration*, No. 69, pp. 325–43; Hudson, J. (1999) 'Informatization and Public Administration: A Political Science Perspective' in *Information, Communication and Society* 2,3, pp. 318–39.
3. www.parliament.uk/
4. www.number10.gov.uk/
5. news.bbc.co.uk/
6. www.no2id.net/

7. The Electoral Commission (2005) *Election 2005: Engaging the Public in Great Britain, an Analysis of Campaigns and Media Coverage*. London: The Electoral Commission.
8. www.edemocracy.gov.uk/
9. Gore, A. (1993) 'Re-engineering Through Information Technology' in *From Red Tape to Results: Creating a Government that Works Better and Costs Less*. Washington, DC, USA: National Performance Review, Government Printing Office.
10. Cabinet Office (2000) *E-government: A Strategic Framework for Public Services in the Information Age*. London: Cabinet Office, p. 11.
11. Cabinet Office (2000) *E-government*, p. 1.
12. Pleace, N. and Quilgars, D. (2002) *housing.support.org.uk: Social Housing, Social Care and Electronic Service Delivery* York: JRF/York Publishing Services; Pleace, N. (2005) 'The Shaping of Electronic Service Delivery: Introducing on-line services in British social housing' *Information, Communication & Society* 8, 4, pp. 524–41.
13. www.direct.gov.uk/
14. Cabinet Office/Performance and Innovation Unit (2000) *e.gov: Electronic Government Services for the 21st Century*. London: Cabinet Office.
15. Loader, B. (1998) 'Welfare Direct: Informatics and the Emergence of Self-Service Welfare', in J. Carter (ed) *Postmodernism and the Fragmentation of Welfare*. Routledge, London.
16. Pleace, N. and Quilgars, D. (2002) *housing.support.org.uk*.
17. Department of Trade and Industry (2000) *Closing The Digital Divide: information and communication technologies in deprived areas*. London: DTI.
18. Department of Trade and Industry (2000) *Closing The Digital Divide*.
19. Scott, S., Knapp, M., Henderson, J. and Maughan, B. (2001) 'Financial Cost of Social Exclusion: Follow Up Study of Antisocial Children Into Adulthood' *British Medical Journal 323, 7306, p. 191*.
20. Department of Trade and Industry (2000) *Closing The Digital Divide*; Livingstone, S., Bober, M. and Helsper, E.J. (2005) 'Active Participation or Just More Information? Young People's Take-up of Opportunities to Act and Interact on the Internet' *Information Communication and Society*, 8, 3, pp. 287–314; Loader, B.D. and Keeble, L. (2004) *Challenging the Digital Divide?: A Literature Review of Community Informatics Initiatives*. York: Joseph Rowntree Foundation.
21. Deacon, A. (2003) '"Levelling the playing field, activating the players": New Labour and the "cycle of disadvantage"' *Policy and Politics* 31, 2, pp. 123–37.
22. Hudson, J. (1999) 'Informatization and Public Administration'; Pleace N. (2005) 'The Shaping of Electronic Service Delivery: Introducing On-line Services in British Social Housing', *Information, Communication & Society* 8, 4, pp. 524–41.
23. The Council of the European Union (2003) *Council Resolution on the Implementation of the eEurope 2005 Action Plan* 5197/03.
24. Chatrie, I. and Wraight, P. (2000) *Public Strategies for the Information Society in Member States of the European Union*. European Information Society Projects/EU: Brussels; European Commission eGovernment Unit (2005) *Signposts Towards eGovernment 2010*. Brussels: European Commission Information Society and Media Directorate General.
25. European Commission eGovernment Unit (2005) *Signposts towards eGovernment 2010*, p. 5.
26. Cabinet Office (2000) *eGovernment: A Strategic Framework for Public Services in the Information Age*. London: Cabinet Office.
27. Margetts, H. and Dunleavy, P (2002) *Better Public Services Through E-government: Academic Article in Support of Better Public Services Through E-government*. London: National Audit Office.
28. Jones, A. and Williams, L. (2005) *What ICT? Providing More Citizen-Focused Services*. London: The Work Foundation.
29. Margetts, H. and Dunleavy, P (2002) *Better Public Services Through E-government*.
30. Margetts, H. and Dunleavy, P (2002) *Better Public Services Through E-government*.
31. Margetts, H. and Dunleavy, P (2002) *Better Public Services Through E-government*.
32. Margetts, H. and Dunleavy, P (2002) *Better Public Services Through E-government*.
33. 3rd Generation cellular telephones that offer high bandwidth web access.

34 Margetts, H. and Dunleavy, P (2002) *Better Public Services Through E-government.*
35 Pleace, N. and Quilgars, D. (2002) *housing.support.org.uk*; Pleace N. (2005) 'The Shaping of Electronic Service Delivery'.
36 Cabinet Office (2005) *eAccessibility of Public Sector Services in the European Union.* London: Cabinet Office.
37 The Electoral Commission (2005) *Election 2005.*
38 Cabinet Office (2005) *eAccessibility of Public Sector Services in the European Union.*
39 Jones, A. and Williams, L. (2005) *What ICT?*
40 The Electoral Commission (2005) *Election 2005.*
41 Pleace, N. and Quilgars, D. (2002) *housing.support.org.uk.*
42 Cabinet Office (2005) *eAccessibility of public sector services in the European Union.*
43 Pleace, N. and Quilgars, D. (2002) *housing.support.org.uk*; Pleace N. (2005) 'The Shaping of Electronic service delivery'.
44 Pleace, N. and Quilgars, D. (2002) *housing.support.org.uk.*
45 Parliamentary Office of Science and Technology (2001) *On-line Voting.* Postnote no. 155, London: House of Commons.
46 6, P., Raab, C. and Bellamy, C (2005a) 'Joined up Government and Privacy in the United Kingdom: Managing Tensions between Data Protection and Social Policy. Part I' *Public Administration* 83, 1, 111–33.
47 6, P., Raab, C. and Bellamy, C (2005a) 'Joined up Government and Privacy in the United Kingdom'.
48 Deacon, A. (2003) '"Levelling the playing field, activating the players"'.
49 The Electoral Commission (2005) *Election 2005.*

Further reading

Hudson, J. (2003) 'e-galitarianism? The Information Society and New Labour's Repositioning Of Welfare' *Critical Social Policy* 23, 2, 268–90.

Pleace, N. and Bretherton, J. (in press) *Sharing and Matching Local Data on Adults of Working Age Facing Multiple Barriers to Employment.* London: DWP.

Rose, R. (2004) *Turnout for the European Parliament: A Comparative Perspective.* London: The Electoral Commission.

6, P., Raab, C. and Bellamy, C (2005b) 'Joined up Government and Privacy in the United Kingdom: Managing Tensions between Data Protection and Social Policy. Part II' *Public Administration* 83, 2, 393–415.

6 The digital republic

Renewing the French state via e-government

Fabienne Greffet

Introduction

This chapter examines the reality of the e-government experience in France. E-government is defined extensively here from an anglo-saxon perspective, but, in fact, it also refers to different areas that are distinct in the French language:[1] e-services to the population, that is to say practices of public administration oriented towards providing services to the public through the Internet; e-management of the administration, such as the use of ICTs to improve the internal efficiency and organisation of the administration; and, to a lesser extent, e-democracy, that is to say practices that involve citizens in the public decision-making process.

Although France is not among the most advanced countries in terms of percentage of Internet users and development of e-government,[2] important progress has been made recently and many initiatives have been undertaken to promote e-government, both at a national and local level. This progress is based on development programmes undertaken by the state and by the EU,[3] Internet initiatives undertaken by local and regional authorities, as well as, of course, the increasing penetration of the Internet amongst the population (52.5 per cent in December 2005, according to Netratings Mediamétrie). These programmes and initiatives will be discussed here, along with concrete examples of Internet opportunities offered to citizens. Some regional and local disparities will also be examined, as well as the problem of the digital divide that still remains a significant issue in France. Rather than judging French e-government according to an 'ideal' of e-administration and e-democracy, this is an empirical study, based upon a wide range of examples.

Beyond this diversity of initiatives and situations, it is necessary to analyse the different concepts of the role of the state, and of the relationship between citizens and the state that appear. The implementation of e-government is linked with ongoing reform of the French civil service, both at a local and national level. Ideas such as better management, a more efficient service and internal organisation, and increased productivity are influencing the public service provision of ICTs. They are some of the aspects of the reform of state and public services which are based on economic rationalism and the desire to reduce public expenditure.[4]

76 *E-government in Europe*

At the same time, official political websites (for example, those of the President, government, Parliament) are mainly devoted to information about the actions and programmes of the governing departments. Transparency and accountability of professional politicians certainly prevails; but measures to associate citizens to government, through online consultations or deliberation initiatives, are an exception. Therefore, it will be shown that whatever aspect is considered (e-administration or communication of political actors), it is a consumerist and professional conception of e-government that is largely being promoted. In other words, the provision of e-government services is being conceived along the lines of an economic rationalist model, where citizens are above all seen as consumers.

The functioning of e-government in France will be explored through three main themes: the implementation process of e-government, the results that have been achieved, both in terms of Internet uses and legal frameworks, and the conceptions of the state that are promoted through the use of ICTs in France.

E-administration and e-democracy: a slow implementation

To consider the implementation of e-government in France, both e-administration, and e-democracy have to be considered at a national and local level. Even if these dimensions are actually linked, the distinction is analytically useful at this stage.

E-government was first promoted in France in the late 1990s, after several official reports in 1996 and 1997. The then Prime Minister, Lionel Jospin, who was appointed in June 1997, mentioned e-administration as a priority for his government. The PAGSI programme (Governmental Action Plan to take France into the Information Society) was launched in late 1997, scheduled to begin in January 1998 and to end in late 2000.

The PAGSI programme was implemented to showcase the national government's involvement in the promotion of ICTs in French society. From the very beginning, taking France into the information age was also claimed to be a way of modernising and reforming the state, as well as showing that the state was establishing a closer relationship with its citizens. Six major areas were highlighted: culture, education, e-business, research, innovation, and the modernisation of the administration. Projects were financed by the PAGSI programme, for a total amount of 9 billion Francs (about 1.38 billion euros).[5] Among the results, 98 per cent of high schools and 89 per cent of junior high schools were connected to the Internet in 2000, compared with 32 per cent and 11 per cent respectively in 1997. A total of 3500 public websites were created between 1997 and May 2001 (although not all were as a result of the PAGSI programme), to promote ministries and administrations, local and regional authorities, libraries, and universities. For example, the website Legifrance (www.legifrance.gouv.fr/), created in 1999, provides the general public with access to the whole of French Law, as well as the French Constitution, free of charge.[6] Created in 2000, the website Service-public.fr (www.service-public.fr/) is a portal that guides citizens in knowing their rights and obligations towards the French state. In addition, a national health insurance computerised system (called VITALE) was implemented in 1998 to digitise health reimbursements. Since that time, every patient is equipped with an electronic smart card that can be read at any doctor's surgery, thus replacing the paper reimbursement form that was previously provided by the doctors that needed to be filled in, signed and sent by the patient to the national health administration. The refund to the insured person now takes approximately five days, instead of two or three weeks using the traditional paper channels.

In terms of e-management, a computing network was created, called AdER (Administration en réseaux, Networked Administration) to allow quick transmission of information and instructions from central administration services and their local offices. In 2000, an official report[7] claimed that France had made up for its late start in implementing new computer and information technologies in its administration,[8] despite internal resistance.[9]

In late 2001, a new step was announced: the complete 'dematerialisation' of all administrative procedures, that is, the replacement of paper forms by electronic documents, by the year 2005.[10] The period 2001/2002, however, was a pre-election period and the e-administration projects were shelved until after the presidential election, when Jacques Chirac was re-elected (May 2002), and the legislative election where the UMP (conservative) majority was returned to Parliament. Jean-Pierre Raffarin became Prime Minister from June 2002 to May 2005. The Raffarin government decided that governmental actions relating to ICTs should be 'less numerous and better targeted', with a focus on the legal framework rather than on big pluriannual plans.[11] The Raffarin government launched two different programmes, the first one being a general plan for France to adapt to the information society, specifically by changing the legal framework; the other being more focused on e-administration, with a similar content to what had been previously proposed under the Jospin government.[12]

The Plan Reso 2007 (presented Nov. 2002, lasting for the period 2002 to 2007) aims to build a 'digital Republic, that would be faithful to the French national motto: liberty, equality, fraternity'. Access to the Internet is reinforced by a number of different initiatives, including wi-fi developments in universities and agreements between the government and computer companies so that students get special prices to allow them to buy computers for 'one euro per day' (200,000 laptops were bought in 2004, and the same number is expected in the years 2005 and 2006). In addition, a charter and a map of 'Internet Public Access Points' (at a local or national level) has been established and is now available online. These access points allow people who don't have home Internet access to get online for free or at a very minimal cost, and in an environment where they can learn how to use the Internet thanks to the presence of competent staff (in libraries, local authorities offices, NGOs and so on). In 2005, there were about 3500 of these Public Access points.[13]

Another aspect of the programme is the 'State role for the development of information society', which includes elements of e-administration. This is outlined in the ADELE programme, launched in February 2004, for the period 2004 to

2007.[14] The budget of the whole programme is 1.8 billion euros but this cost needs to be set alongside the 5 to 7 billion euros that are expected to be saved from 2007 onwards as a result of increasing productivity due to the development of e-administration. The ADELE programme is implementing 140 concrete measures up until 2007, including, for example: the implementation of a pension rights' website that allows net-users to get precise and personalised information about the size of their pensions, an online service to inform the various administrations of a change of address,[15] a special website for companies and NGOs to apply for European structural funds, and a special phone number for citizens needing administrative information. Again, 'dematerialisation' is central here, for example with the digitalisation of all procedures of government, local, and regional procurement on the website www.marché-public.fr. Also planned is the creation of an electronic identity card, as well as the personalisation of an Internet account for each e-administration user (mon.service-public.fr). A governmental agency called ADAE (Agency for the development of e-administration), created in May 2003 to implement and co-ordinate e-administration practices, is now in charge of the realisation of the ADELE programme.[16] The ADAE had about 200 employees in 2005, that were integrated into the 'reform of the state' agency in early 2006.

e-Administration has also spread at the local level since the middle of the 90s, and enabling access via the Internet has increasingly become a priority for public administrations. All regional and county councils, as well as most of the municipalities, have websites. For instance, in the Ile-de-France region, more than 80 per cent of towns of more than 10,000 inhabitants had websites at the end of 2003,[17] the exception being small villages (less than 2500 inhabitants), with only 10 per cent of them having websites. A growing number of websites offer online services to the citizens, for instance the delivery of registry documents. A few towns, like Issy-les-Moulineaux (www.issy.com/), have greatly developed both e-administration and e-democracy. On the one hand, inhabitants of the town can get a number of services online, such as getting registry office documents, getting in contact with the national health system services, or even reserving a book from the library. On the other hand, they can also watch 'interactive local council meetings' on the web, and ask questions online to local councillors, thus getting involved in the decision-making process.

Furthermore, several regions are financing programmes to improve citizen access to the Internet. For example, the programme 'Cybercommunes Bretagne' that has been co-financed by the Brittany regional Council and the municipalities since 1998, aims to provide all citizens with Internet access, no further than 20 kilometres away from their home. More than 400 villages and towns have created such cyberspaces. Since 2005, the law encourages council and regional authorities to get even more involved in the development of the Internet; they can now lead electronic communication networks, and provide e-communication services (for example e-mail addresses).

Some internal changes in the functioning of local administrations have also been adopted, even if they remain a marginal phenomenon. For example, both the town administration of Parthenay and the County Council of les Deux-Sèvres have replaced the traditional paper wage-slip for their staff with an electronic version.[18]

All these developments in e-administration do not necessarily mean an expansion and deepening of e-democracy, in a sense that 'the governed' would become more involved in the decision-making processes of those who govern. Compared with the potential e-democracy experiences,[19] e-democracy seems to be relatively weak in France.

Official political actor websites are now very numerous but still mainly informative – the general scheme of communication still being top-down, with few opportunities for interactivity. All institutions have their own main website, and often provide links to other websites. For instance, the Prime Minister's website (www.premier-ministre.gouv.fr/fr/) is also a portal for all governmental websites, as well as a discussion website (www.forum.gouv.fr). The website promotes governmental projects, and contains the biographies of the members of cabinet, a newsletter and since December 2004 bulletin boards to facilitate public discussion. On other ministry websites, 'chats' with politicians are organised on certain subjects in the news. Political party websites also offer 'limited and supervised' participation.[20] Their websites are largely top-down communication instruments, used to inform people and enhance the image of the party and its leaders.[21] However the amount of information available online is increasing, responding to citizen demands for transparency and accountability.

Citizens themselves undertake many 'bottom-up' Internet initiatives, especially during election campaign periods. The European Treaty referendum campaign in May 2005 was a situation where approximately 12,000 weblogs and websites developed, with a clear majority in favour of the 'No'[22] side. Maybe this is why Catherine Collonna, the French European Affairs Minister, announced the creation of a new government interactive website on the future of the construction of the European Union in spring 2006.[23] The URL of this site has not been announced at the time.

In terms of online electoral participation, however, limitations still prevail – particularly at national level. Internet voting is not possible in France for national political elections, but certain organisations (such as political parties or professional organisations) use it for internal voting.[24] In addition, French nationals living abroad can elect their consultative representatives (Assembly of the French living abroad) via the Internet, but the extension of this procedure to political elections, particularly the Presidential election to take place in 2007, will only be debated by the Parliament during 2006.

Electronic voting at local and regional level is more open. It has been possible at local elections in certain municipalities since March 2004, but it is not generalised. At the last EP elections in June 2004, a few towns encouraged electors to use 'e-voting machines' (for example Issy les Moulineaux, Vandoeuvre) to cast their votes. Turnout was slightly higher in the places using machines, but the difference was still minimal (about two points between the turnout in offices equipped for e-voting compared to those places that were not equipped for e-voting). In May 2005, for the referendum concerning the European Constitutional Treaty, around

50 towns offered electronic voting as an option. However the consequences of this major change to the 'voting ritual' were not really monitored.[25]

The involvement of citizens in discussions and deliberation is even more limited. At the parliamentary level, no public deliberation has been organised to date. At the local level, a few projects – such as, for example, the creation of a third airport near Paris[26] – have included electronic dialogue procedures, but participative and deliberative practices remain the exception rather than the rule. In 1999, a study of 80 town council websites[27] showed that if the content analysis of websites was restricted to political communication (that is to say, not to 'practical' information or services to the citizens), one could conclude that the use of ICTs for local democracy was largely insignificant.[28] About 18 per cent of town council websites were providing political information, such as the agenda of the meetings of local councillors, the minutes of these meetings, or the party affiliation of each politician. Approximately 12.5 per cent were developing dialogue initiatives such as the possibility of participating in a virtual meeting or of chatting with local councillors or mayors. Furthermore, 0.4 per cent of the websites provided spaces for discussion for other local actors such as NGOs, trade-unions, political parties, the media, churches etc, or even hyperlinks to those actors. In 2002, progress had been made with regard to the information online (all towns have a website), but the content provided is still very top-down and information-oriented, the participative and expressive opportunities being limited.[29] For example, only 14 per cent of local council websites have open discussion forums. This can be linked with the fact that other local participative mechanisms exist in the real world, along with the high costs of forum moderating and the risk that only small minorities of activists are mobilised around such forums.[30] In any case, given this quite limited experience of e-democracy there has been no specific monitoring of progress made, which explains why, in the following pages of this chapter, e-government means much more e-administration than e-democracy.

Results: disparities of use and an incomplete legal framework

After a long implementation process, e-government in France has now reached a mature stage. However, there are still disparities in Internet use, which can be perceived not only through statistical results, but also through the evolution of the ICTs legal framework.

Regarding access to the Internet, the digital divide still exists in France. In December 2005, 52.5 per cent of the population aged 11 or more said they had been connected to the Internet at least once in the last month.[31] 37.7 per cent of the households had an Internet connection, 49.1 per cent had a computer. These results show that almost half of the population did not regularly use or have access to the Internet. The non-Internet user population is, as in other countries, also the least educated, poorest and oldest part of the population.[32]

Regarding e-government, its use also reflects the digital divide. According to a study in March 2005,[33] those who use e-administration are more often male (30 per cent of men, 24 per cent of women).[34] The use of e-administration is more frequent amongst the upper and middle classes (respectively, 43 per cent of upper-class and 54 per cent of middle class use e-administration, compared to only 23 per cent of the working class), and also amongst university degree holders (55 per cent use the e-administration, compared with 18 per cent of those without qualifications). Younger people are more likely to use e-administration than older people (with usage running at 47 per cent among 18–24 and 25–34 year olds, compared with 19 per cent among the 50–64, 2 per cent among those 65 and over). There is also a tendency where people living in towns of more than 100,000 inhabitants are over-represented (41 per cent of them are e-administration users). In other words, Internet Public Access points don't have a major impact on helping non-users to become Internet users, but rather on helping those wanting an Internet connection to get one,[35] confirming that the use of a certain technology depends on social and cultural factors rather than on the mere access to the technology.[36]

Nevertheless, a recent official report assesses the extent to which e-government has successfully been achieved in France, both at a national and local level.[37] There are now 7000 public Internet websites, with 90 per cent of public forms available online, one in two health reimbursements processed by computer (via the electronic health insurance system VITALE), and 17 per cent of people moving house using the electronic change of address service.[38] New sites implemented include www.retraites.gouv.fr (launched in 2002), which informs people about pension reform and provides interactive services, including one that allows an employee to calculate his/her future pension online; and www.journal-officiel.gouv.fr (launched in 2004), which replaced the daily printed journal that published all official decisions of the government and administration since 1848. Certain e-administration services have already been a great success. Thanks to the Copernic information system, and the website www.impots.gouv.fr, 3.7 million French filed their tax returns online in 2005 (150,000 in 2002), which represents 11 per cent of all taxpayers,[39] the objective for 2006 being for 10,000 million tax returns completed online. Moreover, 7.5 million users used the online facility to calculate the amount of tax owed, even despite major difficulties in getting access to the Ministry of Finance website in the last days before the deadline, as was reported by the media.[40] The public administrations have also planned to expand their e-practices in 2006, with the digitalisation of customs procedures as well as the possibility to obtain birth certificates online. As planned in the ADELE programme, the portal service-public.fr should also become more personalised, with the option given to users to store personal data so that they can obtain certain outputs, such as identity papers or social security registration through the website www.mon.service-public.fr.

At a local level, the local, county and regional councils, together with the national administrations, have developed innovative uses of the Internet, for example a website devoted to public transport, traffic and air quality in the Ile de France region (www.sytadin.tm.fr/), in the Bouches-du-Rhône county (www.lepilote.com/), an innovative information system that provides a 'virtual office' to each school pupil as well as an information tool that can send SMS messages to parents so that they are immediately informed of the absence of their child at school in the Lorraine region (www.prisme-lorraine.net), and the Calvados council (www.cg14.fr/sig/index.asp) have set up an electronic mapping system, so that one can establish his/her property rights. Though these initiatives have not spread out to all of France, notable examples can be observed.[41]

While these outcomes place France in a respectable position amongst countries that use e-government, France does not do so well when compared to other leading countries (see Table 6.1). Even if classifications are always partial and subjective, and the development of e-administration difficult to monitor in a comparative perspective,[42] reports underline the same weak aspects of e-administration in France.

The Accenture study recognises the large amount of information and public forms online, but also shows that Internet initiatives are not part of a global strategy, which decreases the impact of e-administration upon the public. There are problems with links between websites (so that net-citizens do not have to repeat the same procedures several times), and on co-ordination between the different channels of communication such as the Internet, telephone, and administration in the 'offline world'. Another shortcoming is in the level of Internet service use: although the French have a positive perception of e-administration, most of them (62 per cent) use phone services rather than electronic services (31 per cent). This confirms the previous study by Cap Gemini, together with the EU Commission, in October 2004. Twenty 'basic public services' were monitored, from job search to birth and marriage certificates or income taxes. Each service was scored from 1 to 4, depending on the degree of sophistication of the online service. Stage 1 indicates that the website only provides information on how to get access to the public

Table 6.1 E-government ranking of France, 2005.

	UN global e-government readiness index, 2005[1]	Accenture report, 2005[2]	Cap Gemini / European Commission study, 2004[3]
Rank of France, 2005	23	3 (equal with Denmark, Singapore, Australia, Japan, Norway, Finland) (rank 8th in 2004)	10
Number of countries in survey	191 (worldwide)	22 countries (Europe, America, Asia)	28 (Europe)

[1] Report available online at, unpan1.un.org/intradoc/groups/public/documents/UN/UNPAN-021888.pdf, but there is no specific comment on France.
[2] Available at www.accenture.com/Countries/France/About_Accenture/Newsroom/News_Releases/2005/504egov.htm
[3] The study was developed within the eEurope2005 project. Report available online at: europa.eu.int/information_society/eeurope/2005/doc/all_about/on-line_availability_public_services_5th_measurement_fv4.PDF.

service in the 'real world'; stage 4, the 'full electronic case handling' is when the access to the public service is entirely handled through the website. In France, 50 per cent of the e-services are fully available online (stage 4), which is close to the European average, but far less than Sweden (74 per cent) or Austria (72 per cent), and a little less than the UK (59 per cent). France scores close to Spain (55 per cent), or Germany (47 per cent). Another study which monitored French public websites also underlined that nearly 80 per cent of French websites are 'informative' rather than offering the option of interactive services and teleprocedures.[43]

Therefore, France can certainly do better in terms of both the extensiveness and quality of e-administration services, and also in getting more people to use them. This is confirmed by the statistics on connections to popular public websites, tested by a governmental service called Stat@gouv.fr (see Table 6.2).

Despite these low rates, French Internet-users seem to be pretty satisfied with e-administration. A study by Cap Gemini/TNS-Sofres in August 2005[44] showed that in the last 12 months, 75 per cent of the French net-users had been connected to a public website. The main reason for using public websites was to get information (49 per cent), but a growing proportion of net-users use them for interactive purposes such as paying income tax online (almost 30 per cent in 2005, 16 per cent in 2004). The main obstacle to using e-administration was the preference for human contact and the lack of confidentiality. Approximately 50 per cent of net-users were expecting improvements, particularly more e-services, up-dated information online, and the development of access to the Internet for free. Some of these improvements would probably require a wider legal framework for e-government to be enacted.

To date, there is no comprehensive legal framework regarding e-government in France, but rather a set of different individual laws responding to certain developments of e-government. The legal evolution has occurred incrementally since the beginning of the 2000s. In 2000, a law (2000–2230) recognised the electronic

Table 6.2 Audience of the 10 French main public websites in December 2005.

	Number of visits[1]	% of Internet users[2]
Légifrance	2,557,550	9.4
Sytadin	2,157,675	7.9
Service Public	1,930,304	7.1
Impôts	1,591,171	5.8
Education	1,465,138	5.4
Intérieur	759,685	2.8
Diplomatie	716,702	2.6
Défense	562,721	2.1
Educnet	542,714	2.0
35heures	504,807	1.8

[1] The number of visits was provided by the service stat@gouv.fr. Unfortunately, this service only monitors certain public websites (about 70), and doesn't include popular services such as the national employment agency.
[2] The percentage of Internet users is calculated with the number of Internet users given by the Institute of measure Médiamétrie (27,210,000, aged 11 and more, in December 2005).

84   E-government in Europe

signature for individuals, considering it as having the same legal value as a handwritten signature. In the e-government field, this law can be applied due to a decree from December 2005 that allowed administrative authorities and citizens to transact with one another legally by electronic means, and that also legalised the use of electronic signatures by administrative authorities. In 2003 and 2004, two laws were adopted, which were indirectly concerned with e-government. Law 2003–1365 further deregulated the telecommunication market, and law 2004–2669 opened up the cable market, which means that access to the Internet became cheaper for consumers.

Finally, a number of laws complete this framework. The new Public Procurement Code (January 2004) mentions the possibility of the digitalisation of procurement procedures (article 56). Law 2004–2575 aims to reinforce confidence towards the digital economy, with better protection for consumers against spamming, the possibility of trading contracts online (but with an obligation to offer to the consumer a second reading of the contract), and a definition of specific rules for public communication online (names of the websites, responsibility of the administration). In addition, local council and regional authorities can lead electronic communication networks and provide e-communication services (such as e-mail addresses), in the absence of a private operator providing the service. Law 2004–2801 'Computing and Liberty' modifies the initial 1978 law on personal data, reinforcing the protection of consumers and citizens against the misuse of electronic personal data.

Making the state efficient through e-government?

Through such developments, a new conception of the state is also being promoted: the image of a more efficient and cost-effective state, which is seen mainly as a professional service-provider to the French population, rather than as a collective project in which citizens can participate.

This can be illustrated in different ways. Firstly, e-government is about implementing a culture of e-business in government. The language and procedures of business management are often adopted in this field of e-government. For example, in a recent book about e-government in France, Jubert, Montfort and Stakowski[45] present three essential strategies for the development of government: the growth strategy, to develop new services that would have been too costly without the ICTs, the strategy of efficiency research, to optimise the organisation and its results, and the strategy of proximity, to bring 'citizens/consumers' (sic) closer to the public services. All strategies are monitored, and the performances of e-government versus non e-government are quantified. Many other reports are also made by business consultant offices, and e-government indicators mainly reflect this business culture. The main French business union, Medef, strongly supports the development of e-government.[46]

This shows the extent to which e-government actually facilitates the importation of a business culture into public services. This might create certain difficulties given the French public service culture. Opposition has been expressed over the last few years. One such protest took place in the context of a reform to the financial administration in 2000. This reform was explicitly referring to an 'intensive model',[47] where ICTs were not an external communication system, but an instrument in a deep transformation of the internal organisation. The objective was to simplify the procedures for the citizens, and to make the service more efficient, to reduce public expenditure. This initial proposal was rejected both by civil servants and their trade unions, as they felt they were being reproached both for a lack of efficiency and the high cost of their labour. They also noted that if the 'user-client' was the centre of the new organisation, the civil servants themselves would be forgotten. The Finance Minister, Christian Sautter, had to resign and this first project was abandoned in 2001. The new reformed Copernic is much slower and the question of productivity is not directly tackled, but trade unions have already expressed their distrust.[48]

Another example of protest is one organised in 2005 against an electronic national ID card project, that in part mirrored a similar debate on the same issue in the UK. Several organisations, such as professional lawyers associations, NGOs, and trade-unions criticised this project, that aims to computerise biometric data (such as fingerprints) and personal information about all citizens. They denounced this as a serious risk for civil liberties, as the state could potentially control any citizen,[49] but the project is still to be brought to fruition in 2006.

Despite these protests, a majority of civil servants seem to be broadly in favour of e-government reform. According to an opinion poll from December 2005: 82 per cent of French civil servants think e-government modernises their work; 86 per cent think that it gives a good image of administration; and 85 per cent that e-government means time gains for everybody, even though only 40 per cent of them think they are well-informed about e-administration.[50]

Additionally, e-government is associated with an image of modernity and reform. The creation of the ADELE agency, for example, as well as the e-government projects, were presented as an aspect of the 'reform of the state'issue, which has been the subject of debate for over 25 years in France and consists of achieving a more efficient, less expensive and more satisfying state for the citizen-consumer. This has become even clearer from January 1st 2006, when a unique governmental service in charge of 'Reforming the State' has been created,named 'Direction générale de la modernisation de l'Etat' (General Directorate for the Modernisation of the State). This service incorporates four previously seperate services, now all placed under the authority of the Ministry in charge of Budget and Reform of the State.[51] Despite specific protests from certain ministries (such as the financial administration, see above), this reform has not provoked significant protest; for many, e-government equates with modernity and a response to the challenge of a new, globalised world, and being against e-government would be like being anti-modern or anti-progress. It is presented as a good and unavoidable process which governments and citizens should embrace.

From a political point of view, it is surprising that this apparent consensus about e-government is not challenged more by raising questions about cuts to government expenditure and the reduction of jobs in the public sector. To some extent, with regard to the French example, a comparison could be made with the transition from the Fourth to the Fifth Republic, when the former regime was presented by most of the political élite as old-fashioned and out-of-date while the new one (which gave less power to the Parliament and reinforced the power of the executive) was promoted as a symbol of a modern and efficient state, a construction that was completely accepted by the public.[52] The same phenomenon seems to be happening in the transition to e-government, in which legitimacy and usefulness don't seem to be greatly questioned, except for very specific reforms such as that of the financial administration noted above. In opinion polls, the Internet is seen by the population as both a tool to reinforce democracy,[53] and as a vehicle to increase the quality of administrative services.[54] In that sense, the two movements of getting a more efficient state, as well as a more democratic state, by using ICTs do not seem to be contradictory but complementary. A 'new state' is emerging, that ICT use can help to bring into existence.

As noted in the earlier Chapter by Nixon, modernisation through e-government is also an EU objective. Through programmes such as eEurope 2005, renewed and extended with the i2010 programme, the Commission views e-government as an opportunity for a major economic boost, because it provides new and better services for all citizens and companies in Europe. The Commission has called upon Member States to express their political commitment to co-operation at European level, spanning both the private and public sector, to accelerate the take-up and development of e-government. Therefore, e-government is also the result of a process of change that is supported by all levels of governance – local, national, and European.

Conclusions

E-government in France is a strong, emerging, reality. Many achievements have been made since 2000, and further projects are in the pipeline – such as the digitalisation of most official forms or the ID electronic card. In addition, procedures of e-democracy are being developed, either through top-down or bottom-up communication schemes. Though the development of e-administration has been emphasised by the state, rather than e-democracy, the two issues seem to be complementary. A strong amount of support from the different levels of government and within the population seems to be apparent, even if some protests have already been expressed. Incrementally, a new state seems to be emerging that could be more efficient, more productive, and could cost less, and that could let citizens express their demands towards the public decision-making process and organisation.

Maybe there is a need to further 'deconstruct' the meaning of these reforms and the apparent consensus they generate. It is not certain that most French civil-servants would support reforms if they mean strong expenditure cuts and a deterioration of labour conditions; it is also not evident that this reform is 'new' in a sense that historically, it can be seen as similar to the passage from one model of a state to another, legitimised by political and economic actors who have an interest in pushing that change. And, as noted earlier, it is possible to see an analogy with the transition from the Fourth to the Fifth Republic. A sociological study of the actors involved in e-government would be useful, because it would probably show the way that certain interest groups and agencies, both public and private, legitimate themselves through this 'ideology' of e-government.

Notes

1 Benyekhlef, K. (2004) 'L'administration publique en ligne au Canada: précisions terminologiques et état de la réflexion', *Revue française d'administration publique*, 110, pp. 267–77.
2 The UN ranked France 23th in 2005 (24th in 2004, 25th in 2003) on a global e-government readiness index in 2005. In Europe, France was 15th out of 42 countries taken into account. UN report available online at unpan1.un.org/intradoc/groups/public/documents/un/unpan021888.pdf
3 Through the programmes eEurope 2005, launched in 2002, and i2010, launched in 2005, that both encourage among other things the development of e-government in the member states. Webpages available at europa.eu.int/information_society/eeurope/2005/index_en.htm and europa.eu.int/information_society/eeurope/i2010/index_en.htm.
4 The reform of the state is a continuing process, that has been contemplated and developed through various reforms since the 1970s, for example via the creation of an agency for the reform of administrative procedures (1983); the movement has been accelerated in the 1990s, with the creation of an agency in charge of the reform of the state (1995), and the adoption of a law about the rights of the citizens towards the administration (2000). See Lacasse, François and Verrier, Pierre-Eric, eds (2005). *30 ans de réformes de l'Etat*.
5 Ducoutieux, C. (2002) Stéphane Mandart. 'Le gouvernement de Lionel Jospin a su accompagner le développement de la Toile', *Le Monde*, April 19th.
6 See the report 'Quatre ans d'action gouvernementale pour la société de l'information', (August 2001), available online at egov.alentejodigital.pt/Page10526/agsi4ans.pdf
7 Lasserre, B. (2000) 'L'Etat et les technologies de l'information et de la communication', *Les cahiers français*, 295, March/April, 17–24.
8 Rollot, C. (2002) 'Internet, une tentative soft pour déboguer l'Etat', *Le Monde*, Feb 5th.
9 Basquiat, J.-P. (2001) "Les administrations et Internet en 2001", *Les cahiers de la fonction publique et de l'administration*, 205, pp. 3–6.
10 See the discourse of the Ministry of State Reform in the Jospin government, Michel Sapin, in January 2002: www.fonction-publique.gouv.fr/article208.html
11 Kahn, A. (2002) 'Le gouvernement entend mener une politique de l'Internet plus "ciblée"', *Le Monde économie*, Sep. 10th.
12 The report on the 'Hyper-Republic', presented to the Raffarin Government in 2003 by Pierre de la Coste, explicitly refers to it, as is presented as the following step of the previous reports presented under the Jospin government. Report available online at www.cri74.org/actualites/articles/2003/hyper-republique.pdf
13 Statistics from the Délégation aux usages de l'Internet (DUI), available at delegation.Internet.gouv.fr/acces/index.htm
14 Van Eeckhout, L. and Landrin, S. (2004) 'M.Raffarin attend 5 milliards d'euros d'économies par an de l'administration électronique', *Le Monde*, Feb. 11th.
15 This service, involving several agencies (tax department, health insurances, labour office, department of social affairs, national service directorate) is considered as a 'good practice' example in the report 'Beyond E-government', available online at www.egov2005conference.gov.uk/documents/pdfs/beyond_egov.pdf, p. 81 and p.109.
16 Interview with Jacques Sauret (2003) 'Les nouvelles technologies ne sont plus un enjeu de pouvoir mais un moyen de mieux servir les usagers', *Journal du Net*, Sep. 11th; available at www.journaldunet.com/itws/it_sauret.shtml

88 *E-government in Europe*

17 Statistics from Artesi-idf, available at www.artesi.artesi-idf.com/public/dossier.tpl?id = 6326&head = 6296.
18 Chirot, F. (2005) 'l'état civil et la comptabilité publique sur ordinateur', *Le Monde*, June 7th.
19 Shane, P.M. (ed) (2004) *Democracy Online: the Prospects of Political Renewal Through the Internet*. London, Routledge.
20 Villalba, B. (2003) 'Moving Towards an Evolution in Political Mediation? French Political Parties and the New ICTS', in Gibson, R., Nixon, P. and Ward, S. (eds) *Political Parties and the Internet, Net Again?* London, Routledge, pp.120–38.
21 Greffet, F. (2001a) 'Les partis politiques français sur le Web' in Andolfatto, D, Greffet, F. and Olivier, L. (eds) *Les partis politiques: quelles perspectives?* Paris, L'Harmattan, pp. 161–78.
22 Study by from the two researchers, Franck Ghitalla and Guilhem Fouetillou, from the Univerity of Compiègne; available online at www.utc.fr/rtgi/index.php?rubrique=1&sousrubrique=0&study=constitution
23 Colonna, C. (2006) 'En avant l'Europe !', *Le Figaro*, Jan. 17th.
24 For example, the elections of the representatives of businessmen and shopkeepers in the local 'trading chambers' were organized both through the Internet and by correspondence in Oct. 2004. The first UMP Congress (main conservative party) in 2002, and the next one in 2006, will also use this technology for the party members to vote on the changes of internal rules of the party and the election of the party President.
25 Ledun, M. and Paniez, P. (2005) *Le vote électronique: des préconisations aux usages de la e-démocratie*. Paper presented at the conférence 'Démocratie et dispositifs électroniques; regards sur la décision, la délibération et le militantisme', Paris, December 2005. See also: Monnoyer-Smith, L. (2005a) *Derrière l'urne, le citoyen: les rituels du vote sont-ils intangible?* Paper presented at the Conference 'Démocratie et dispositifs électroniques: regards sur la décision, la délibération et le militantisme', Paris, December 2005.
26 Monnoyer-Smith, L. (2005b) *Nouveaux dispositifs de concertation et formes de contreverses: le choix d'un troisième aéroport pour Paris*. CNRS, Final Report, Paris.
27 Loiseau, G. (1999) *Municipalités et communication numérique. Les sites Internet des grandes villes de France en 1999*, rapport LOCAL/AMGVF, Université Paris I. see also Loiseau, G. (2000) 'La démocratie électronique municipale française: au-delà des parangons de vertu', *Hermès*, 26–27, 213–32.
28 Loiseau, G. (2000) *La démocratie électronique municipale française*, 222.
29 Loiseau, G. (2003) 'L'assujettissement des sites Internet municipaux aux logiques sociétales', *Sciences de la société*, 60.
30 Wojcik, S. (2003) *Les forums électroniques municipaux, espaces de débat démocratique?* Paper presented at the DEL research seminar, University Paris I.
31 Mediamétrie/Net ratings.
32 Norris, P. (2001) *Digital Divide: Civic engagement, information poverty, and the Internet worldwide*. Cambridge, UK, Cambridge University Press.
33 Barometer ADELE/BVA, Marc 2005, available at www.adae.gouv.fr/IMG/pdf/barometre_adele_2005.pdf
34 The percentage of e-administration users is 27 per cent.
35 Arnauld, M. and Perriault, J. (2002) *Les espaces publics d'accès à Internet*. Paris, Presses Universitaires de France, p.199.
36 Wolton, D. (2000) *Internet et après*. Paris, Flammarion.
37 Official Report (2005) 'La société de l'information en France en 2004', Cabinet du Premier ministre, available online at www.premier-ministre.gouv.fr/IMG/pdf/societe_information_2004.pdf
38 This statistic (December 2005) is from the ADAE service, available at www.adae.gouv.fr/IMG/pdf/Communique_ADELe-1.pdf
39 Statistics from the report 'Beyond e-governement', available online at www.egov2005conference.gov.uk/documents/pdfs/beyond_egov.pdf, p. 103. See

also Franko, C. (2004) 'La conduite du changement par les TIC' for an analysis of the implementation of the Copernic system.
40 See for example the online newspaper ZDnet, available at www.zdnet.fr/actualites/Internet/0,39020774,39216771,00.htm
41 A list has been established, see Caisse des dépôts et Consignations (2005) 'Les services numériques'.
42 Lau, E. (2004) 'Principaux enjeux de l'administration électronique dans les pays membres de l'OCDE', *Revue française d'administration publique*, 110, 225–43.
43 Alcaud, D. and Lakel, A. (2004) 'Les nouveaux visages de l'administration sur Internet: pour une évaluation des sites publics de l'Etat', *Revue française d'administration publique*, 110, 297–313.
44 Study 'e-Administration 2005', results available online at www.fr.capgemini.com/m/fr/n/pdf_e-Administration-2005-l-ann-e_du_changement.pdf
45 Jubert, F., Montfort, E. and Stakowski, R. (2005) *La e-administration, levier de le réforme de l'Etat*. Paris, Dunod, pp.18–20.
46 Lemoine, P. (2004) 'Le MEDEF et l'administration électronique (entretien)', *Revue française d'administration publique*, 110, 359–62.
47 Flichy, P. and Dagiral, E. (2004) 'L'administration électronique: une difficile mise en cohérence des acteurs', *Revue française d'administration publique*, 110, 245–55.
48 See *La lettre de la modernisation de l'Etat*, no.12, May 30th, 2005.
49 Foucart, S. (2005) 'Polémique contre la carte d'identité électronique', *Le Monde*, May 28th.
50 www.adae.gouv.fr/IMG/pdf/CP_Forum-LH2-def.pdf.
51 The new service includes the e-administration agency, the direction of the public budget reform, the delegation in charge of the relationships with the administration users and simplification of administrative procedures, and the delegation in charge of modernizing the public management and the state structures.
52 Dulong, D. (1997) *Moderniser la politique. Aux origines de la Ve République*. Paris, L'Harmattan.
53 An opinion poll from September 2005 shows that 68 per cent of net users consider the Internet as a good tool to improve democratic function. See www.forum-edemo.org/article.php3?id_article = 505
54 For example, in an August 2005 poll, 71% of the French think e-administration would bring citizens closer to their administration, and 65 per cent of the French consider e-administration as a good way to decrease the public expenditure. See www.adae.gouv.fr/article.php3?id_article = 863

Further reading

Caisse des dépôts et consignations (2005) 'Les services numériques: une nouvelle dimension pour le département', *Les cahiers pratiques du développement numérique des territoires*, 6. Paris, La documentation française.

Franko C. (2004) 'La conduite du changement par les TIC: l'exemple de l'administration des impôts', *Revue française d'administration publique*, 110, 327–36.

Lacasse, F. and Verrier, P.-E. (eds) (2005) *30 ans de réformes de l'Etat: expériences françaises et étrangères*. Paris, Dunod.

7 E-government in Germany

Tina Siegfried

Introduction

After initial steps made in the 1990s, experimenting with electronic signatures and creating portals with applications for citizens and enterprises, the perception of e-government in Germany has changed considerably. E-government today means modernising the public sector and developing new forms of public service delivery. To achieve this goal, we need to exploit the technical potential of ICT and consider new organisational forms within public administrations. New 'virtual' administrations are imaginable if the potential of ICT is realised. The following text will describe the development of e-government in Germany and the current status of public online services. Finally, it will give an impression of the potential and difficulties of using ICT for a transformation of the public sector.

The informatisation of the public sector in Germany

The informatisation of the public sector can be considered as an ongoing process, the roots of which go back to the 1960s and 1970s and the beginnings of automated electronic data processing and the development of data bases and storage media.[1] In the 1980s the dissemination of PCs increased substantially, although back in those days, PCs were mainly used as a form of electronic writing machine that facilitated the secretary's office work. They were not considered as tools offering the ability to facilitate office communication and organisation, nor were they seen as tools to create co-operative working forms or tools that offered the possibility to work on a subject at different times and in different places. The era of a new orientation towards using ICT started in the 1980s and is characterised by the decentralisation of data processing and storage, raising expectations regarding informatisation possibilities, the beginnings of networking and co-operative work, new concepts for integration of data and information and testing newly developed expert systems. The automatisation of data processing and electronic data transfer had already been fairly well advanced since the 1970s, but it was only the advent of the Internet that brought a new level of quality to the use of ICT within public administration. For the first time, communication between public agencies and customers or public bureaucracies and private enterprises could take place over the Internet.

The development of e-government in Germany

The term e-government emerged in the late 1990s. By then, German e-government projects focused mainly on the question of how new developments in the field of ICT and new technologies such as electronic signatures could open new markets. The first multimedia project of the federal government in Germany was started in 1998 by the Ministry of Economic Affairs. It was called *MEDIA@*Komm and it was originally designed with the intention of introducing electronic signatures to legally-binding transactions. In 1999 the Ministry of the Interior adopted a programme with the aim to modernise public administration. Key aspects of this recently updated programme were, and still are, creating a more efficient administration, reducing bureaucracy and increasing the number of public online services.[2] The first steps in implementing e-government within the public sector were taken when the first portal sites were created; portals that at first contained mainly information and communications and later also provided application forms for online transactions. In the late 1990s, a search for the term e-government on the Internet using search engines generated only a few hits. Today, trying 'e-government' in Google alone will produce almost 8.5 million hits.

The term e-government has never been defined properly and is still not used consistently. Early on, the term was rather narrowly defined and mostly used in analogy to e-commerce. Back then, e-government was more or less an umbrella term for the so-called virtual city halls,[3] used to describe the administration's activities to offer electronic means for information gathering and distribution, communication or creating electronic customer-oriented applications via the Internet. A more advanced image of e-government was discussed with the establishment of call centres and the creation of common service shops as access points for customers, where they can handle administrative procedures either electronically or in the conventional way.[4] In most cases, however, the newly created e-government services were nothing more than 'digitised' forms of already existing administrative procedures, such as application forms, simply presented via static html websites on the Internet.

In Germany, the federal government, the governments of the 16 federal states and many municipalities (mostly the bigger cities) created Internet portals that served as a kind of shop window, where the government presented its goods and services. The portals of many public authorities were designed to provide information and to allow electronic communication via e-mail. The idea was to create a 'virtual' image of the 'real' public administration, and to provide a platform for electronic customer-to-government interactions. The aim was to provide as many online services as possible and thus improve customer services.

A rather visionary view and broader comprehension of e-government was published in 2000 by the German computer society (Memorandum e-government 2000). In this document was a broadly accepted definition that e-government comprises several aspects of governance and government, including aspects such as public decision-making, service provision and participation, supported by ICT. In this view, the adoption of ICT provides a basis for the re-organisation and modernisation of the public sector in Germany.

Today we have a great number and a wide variety of different portals on several state-levels (central, regional and local – mirroring the importance of the devolved nature of German government and the role of the Länder in federal governance) and there are a lot of portals provided by enterprises or special interest groups. Many of them offer identical content. All portals run by the government are similar in that they provide information and communications, with the number of possible transactions still growing. There are also a great number of online applications that were designed in order to facilitate services for the customers and to facilitate contact between customers and their local administration. Life events such as the birth of children, education, looking for jobs, house building and so on, or special services for enterprises such as calls for tender, e-trading or licenses were created on national and regional or local levels (depending on responsibilities).[5]

Internet users

The number of Internet users in Germany is continuously increasing. In 2005, 35.7 million (or 55 per cent) of the German population older than 14 years had Internet access. The number of people using the Internet has therefore considerably increased: in 2005 about 1.7 million more people were online than was the case in 2004, this being a total increase of 18 per cent within the last 5 years. A difference in the level of ICT usage between men and women still exists, although more women than ever are online today. More than 63 per cent of men and almost 48 per cent of women claim that they go online. We can also see a rapid growth in ICT use by the older generations. More than 50 per cent in the age range 50 to 59, and almost a third of people in the age range 60 and 69 (29 per cent) are now using the Internet regularly (see Table 7.1).[6]

A joint national e-strategy: Germany On-line

'Deutschland On-line' (www.deutschland-on-line.de/Englisch/english.htm) is the official joint e-strategy adopted in June 2003 by the federal government, the federal-state governments and municipalities. It aims at bundling the different initiatives on all levels and to work on co-operative structures. The Deutschland On-line strategy draws on the strengths of federalism: on the one hand, some partners are taking the lead with model solutions according to the 'some for all' principle. Public services such as registers of trade, car registers, registration of residents or applications for statistics, geo-data and geo-information systems were chosen and are currently designed as model solutions.[7] On the other hand, suitable projects will be carried out in co-operation. The federal government, state governments and municipalities will develop a joint business model. This model will be used to offer e-government applications developed by the federal

Table 7.1 'Onliners' and 'nonliners' in Germany 2005.

Age	Onliners	Nonliners
14–19	84.8	7.4
20–29	81.4	12.3
30–39	75.8	16.9
40–49	66.7	25.9
50–59	53.2	40.1
60–69	29.1	64.7
70+	9.8	87.7
Total	55.1	38.6

Source: tns infratest/Initiative D 21 (2005).

government, state governments and municipalities to other regional and local authorities for their use. The Deutschland On-line strategy provides the framework for co-operation between all administration layers, based on the following five priorities:

- Development of integrated e-services for citizens and businesses: the most important cross-level administrative services will be made available online to citizens and business. The fields 'register queries' (commercial registers, Federal Central Criminal Register), 'citizens' registers' and 'civil status registers', official statistics, vehicle registers, Federal Education Assistance Act, and unemployment and social welfare assistance will be regarded as priority model projects.
- Interconnection of Internet portals: access to public services will be enhanced by implementing the required interoperability of Internet portals.
- Development of common infrastructures: joint e-government infrastructures will be established and developed in order to facilitate the exchange of data and to avoid parallel developments.
- Development of common standards: the federal government, state governments and municipalities will create joint standards as well as data and process models for e-government.
- Experience and knowledge transfer: the transfer of e-government solutions between the federal government, state governments and municipalities will be improved, know-how will be multiplied and parallel developments will be avoided.[8]

When the initiative began, a controversial debate arose about the aims of the strategy and what would be considered as success. Representatives of municipalities and of the Länder appreciated the need for interconnecting portals and for efforts to jointly develop standards, but they stressed the point that the national government should provide financial resources for this project, because the Länder and the regional and local level institutions would be in charge and had the major burden of implementing the strategy given to them.

Government services online

The German federal system is a complex one. It endows each level of institution with different responsibilities, and therefore comprises a very heterogeneous system of actors. The federal government, 16 state governments of the Länder, more than 300 regional authorities and last but not least approximately 15,000 municipalities actually provide online services. The local level is certainly the one with the most contacts between customers and the administration, but it cannot provide all services. If one takes the example of registration services for citizens; these are, mostly, provided on a local level, but several services such as pension approval certificates, the handling of loan programmes or import licenses are within the responsibility of national authorities. Therefore, we have a wide variety of Internet portals providing several services for several target groups, including information, communication and sometimes transactions.

Nevertheless, in European benchmarks regarding online services, Germany is very often seen to be scoring only slightly above average – and sometimes scoring at the bottom – depending on the survey. In the years 2001 to 2004, the EU Commission ordered several surveys with the aim to scan online available public services for citizens and enterprises, to enable participating countries to analyse progress in the field of e-government and to compare performance within and between countries.[9] The essential and structural weakness of these benchmark studies is that they do not take into account the changes in the awareness of policy makers or changes in programmes and strategies of public administrations. In 2003, Janssen, Rotthier and Snijkers analysed 18 different international benchmark studies.[10] They found that all the studies differed in focus, scope and in the type of measurement criteria that were used. Even the definition of e-government differs and some studies were limited to counting online applications. None of the studies focussed on the integration of back-office processes, on cross-organisational processes or on data sharing. Last but not least, the benchmark surveys almost never took into account the customers' needs. Most surveys have a dearth of research questions that asked about customers' needs and desires.

The German experience is that an average customer contacts the administration only twice a year, which brings up the question if the limited resources within the public sector should be used to create online applications or if one should rather concentrate on how to gain more efficient use of labour and other resources. Some municipalities such as the cities of Bremen (www.bremen.de), Nürnberg (www.nuernberg.de), Dortmund (www.dortmund.de), Köln (www.koeln.de) and Düsseldorf (www.duesseldorf.de) created Internet portals and online services for different target groups. Lawyers, tax consultants and enterprises are big and important special target groups, and in Bremen they can get specialised information and can handle their transactions with the administration online. In this case, the internal processes within the administration have been redesigned and were arranged specifically for the special needs of this special customer group.

However, in general, with the exception of some cities such as Bremen and Dortmund that are more pioneering, the administrative processes in Germany haven't really been radically changed yet through the use of ICTs. One-stop government is still rare, because ICT has been seen only as a form of technical tool being used with the aim to re-design or indeed provide completely new services; therefore using it for a modernisation of the public sector has hardly been realised. This technology-driven approach has to be changed, and the still-prevailing intra-organisational view in designing online services must be overcome. ICT offers a great deal of potential for co-ordination, co-operation and networking as well as the potential to change the public sector itself.

One of the most essential characteristics of ICT is its independence from space and time. The 'ubiquity' of data allows access to stored data and information at any time and in any place. The previous dependency on information that was stored in offline records and files, and the restrictions caused by having that information stored in disparate locations, can now be handled more efficiently or in some cases completely overcome by using ICT. Multiple collection of the same or similar data is no longer necessary now that ICTs offer the possibility for collected data to be easily transferred to, and used by, any other linked electronic system user. This allows parallel work on subjects by different officials, although they may be working in different places and indeed for potentially differing purposes. Workflow management systems offer automatically activated procedures, with work that formerly had to be executed by people now being often open to automation. Information and communication can be handled faster and much more efficiently by using electronic communication systems. Finally, computer supported co-operative work systems support co-operation and teamwork, as does the increasing use of specially-designed project management software.

ICT potentials for co-operative work

Using ICT supports modernising efforts because of its potential to create new flows of work and facilitate the creation of new services. This concerns both the internal view of administrations and the view of customers whose needs should be considered carefully when designing new processes. ICTs have the potential to remove spatial boundaries and to enable people to access data and information wherever and whenever they choose to do so. It also provides an option for different people to be working on the same subjects and even on same documents at the same time for differing purposes. Even routine jobs can be automated by machines and the staff can use the time saved for other work or for customer services. Thus, rising efficacy and efficiency is a big issue. Having access to any data and/or knowledge system might save large amounts of time, presenting the authorities with a clear choice to save that time and reduce costs through efficiency or to re-invest those time savings for greater and more thorough investigations into the facts and details of any given case. In other words, ICT might save time, raise efficiency and therefore save costs, or it can be used to allow government to operate at a more thorough level.

The deployment of ICT might even lead to new co-operative forms of networking within administrations. Using group-ware, joint editing systems or whiteboards allows several people to work on single documents in a collaborative sense although stationed in different places. New computer supported co-operative work systems provide functions such as mail, telephone or video conferencing via the Internet, chat-tools, discussion-forums and so on, that can be used for parallel working. Workflow management systems and document management systems have also influenced traditional working procedures because they transmit files; the worker need not physically retrieve any necessary files from a central store but will receive them in his/her mailbox automatically. These systems already exist and have already played a role in altering working practices within German government. There can be little doubt that they will have a strong influence on how working procedures will be organised in the future. With the advent of mobile-based applications one can foresee a rapid change in working practices in German government across all levels. When one takes into account the mobile applications that are already implemented to date, one can easily imagine that in future it is not the customers that will have to make efforts to contact their local administration, but that it is more likely that the administration will contact the customers by engaging and interacting with them at the places where they live, where they shop, in other places that are open to the public (such as libraries) or indeed even on public transport.

The traditional internal organisation within administrations in Germany has followed hierarchical principles and was divided on a functional basis. The customer only rarely exists in this principle of organisations. It is a problem for the customer to find out precisely which authority is responsible for their request and, very often, it is always the customer who has to take care that their applications will be handled properly. It might be that a customer has to contact several authorities or departments in order to get specifically-required confirmations. No wonder, then, that sometimes people can get lost in this jungle of authorities. ICT can help to overcome this outdated behaviour of authorities and help to create new and better services. A broader comprehension of e-government will not only ask how ICT can improve the internal organisation by supporting internal production- and decision-processes; it is much more important to ask how ICT can be used to support and to improve customer services.

In order to take advantages of the potential of ICTs, the business processes have to be analysed and redesigned. It is not enough to simply speed-up existing processes by using ICT, it is also important to create new processes in order to gain the maximum benefit from the potential of ICTs. It is not only a question of how to design a process; rather, the results of business processeses should be anticipated. E-government means to create new processes instead of trying to improve existing processes.[11] But business process engineering is only one direction to consider. There ought also to be a realisation of the special nature of some governmental administrative processes. Simply transferring reference models from the business world into the world of public administration won't work, because administrative processes are much more diverse. Administrative processes are not only characterised by decisions, they also deal with information and consulting and – most importantly, and unlike the business world – there are several options and greater scope for decision-making.[12] The crux is that thinking in administrative business processes will almost always lead to regarding only the internal view and concentrating on internal processes. But ICT use offers the chance to also consider the customers, as well as other authorities or even the employees, and it offers the chance to design transactions that will overcome the still-existing barriers between these groups. Therefore, it might be helpful to consider administrative processes from a different point of view and to consequently design new processes that will consider the needs of all players involved. The aim should be to implement a single-window approach (or 'one-stop shop') where the customer will have only one contact point, from where his or her request will be electronically transferred to the appropriate authority. This front-end can be designed online as well as in the form of 'physical' desks in a town hall. Service shops or call centres might also serve as additional access points. Offline access to public administration might be especially necessary for those who don't have access to the Internet, or are for other reasons not able or not willing to deal with electronic services – although over time it is felt that such resistance to new technologies will decline.

Germany's public administration's activities were – in the beginning of the drive towards e-government – focussed on creating online services for the customers; everyone tried to create online transactions via the Internet and to provide information about authorities and responsibilities. Now, the focus has changed and the idea that e-government might be seen as an instrument towards modernising public administrations is becoming more and more important. E-government leads to fundamental changes in organisational form, often in respect of personnel changes.

E-government definitely raises technical questions, and also questions of change management within the public sector. E-government affects many aspects of German governmental life, such as strategic action planning, staff qualifications, organising communication and knowledge management, organisational culture, building up partnerships, planning on financial and personnel resources and so on.[13] ICT can thus be considered as an enabler but not as a purpose within itself. Above all, e-government has a potential for transforming governmental organisations because of its potential for changing institutions.

ICT – potential for a transformation of the public sector

We can envisage that organisational boundaries can easily be overcome using ICT, and that inter-organisational service provisions are possible. Re-engineering for e-government is not only a problem for single authorities having to deal with setting up internal networks and installing new technologies but also for how they relate to other organisations in terms of problems of overlap and function. Moreover, the question arises how to overcome split competencies and responsibilities, how to set up cross-organisational services including several authorities on a municipal and regional level (horizontal networking). We can predict that there will be increased prospects for networking with different authorities – even private institutions – on different state levels, thus offering the opportunity to create vertical networks across the public sector. At the very least one can see options for a transformation of state-wide structures, procedures and functions; a new perspective for a fundamental re-organisation of co-operation within the public sector arises.

Using ICT allows modularisation of processes and the separation of front-end and back-end services. It is now possible to separate production and distribution of customer services, in either spatial or organisational respects. This leads us to the question of whether it is possible to outsource processes or parts of processes simply because different organisations (even private ones) may have better results in service production, meaning they can work easier, faster or cheaper. This obviously brings up the further question of what services should be provided by public administration at all?

A critical discussion of the need for certain public services will also have to address the questions of how to organise an effective provider mix (or 'delivery network')[14] and of how to tackle the corresponding steering and control problems.[15] In stark contrast to the experience of private sector corporations, in the context of e-government the concept of virtual organisations[16] in the public sector have only been weakly developed. E-government is still primarily organised within the confines of individual administrative units or levels (such as local, regional or federal agencies), whereas public–private partnerships or significant outsourcing of public services is still relatively unheard of. As a consequence, we are still a long way from a more flexible and dynamic 'organisation without boundaries'[17] that is independent of geographical locations but focused on specific missions and tasks. From a more normative perspective, however, it seems worth asking whether this type of virtual organisation is something to be desired or not. Does the citizen, in whose name all such changes are enacted, really desire a shift from the present notion of spatially-oriented German public administrative structures? What might be the consequences for the German democratic system if such a shift were to occur? In theory, modern ICT clearly has the potential to change the traditional division of labour between the local, regional and federal levels of government. Undoubtedly, this technological potential calls into question the rationale for administrative decentralisation which presently rests on the assumption that services ought to be delivered where they are closest to the citizens, that is to say primarily at the local level.[18] Seen from the angle of e-government, however, very little, if anything, stands in the way of redrawing these lines of the established division of labour according to budgetary or efficiency criteria – resulting in a shift away from traditional providers to other public or private delivery organisations.

Prospects

Our current research findings[19] underline the thesis that it would be better to drop the 'e' in e-government and to concentrate on analyzing and re-designing processes in order to create better services for customers and to create integrated or seamless government services. The main fields for future activities are the integration of information and the integration of processes, as well as integrating the customer and his/her special needs. Compiling data and knowledge, the standardisation of data and data exchange, interoperability, the design of inter-organisational workflows and questions of liabilities and sanctions are the future tasks in e-government and in modernising the public sector.

We also need to start a broad discussion about options and the outcomes of e-government. The options are multifarious: the realisation of the one-stop-government-principle, designing decentralised front-office processes, implementing a multi channel management, re-engineering back-office processes, creating cross-organisational services, the inclusion of private organisations and the creation of interoperability and standardisation are catchwords to describe the potentials and the organisational diversities. The technical obstacles seem to be marginal compared with the challenges that will emerge when trying to change approved organisational cultures and to overcome the financial or legislative obstacles. We can certainly expect a reluctance to change long-lasting cultures and behaviours.

If one realises the enormous potential of e-government as a tool of reorganising public administration, the revamping of structural features of public organisation is almost a logical consequence. This is particularly true if the aim of reform is not the mere fine-tuning of internal administrative processes, but the improvement of inter-organisational service production and delivery. Before embarking on such far-reaching reform projects, however, we also have to consider political and administrative implications, asking ourselves whether it makes sense to introduce new procedures only because it is technologically feasible. At the same time, we need to be prepared to face typical patterns of organisational resistance and to anticipate concerns from organisational members.

It follows from this that successful e-government reformers need to be able to think outside the box. A new way of conceptualising service production and delivery beyond established lines of administration; demarcation is a necessary prerequisite for reform. On top of that we have also to take budgetary and efficiency-oriented considerations into account. In view of tight budgetary restrictions, we need to be careful not to duplicate too many reform approaches and not to pursue contradictory or incompatible reform strategies. How heterogeneous a reform landscape can Germany economically afford? How many different local databases can we really justify? Most importantly, any thorough re-conceptualisation of provider networks in the delivery of public services with regard to the vertical division of labour between the various levels of public administration calls into question the established political and administrative order. In a nutshell, the federal structure of Germany, as well as the status of local government within it, is at the centre of the debate. To be sure, there is no need to throw the baby out with the bathwater and to discard federalism altogether. Rather, a more strategic question is at stake: To what extent, if at all, are we ready to foster co-operation in the delivery of government services between local, state and federal authorities by the way of e-government, and what concrete form and shape will this cooperation take?

Today, only a few researchers, politicians and senior managers are dealing with the question of how to create a new and innovative service production of public administration. Certainly, we do need new ideas, new strategies and new tools for innovative processes. In order to get an idea of how to modernise the public sector we have to analyse possible impacts of new procedures and we have to assess which impacts are tolerable, which ones are desired and which ones are possibly not. 'Innovation impact assessment' and 'open choice' are two currently discussed approaches in this field, dealing with both strategic and technical questions.[20]

Modernising the public sector is inextricably linked to e-government, but e-government is a field where more knowledge is required. Developing ideas for integrative e-government and designing the future of the public sector requires more research and more information about strategies and tools for a public sector reform, about obstacles or 'stumbling blocks' of innovation processes and the contextual factors that decide about success and failure in their respective countries. We know that reform processes are long-lasting processes and that it is much more difficult to bring such reforms to a lasting success.[21] We have to know more about the conditions under which reform processes could be successful. We need to examine the influence of the different actors or sets of actors who influence the processes and results, according to their own preferences. At the same time the willingness of the public and the private sector to invest in e-government activities is declining because of the lack of generalising results. The current German research funds are too limited at the moment, and more investment in applied research to obtain more knowledge is required.

As a consequence, in February 2006 German e-government researchers met in Berlin and decided to found a national e-government society. The future tasks of this national society are currently under discussion, but the memorandum of understanding includes the following aspects:

- to determine future research fields and activities;
- to intensify networking across different disciplines dealing with e-government;
- to create a hub and act as an intermediary for information and communication for researchers and practitioners;
- being in charge of knowledge transfer;
- lobbying, that is to say to address policy makers with one voice and to emphasise increased requirements for research towards policy programmes;
- the evaluation of e-government programmes and projects;
- promoting young researchers in the field of e-government; and
- promoting networks on an international level.

Conclusions

The move towards e-government has certainly contributed to starting a debate about the potential of ICT and the potential to modernise the public sector, but we are still at the very early stages of that debate. There are still many goals to achieve, a change in management within the administration, for example, is still essential, as is an upgrading of the qualifications and training of the employees. Virtual administrations in the future will overcome the fragmented responsibilities of today and offer customer-oriented services. Data sharing across administrational borders will be taken as a matter of course and some day even standardised processes will be exchanged across public and private institutions. This kind of integrative e-government will almost certainly raise questions of new institutional designs within the public sector and questions about institutional structures of government, but we have to tackle this future challenge. Last but not least, more knowledge and more research are required in order to manage the innovative process of modernising the public sector.

Notes

1. Lenk, K. (2004b) *Der Staat am Draht*. Berlin, p. 26 (edition sigma).
2. www.staat-modern.de
3. Siegfried, T. (2001) *E-government and e-Commerce – German Experience in the Construction of Virtual Town Halls and Market Places*. Berlin, German Institute of Urban Affairs.
4. Lenk, K. (2004a) *Verwaltungsinformatik als Modernisierungschance. Strategien – Modelle – Erfahrungen*. Aufsätze 1988–2003, Berlin (edition sigma).
5. For a complete survey, see www.bund.de/nn_174036/DE/Startseite-knoten.html – nnn = true provides a survey in English, French and some other languages.
6. tns Infratest/Initiative D 21 (Hrsg.) (2005) *(N)On-liner-Atlas 2005 – eine Topographie des digitalen Grabens durch Deutschland*. S. 12, available at www.non-liner-atlas.de/pdf/dl_NON-LINER-Atlas2005.pdf (accessed 20/01/2006).
7. For a survey (in German only), see www.deutschland-on-line.de/Downloads/Dokumente/031114%20DeutschlandOn-line%20Bericht%20MPK%20final.pdf
8. European Commission (2005) *E-government Factsheet – Germany – Strategy*. Available at europa.eu.int/idabc/en/document/1350/396 (accessed 20/01/2006).
9. For example, Cap Gemini, Ernst & Young (2004) *On-line Avaliability for Public Services. How is Europe Progressing?* Available at europa.eu.int/information_society/eeurope/2005/doc/highlights/whats_new/capgemini4.pdf (accessed 25/01/2006).
10. Janssen, D., Rotthier, S. and Snijkers, K. (2004) 'If You Measure it They Will Score: An Assessment of International E-government Benchmarking', *Information Polity* 9, 121–30.
11. Gaitanides, M. (1995) 'Je mehr desto besser?', *Technologie & Management* 2, 69ff.
12. Lenk, K. (2004b) *Der Staat am Draht*.
13. Grabow, B., Drüke, H. and Siegfried, T. (2004) 'Erfolgsfaktoren des kommunalen E-government', in *Deutsches Institut für Urbanistik*. Berlin, Deutsche Zeitschrift für Kommunalwissenschaften, 2004/II, pp. 64–93.
14. Reichard, C. (1998) 'Institutionelle Wahlmöglichkeiten bei der öffentlichen Aufgabenwahrnehmung', in Budäus, D. (Ed.) *Organisationswandel öffentlicher Aufgabenwahrnehmung*. Baden-Baden, p. 121–53.
15. See Brueggemeier, M. (2004) 'Gestaltung und Steuerung öffentlicher Leistungsnetzwerke im Kontext von Electronic Government', in:Reichard, C., Scheske, M. and Schuppan, T. (eds) *Das Reformkonzept E-government*. Münster, pp. 188–209.
16. See Reichwald, R., Möslein, K., Sachenbacher, H. and Englberger, H. (2000) *Telekooperation. Verteilte Arbeits-und Organisationsformen*. Berlin, p. 241.
17. Picot, A., Reichwald, R. and Wigand, R. (2001) *Die grenzenlose Unternehmung. Information, Organisation und Management*. Wiesbaden, p. 387ff.
18. Lenk 2004b, *Der Staat am Draht*. p. 87.
19. See various case studies of the Research Project 'Organisatorische Gestaltungspotenziale durch E-government', available soon (in German) at www.orggov.de
20. See Brüggemeier, M., Dovifat, A., Kubisch, D., Lenk, K., Reichardt, C. and Siegfried, T. (2006) *Organisatorische Gestaltungspotenziale durch e-government*. Berlin.

21 Lenk, K. (2005) 'How to Bring About Public Administration Reforms with E-government', in Wimmer, M.A. (ed) *E-government 2005: Knowledge Transfer und Status*. Vienna, Oesterreichische Computer-Gesellschaft, pp. 317–24.

Further reading

Deutschland On-line: Bericht über die Zusammenarbeit von Bund, Ländern und Kommunen im e-government, available at www.deutschland-on-line.de/Downloads/Dokumente/031114%20Deutschland-On-line%20Bericht%20MPK%20final.pdf (accessed 28/02/2006).

Federal Minstry of the Interior (2004) Deutschland On-line – the joint e-government strategy by the federal government, federal-state governments and municipalities, available at www.deutschland-on-line.de/Englisch/Dokumente/Broschure_english.pdf (accessed 20/01/2006).

Memorandum on e-government (2000) Electronic Government als Schlüssel zur Modernisierung von Staat und Verwaltung. Ein Memorandum des Fachausschusses Verwaltungsinformatik der Gesellschaft für Informatik e.V. und des Fachbereichs 1 der Informationstechnischen Gesellschaft im VDE, Available at www.gi-ev.de/informatik/presse/presse_memorandum.pdf

8 Re-organising government using IT
The Danish model

Kim Viborg Andersen, Helle Zinner Henriksen and Eva Born Rasmussen

Introduction

This chapter investigates the adoption and exploitation of IT in the Danish government. The Danish case is interesting due to the strategic commitment to face challenges and formulate explicit milestones for the success of e-government strategies. Through a presentation of four cases of successful e-government implementation (taxation, the health sector, case handling and procurement), this chapter examines the governmental policies through the lenses of normative actions, economic incentives, knowledge transfer, and management practice. The chapter identifies a remarkable shift from using primarily knowledge transfer mechanisms towards direct normative policies.

The wide dissemination of the Internet has led to an increasing interest in opportunities for government departments to leverage technology to offer better and more efficient services to citizens, companies, and other parts of government. This is particularly attractive in the current climate of severe budgetary constraints in government, due to the expectation that the implementation of IT can lead to cost savings. The drive to accomplish more with fewer resources has led to investments in IT to digitise internal and external processes within Danish government. The Danish case is fascinating for two reasons: the long timespan of adoption and exploitation of IT prior to the current e-government wave, and the strategic commitment to face challenges and formulate explicit milestones for the success of e-government strategies.

The high degree of computerisation of Danish government did not happen overnight or by adding instant doses of technology and organisational transformation. Rather, the Danish story is the evidence of the value of building on top of solid groundwork. E-government in Denmark is in what can be considered as the next stage in a 30-year-long trend where digital exchange of messages, issues of interoperability, and semantic challenges have been addressed long before the era of e-government. With 60–70 per cent of the Danish gross domestic product (GDP) being re-allocated through government and about one-third of the workforce employed in the public sector, it is hard to find another case where the public sector plays such an equally critical role in an economy that has, at the same time, managed to stay efficient in the global economy. An unemployment rate of 5 per cent, a surplus in the foreign exchange balance and in the state budget, and a GDP per capita ranking in the top-five of the OECD-countries[1] is all evidence that the Danish model is very successful.

The second reason to focus attention on the Danish case is the unique strategic commitment to ensure that the use of IT must create value for citizens and companies, directly via online services and equally directly via a more efficient public sector. The policy commitment to use IT to transform the public sector is backed by explicitly-defined criteria for successful implementation of e-government solutions. Facing challenges in reaching the strategic objectives, e-government implementation policies have shifted from a knowledge transfer and standard setting perspective towards direct enforcement that forces companies to deliver invoices in digital format and abandon physical salary transfer notices for public employees.

The objective of this chapter is to present the content of the Danish model and to provide some illustrative cases on how it has been used as a lever for an on-going improvement of governmental services.

Our analytical framework

Institutional frameworks have been found to influence and facilitate – or sometimes even to retard – processes of technical and structural change, co-ordination, and dynamic adjustment.[2] Regulatory intervention of different descriptions makes up an important set of institutional factors in this sense. Such intervention may indeed influence innovation at the organisational level and may be expected to be especially important in influencing the diffusion process. This chapter emphasises the significance of institutional intervention at the government level rather than on the diffusion of innovations viewed at the micro-level. One implication of this choice is that it bypasses the analysis of potential adopters as well as of innovation attributes that usually require attention in diffusion studies.[3] While it is acknowledged that the individual and organisational characteristics of potential adopters cannot be completely neglected when impacts of institutional intervention are analysed,[4] the present analysis will nevertheless focus on how institutional instruments are designed to initiate a diffusion process in a social system.

Damsgaard and Lyytinen[5] suggest that institutional intervention can be classified into two overall categories: influence and regulation. *Influential initiatives* aim to change the behaviour of those under the institutions' sway. No direct force or command is applied when institutional intervention is used to influence behavioural change. The means of influence may, for example, be knowledge dissemination in the form of knowledge building or knowledge deployment, where initiatives may be subsidised. In contrast to influential initiatives, *regulation* is expected to directly affect the behaviour of entities that fall within the institution's formal jurisdiction. This could, for example, be in the form of explicit directives or of other measures that limit options of behaviour. Regulatory initiatives in this sense may, for example, involve compliance to mandatory standards or adherence to the specifications of innovation directives.

Following on from the Damsgaard and Lyytinen dichotomy, we distinguish between direct and indirect actions in order to gain an understanding of the structural features of institutional intervention. Using the example of interventions related to the uptake of e-government, illustrations are provided in relation to direct and indirect actions. Direct actions are those that target e-government usage by subsidising the direct investment necessary for e-government use; funding the definition of protocols for a certain user group is an example of this. Indirect actions comprise initiatives that aim to increase e-government 'awareness' or acceptance, thereby enabling 'smoother' use of e-government.[6] This can be accomplished through the introduction of public e-procurement or by participating in task forces, councils, international committees or special interest groups.

Both direct and indirect actions can be viewed as involving four modes of intervention: regulation and legislation, economic incentives, knowledge diffusion,[7] and organisational management.[8] Prohibitions and commands characterise interventions based on regulation and legislation. Intervention, in this case, involves the enforcement of regulatory objectives. Economic interventions are, contrastingly, expected to influence what potential adopters find advantageous to do. Through economic interventions, organisations are rewarded for certain behaviours or are punished for others. The third mode of intervention involves knowledge diffusion. It is characterised by information campaigns initiated by governmental units and larger associations where the aim is to influence the opinion of a given group of potential adopters. Eckhoff[9] argues that information is a must in most cases where economic and regulatory interventions are brought into play. However, information in itself can be used as a means of intervention. Information can be used to influence opinions and values thus making individuals more motivated to perform certain types of actions recommended by governmental units or business associations. The fourth mode, the organisational management, focuses on the work processes in the public sector's own organisations and level of government. Organisational management is especially relevant in our analysis given the prominent role that the public sector played in Danish IT policy during the 1990s.

Below, we briefly relate the four modes of interventions to e-government initiatives that have taken place abroad. Knowledge diffusion initiatives include seminars for practitioners and the dissemination of information about e-government, as well as the support of e-government related research at universities and international research communities.

At the supranational level, there has been an extensive use of knowledge diffusion initiatives related to e-government. The UN, OECD and EU are among supranational agencies that have published agendas and statements supporting such knowledge diffusion. This has influenced most national governments that have launched plans for the implementation of national e-government initiatives. Many of these action plans and e-government agendas are, however, general in nature and present more of a catalogue of what is possible through the means of IT than what is actually realistic and advantageous to do in the long run. Another feature is that much of the responsibility for successful implementation has been placed on the end users, typically the citizens or businesses who should ultimately benefit from the provision of the digital services. However, they are first expected to move to adopt the Internet and to change their behaviour by servicing themselves through digital means. This is certainly true in the Danish case. The first ten years of IT policies were characterised by several agendas that were generalised and with high expectations, particularly towards the business sector, that the user should take the lead in the diffusion of digital government.

Another source within the realm of knowledge diffusion initiatives which has strengthened the e-government discourse is the growing interest in studying the phenomenon in academia. During the period 1998 to 2003 there has been a steady growth in the number of academic papers that have found their way to the established academic outlets.[10] Additionally, a number of new academic journals focusing on e-government have seen the light of day (for example, the *International Journal of Electronic Government Research* and the *Electronic Journal of E-government*). Finally, there has been an increase in academic conferences focusing on e-government. According to the knowledge diffusion perspective these activities are all means of fuelling the diffusion of a given phenomenon.

Economic initiatives involve the provision of favourable, often subsidised, software or web-solutions. They may also involve the direct subsidisation of e-government activities either as 'pilot projects' or on a more long-term or even permanent basis. In the Danish context, national boards and councils have distributed limited resources for development of software in pilot projects[11] and at the supranational level the EU has tended to favour projects focusing on development of IT-applications in the fifth and sixth framework of the IST programme, hence indirectly subsidising the diffusion process. One of the most well-known examples of economic initiatives is the French Minitel initiative that took place in the 1980s.[12]

The third mode of institutional intervention is that of regulation and legislation initiatives in the e-government context. The model involves a wide set of directives and legislation, the subject of which may concern syntax rules, data dictionaries, or the document standards that are utilised in business transactions with the public sector.

An example of this mode of intervention is the Singaporean TradeNet that was launched as a mandatory initiative by a governmental agency, The National Computer Board. Companies involved in the export sector were required to implement EDI in their exchange of export documents with the public authorities. The electronic infrastructure was launched in 1989. The Singapore experiment can be seen as a success in diffusion of EDI in a business community, where it has achieved or surpassed its goals.[13]

Finally, the fourth mode, organisational management, focuses on work processes in the public sector's own organisations and level of government. The politics of e-commerce management can be significantly more complex in the public sector due to a broader range of special interests. Klein showed in an analysis of the TEDIS project that the public administrations' use of EDI represents a significant special case, observing that:

On the one hand the government departments responsible represent a monopoly, so at the local level they do not have to co-ordinate the introduction of electronic trading with any other equivalent body. However, public administrations lack the commercial pressures to seek efficiency improvements through IT innovations faced in the private sector.[14]

Table 8.1 illustrates that the first three modes encompass the traditional actions used by governments. But organisational management may be as important as these three other modes, as, in many countries such as Denmark, the public sector itself may be a more eager user of e-government applications. As an illustration, more than one third of the work force is employed by government, so private agencies saw the opportunity of creating a good market having the public sector as their primary customer relatively early in the history of computing in the public sector. Therefore, the public sector is in the situation where applications suiting its needs have been developed along with the general development of IT. The public sector was therefore in a situation where it could deploy ICTs at an early stage.

The early use of e-mail within the public sector in Denmark was characterised by a high level of internal use, rather than direct communication with citizens. Consequently, government actions may affect both the demand-pull as well as the supply-push for e-government in the private sector. Accordingly, when we address the impact of institutional intervention, both the public sector's diffusion and the private sector's adaptation are of equal interest. In addition, the variety of instruments outlined in Table 8.1 reflects how many means government have at their

Table 8.1 Classification of governmental actions related to e-government diffusion

Mode of Intervention	Direct actions	Indirect actions
Knowledge diffusion	Knowledge deployment Innovation directive Transfer of e-government technology	Mobilisation Developing new technical knowledge Knowledge building and dispersing e-government councils Co-ordination of supranational e-government initiatives Targeting public opinion to create demand-pull Discursive initiatives
Economic	Direct subsidy of e-government projects	Subsidy for educational e-government projects and general IT learning Subsidy for information infrastructure Provision of favorable charging modes for network services Subsidising innovation processes
Regulation & legislation	Innovation directive Standard setting Legislation on electronic signature and e-government	Innovation directive Standard setting Public procurement

disposal to stimulate the diffusion of e-government. For example, the TradeNet in Singapore did not achieve success merely by bottom-line analysis and top-down steering. Instead, this example showed the need to stimulate and evaluate e-government diffusion in its organisational context, whether it is in the public or the private domain.

A further important point is that local government and quasi-governmental organisations might be just as, or even more successful than central government in initiating low-cost e-government solutions. We believe this is a very important observation given that governments have multiple forms, and that the distinction between private and public institutions is no longer as clear-cut as it was a century ago. Moreover, the spread of semi-public companies is changing the roles of politicians, managers and staff in the public sector, and these same public institutions are influencing the constitution of the private sector.

In this section we have presented our analytical framework that will guide the further presentation of possible explanatory factors for the successful Danish model.

Key features of e-government in Denmark

The key characteristics of the historical background for what has made the e-government initiatives in Denmark unique can be summarised as having a long tradition, small size, decentralised use of IT, on-going structural changes, central state IT initiatives, and cross-agency dependencies.

There has been a long tradition of the use of IT in the public sector. Denmark has, over time, created a strong national data infrastructure based on unique identifiers of citizens, of businesses, of buildings and of property. The Danish systems of taxation are very advanced, with electronic communication to almost all the parties involved. Close to 100 per cent of all information in the tax system is collected and exchanged electronically. In addition, the financial sector in Denmark has established a very efficient infrastructure for electronic exchange of financial transactions. The public sector benefits from these services and, today, very few payments are made manually. Key initiatives include the compulsory demand for digital communication between two public authorities ('eDag') and the compulsory establishment of an individual account for each citizen in order to be able to receive any payment from the government such as wages, benefits and so on ('NemKonto').

The implementation of this national data infrastructure in Denmark has first of all been possible due to the ability to experiment with the use of IT in the public sector, within a small population (5 million inhabitants) living in a relatively small geographical area.

There has, in Denmark, been a long tradition of strong local government. Over the last 30 years, the local authorities at the municipal and regional levels have been given a steadily-increasing functional responsibility for, and fiscal control of, for example, schools, hospital, roads, and so on, which has required extensive use of IT. The use of IT in the public sector has been perceived as the responsibility of the individual institution and has over time been gradually adapted to support this decentralised government structure. The use of IT has been dominated at the municipal level by one central provider, established in the 1970s as a shared IT-service provider, offering a wide range of shared services supporting most of their activities.

The 275 municipalities and 14 counties that existed in the 1970s have over time been reduced and will after the latest changes become 99 municipalities and 5 counties in 2007. These mergers of local government have been a key driver for an increased awareness of the need to ensure that such changes can be supported by the use of IT.

The central state control of the local authorities since the 1970s has been characterised by efforts to 'streamline' and simplify the many central regulations and 'rules'. At the same time, central IT initiatives have attempted to ensure a common IT strategy for the many decentralised IT initiatives. For example the Ministry of Finance has over time offered shared (and compulsory) services on accounting, payroll and budgeting which are used by all government organisations.

For more than 40 years Denmark has experimented with establishing (and closing) central government agencies, entrusted with carrying out specific tasks based on 'contract agreements'. Many business services offered by one agency require cross-agency support to be carried out by another. This has increasingly required advanced and smooth integration between the decentralised IT systems – a challenge not easily met and as such an on-going challenge for e-government in Denmark.

These characteristics have resulted in an overall dilemma: on one hand the decentralisation has been the background for the development of many user-centred and advanced IT services offered by the various (central and local) public authorities; on the other hand there has been a costly and time-consuming duplication of efforts in the initiatives, resulting in an increasing need for re-alignment initiatives from the centre.

This dilemma has recently led to an increasing acknowledgement of the need to ensure a common framework for the use of IT in the public sector to ensure operational efficiency and interoperability of the local solutions and to support local competencies. This includes the need for an open process driven by unity among the main stakeholders for IT in the public sector about the targets, in a dialogue with, among others, the IT sector, international partners and standardisation groups, the Ministry of Finance with their budget and administration policies, the Ministry of Science, Technology and Innovation, as well as various business organisations and professional organisations, and the regional and municipal public authorities.

Computing in government

The first computer in Denmark was an arithmetic sequential calculator (DASK) with a RAM of 5 kilobytes and a hard disk of 40 kilobytes. DASK was donated via Marshall Aid in the 1950s and was in use from 1958 to 1968. The foundation for the streamlining of processes between government and citizens was laid during the late 1960s and 1970s with the development and deployment of central registers for citizens and buildings IDs (the CPR and BBR registers respectively). The computerisation wave in Scandinavian government did not take place earlier than in, for example, the US, but it was more radical and much more comprehensive than, for example, the US Social Security Register designed in the 1930s, or the French citizens register developed in the 1940s.

Within government operations, the document and record management systems were developed by companies such as Scan·Jour Inc. During the 1980s Scan·Jour Inc. was by far a leader in respect of innovation, and the diffusion of their systems within the Danish administration to all key administrative tasks was much more widespread than in most other countries in the world.

Digital front-end services and digital procurement were not invented by the moves to adopt a specific policy of e-government. Touch-tone services and e-mail communication with government existed long before the e-government application. Private companies and public sector authorities exchanged orders and invoices electronically, often through third-party vendors.

If one examines the international rankings on e-government, Denmark can be seen to be not only good, but world class. See, for example, Table 8.2 where we have listed the rankings from Cap Gemini, Accenture, The Economist, UN, EU, and OECD, where Denmark is in the top five in all the listed rankings.

The main challenge with the international rankings is that they almost exclusively focus on the supply of service, and therefore fail to look at the demand side of service and ignore the governance/governing part of e-government. In addition, the international rankings measure mainly what's online, not back-office integration and interoperability. Denmark is, in our view, at world-class level on both dimensions.

The rankings provide 'an average picture' of e-government. Clearly there is massive innovation in e-government applications that is taking place outside Scandinavia. For example, the MyKad in Malaysia with the Government Multi-

Table 8.2 International rankings on Danish e-government, 2005

Source	International ranking
Cap Gemini[1]	2
Accenture[2]	5
Economist[3]	1
UN[4]	2
Eurostat[5]	4

[1] Cap Gemini (2005). Online availability of public services: How is Europe progressing? EU: DG Information and Media. Available at e.gov.dk/
[2] Accenture (2005). Leadership in Customer Service: New Expectations, New Experiences. Available at www.accenture.com
[3] Economist (2005). The 2005 e-readiness rankings: A white paper from the Economist Intelligence Unit. Available at e.gov.dk/
[4] UN (2005). UN Global E-government Readiness Report 2005. Available at www.un.org
[5] Eurostat (2005). Eurostat. Available at europa.eu.int/comm/eurostat/

purpose smart Card – GMPC – has integrated passport, ID, driver licence and so on into one chip-based card. In countries such as Myanmar and Bhutan, online visa applications are being installed, e-voting in Estonia and India, and digital facial recognition in Pakistan are all innovations in government that have become world class innovations. These international innovations exemplify the myriad problems that can be tackled by e-government solutions using IT. The reason why facial recognition is implemented in Pakistan is to prevent fraud. The MyKad was developed because of pressure on government to be more efficient and was part of the ambition to turn Malaysia into a 'smart nation'. The challenge for e-government in Denmark is at a different level. The challenges are not to link government or digital identifiers to buildings, companies, and citizens; this wave was developed and implemented during the 1960s and 1970s. The objective now is more of a semantic and ontological character and to exploit the technologies for operational and strategic benefits.

The rankings reflect, as mentioned above, how well the Danish government performs e-government at the front end to the citizens and businesses rather than how well it fares in back-office integration that can ultimately reduce workloads in public administration and lead to increased efficiency. To illustrate how the Danish government has actually gone some way in its effort to streamline work processes through the means of ICTs, the next section provides four examples of successful e-government projects in Denmark.

Four cases of successful e-government projects

Case handling and electronic communication with citizens and companies

Emailing among public sector agencies and between government and citizens has progressed rapidly during the late 1990s and the first five years of the new century. However, it was not until September 1st, 2003, with the launch of 'eDay 1' that it was explicitly stated that 'all public authorities have a general right to communicate electronically with each other and are encouraged to use e-mail etc. instead of paper', unless the documents are specifically excluded for privacy or security reasons. One and a half years later, 'eDay 2' was launched on February 1st, 2005. This marked the day where all public entities took an important step in the direction of e-government and secure communications. From that day on, 'sensitive, personal data could be sent by secure e-mail between authorities and citizens and companies, if they have a digital signature'. A significant portion of the mail which is transmitted today in paper format can be sent electronically. Therefore, the overall objective of eDay2 was to replace 40 per cent of the physical-letter mail by electronic mail by November 2005. At this point in time it is too early to assess if that objective has been achieved. However, there has been a growth in the share of cases that are processed digitally during the period 2002 to 2004 (see Table 8.3 below).

As of 1st February 2005 at the latest, all public entities had to have implemented secure email using digital signatures and ensure that the handling of secure email was appropriate. With the two eDay initiatives, the Danish government has taken a huge step towards a paperless public administration. Most importantly, it has led to a shift in attitude to what can be done electronically.

Accordingly, the public sector institutions have, in 2005, implemented that all public employees receive their pay-check information electronically through an electronic mail box ('e-boks') that can only be accessed via the Internet. Some of the unions have argued that not all public employees have access to a computer at their workplace and are therefore disadvantaged by the new system. The political change is that digital divide arguments are put aside and rational arguments are in pole position. The e-boks application is designed so the users do not have to pay to use it and that the documents mailed to the e-boks can not be altered or deleted for five years. This initiative was to prevent arguments deriving from lost or altered documents, and so on.

Another example of the digitalisation of electronic communication is The Danish National Board of Industrial Injuries, which is a financially autonomous agency under the Ministry of Social Affairs that deals with individual work-related injuries. The work process involves retrieval of data, checking of legal data/reference materials, and co-working with other colleagues in the office before an insurance amount can be paid to an injured person.

In 1995, the Board received 327,000 letters, while they sent off 375,000 letters. They received 46,000 notifications of injuries and made 90,000 decisions. In 1997, the insurance companies and the Board started using EDI. The insurance companies are required by law to use the board in cases of worker compensation related to injuries. The board needs to check insurance numbers and the insurance companies need to check social security numbers. By using EDI, the two partners bypassed a legal barrier that prohibits insurance companies from obtaining direct access to centrally-stored personal data. The web interface and subsequent obtainment of the digital signature have now allowed the clients to trace their records and send e-mails that have legal proof status.

The three examples of case handling and electronic communication with citizens and companies illustrate that the Danish public sector has been able to change back-office procedures by adopting IT. By issuing the directives on digital communication

Table 8.3 Number of cases processed digitally in central government, 2002–2005

	2002 (%)	2003 (%)	2004 (%)	2005 (%)
More than 50% of the cases are processed digitally	26	34	40	43
25–49% of the cases are processed digitally	13	15	10	16
Less than 25% of the cases are processed digitally	51	40	42	27
Do not know	10	11	8	14
Total	100	100	100	100

Source: Statistics Denmark, 2006.

within the public sector, reams of paper have been replaced by electronic files. One implication is that it has become easier to obtain, access, and store information. By expanding the digital communication to employees in the public sector with respect to the delivery of the monthly salary statement, a new routine has been implemented. It is a routine that is beneficial both for the public sector and the employees in the long run. As for the third case presented, there has been a streamlining in the processes internally in the case handling, ultimately leading to shorter administrative procedures that is clearly of benefit for the injured party. Generally, the three initiatives have supported the growth in the number of cases which have been handled electronically. The numbers in Table 8.3 presented above reflect this growth.

Public procurement

In 1997, National Procurement Ltd. introduced an EDIFACT-based[15] database which encompassed all goods and services in the then-current paper-based purchasing system. In addition, an electronic public purchasing system was designed in co-operation with the national and local public network operators.

These two systems are completed with EAN location numbers for all subscribers, as well as a set of EDI documents and standards which form the backbone of a thorough public trade environment. This is combined with an open interface to other 3rd party goods and services databases and administrative systems used in the public sector.

In 1998, all public authorities were able to commence transactions via EDI. Together with National Procurement, Ltd., the Agency for Financial management and Administrative Affairs developed a basic procurement system for public economic management systems. The procurement system became operative for municipal and central government users as of February 15th, 1998. As an instrument to speed up the diffusion of e-procurement, government mandated all suppliers by law to deliver their invoices in electronic format by February 2005. Though it has been a challenge especially for the small suppliers, e-invoices have been imperative since the implementation of the law (see Table 8.4).

Taxation

The Danish Central Customs and Tax Administration aims to receive all documents electronically. While similar ambitions are held in all other European countries, the Danish quest to achieve this goal dates back to 1988 when the Tax department started mailing pre-formatted tax forms with pre-filled data necessary for calculating taxation (for example, statements from workplaces concerning accurate income and statements from banks about interest earned during the year) to citizens, which they would approve and mail back. The forms were then scanned and processed electronically.

During the 1990s, the Danish Central Customs and Tax Administration's EDI strategy consisted of two major elements: firstly, a strategy for the handling of all incoming data from companies electronically through an alliance with the Statistics

114   *E-government in Europe*

Table 8.4 Electronic procurement integration with accounting system or digital invoicing, 2003–2004.

	Total	Central gvnt	Counties	Municipalities		
				Total	< 15 K citz.	15 K + citz
Integration of e-procurement and accounting system						
2003	12	7	25	13	9	21
2004	16	13	40	17	11	28
2005	29	22	55	31	30	31
Integration of e-procurement and e-invoicing						
2004	19	9	40	22	21	25
2005	69	68	73	69	70	66

Source: Statistics Denmark (2006)

Denmark and the Danish Commerce and Companies Agency, Ministry of Business and Industry; secondly, enabling citizens to deliver their advance tax assessments and income tax statements via the Internet and voice-response.

The new EDI interface enabled companies to deliver their declarations regarding VAT and individual article tax electronically, a service that many companies took advantage of. In 1997, more than 20 per cent of all Danes made use of the service to enter and transmit information for advance tax assessment and income tax return by telephone using the touch-tone system. Less than 1 per cent used the Internet for this task in 1997. By 2005, 80 per cent of the citizens and 86 per cent of the companies used the Internet for their transactions. The case of taxation is interesting not only due to its Internet interface but also due to an explicit goal of having as few 'hits' as possible. The reason for this goal is that tax handling should be seamless and hence not be subject to inquiries from citizens and businesses wherever possible.

Health sector

The Danish healthcare sector is considered to be one of the most automated in Europe. In 2001, 15 per cent of discharge letters, 7 per cent of laboratory results, and 10 per cent of pharmacy prescriptions on average were handled by EDI. In 2005, discharge letters, laboratory results and pharmacy prescription were totally digitalised.

In 1992, Fuen County initiated the development of the 'Fuen health data network' using the acronym MedCom. Communication was established via an electronic mailbox connecting hospitals, general practitioners (GPs), pharmacies, and the regional health insurance. The health data network involves communications such as letters of discharge from hospitals to GPs, laboratory and radiology reports to the GPs, prescriptions from GPs to pharmacies, current information on the occupancy levels of hospital departments, waiting lists, treatment procedures and so on from the hospitals to the GPs, reimbursement forms from GPs and pharmacies to the regional health insurance authorities, and medical information from

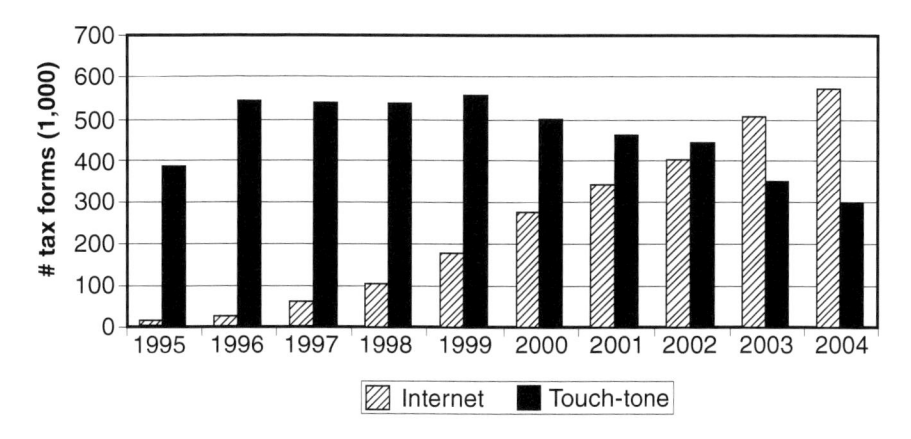

Figure 8.1 Take-up of digital tax form reporting, 1995–2004.
Source: www.tastselv.toldskat.dk/

wholesale suppliers to pharmacies and/or doctors. The communication follows the EDIFACT format.

The diffusion of the health data network points to local and corporate autonomy as essential in making ongoing innovations and securing some degree of competition in a mostly publicly-financed health sector where a number of tasks are undertaken by private players, as is the case with pharmacies and GPs, both of which are private businesses in Denmark. In Fuen, the number of GPs and pharmacies being connected is the engine behind the development. The relatively small scale of the network makes changes and quick feedback possible. National systems might be too tardy, address misleading or wrong issues, and be hard to change. The MedCom case suggests that a bottom-up organisational process for such systems is much more flexible and hence also more attractive. Thus, a network should emerge at the lowest level possible (in this case at the county level), initiated by local actors and interests, although this could challenge the control and autonomy of the Ministry of Health.

Figure 8.2 illustrates the steady increase in the deployment of the MedCom network during the period 1998 to 2005. Measurement is based on the number of EDI messages exchanged via the network distributed on different types of messages. Discharge letters from hospitals and laboratory letters show a high level of usage. This suggests that the initiative has achieved acceptance both from public (hospitals) and private (laboratories) players.

Discussion

The cases presented above have provided insights into different areas in Danish public administration where change has taken place as a result of the implementation of ICTs as a tool for streamlining back-office processes. The cases

Notes

1. Statistics Denmark (2006) *IT in the Public Sector, 2005*. Copenhagen: Statistics Denmark.
2. King, J.L., Gurbaxani, V., Kraemer, K. L., McFarlan, F. W., Raman, K. S., and Yap, C. S. (1994) 'Institutional Factors in Information Technology Innovation', *Information Systems Research* 5(2), 139–69.
3. Rogers, E.M. (1995) *Diffusion of innovations* (Fourth ed.). The Free Press; Tornatzky, L. G., and Fleischer, M. (1990) *The Process of Technological Innovation*. Lexington Books.
4. Henriksen, H.Z. (2002) *Performance, Pressures, and Politics: Motivators for Adoption of Interorganizational Information Systems*. Copenhagen: Copenhagen Business School.
5. Damsgaard, J., and Lyytinen, K. (2001) 'The Role of Intermediating Institutions in Diffusion of Electronic Data Interchange (EDI): How industry associations in the grocery sector intervened in Hong Kong, Finland, and Denmark', *The Information Society* 17(3), 195–210.
6. Andersen, K.V. (1998) 'Health Data Network: Organizational and Political Challenges', Proceedings of the 31st Hawaii International Conference on System Sciences (HICSS).
7. Eckhoff, T. (1983) *Statens styringsmuligheter*. Oslo: Tanum-Norli.
8. Andersen, K.V., Juul, N.C., Henriksen, H.Z., Bjorn-Andersen, N. and Bunker, D. (2000) *Business-to-Business E-commerce, Enterprises Facing a Turbulent World* (First edition). Copenhagen: DJØF Publishers.
9. Eckhoff, T. (1983) *Statens styringsmuligheter*.
10. Andersen, K.V. and Henriksen, H.Z. (2005) 'The First Leg of E-government Research: Domains and Application Areas 1998–2003'. *International Journal of Electronic Government Research* 1(4), 26–44.
11. Henriksen, H.Z. (2002) *Performance, Pressures, and Politics*.
12. Hill, R. (1997) 'Electronic commerce, the World Wide Web, Minitel, and EDI', *The Information Society* 13, 33–41.
13. Thong, J.Y.L. (1999) 'An Integrated Model for Information Systems Adoption in Small Businesses', *Journal of Management Information Systems* 15(4), 187–214.
14. Klein, S. (1995) 'The Impact of Public Policy on the Diffusion and Implementation of EDI: An Evaluation of the TEDIS Programme', *Information Economics and Policy* 7, 147–81.
15. Electronic Data Interchange for Administration, Commerce and Transport developed by the UN and approved by the International Standards Organization (IOS) and Comite European de Normalisation (CEN).
16. Henriksen, H.Z. and Andersen, K.V. (2004) 'Diffusion of e-Commerce in Denmark: An Analysis of Institutional Intervention', *Knowledge, Technology, and Policy*, 17(2), 63–81.

Further reading

Accenture (2005) *Leadership in Customer Service: New Expectations, New Experiences*. Available at www.accenture.com

Cap Gemini (2005) *On-line availability of public services: How is Europe progressing?* EU: DG Information and Media. Available at e.gov.dk/

Economist (2005) *The 2005 E-readiness Rankings: A White Paper from the Economist Intelligence Unit*. Available at e.gov.dk/

Eurostat (2005) *Eurostat*. Available from europa.eu.int/comm/eurostat/

United Nations (2005) *UN Global E-government Readiness Report 2005*. Available from www.un.org

9 E-government in the Netherlands

From strategy to impact – the pursuit of high-volume, high-impact citizen e-services in the Netherlands

Martin van Rossum and Desirée Dreessen

Introduction

Despite being one of the smaller countries in the EU, with just over 16 million inhabitants, the Netherlands has experienced a long tradition of industrial activity that predominantly revolves around food processing, chemicals, petroleum refining and electrical machinery. In addition, the country enjoys a highly-mechanised agricultural sector as well as transport and banking sectors. With regard to the information society, the Netherlands is one of the most developed countries in the world.[1] There is a dense cable network infrastructure and the amount of Internet connectivity is comparatively high, with 78 per cent of Dutch households connected to the Internet as of 2005. A majority of 54 per cent of these were broadband connections, which is the highest percentage in the EU (for businesses these numbers are 88 per cent and 71 per cent respectively).[2] These figures are not overly surprising when one takes into account that until 2004, PC ownership was promoted among citizens by means of a so-called 'PC-privéregeling' ('private PC scheme'). Through this scheme, employees and students received tax benefits when they bought a new PC via their employers or universities.

Partly as a result of these favourable social conditions, e-government in the Netherlands started to develop relatively early, with the first policies commencing in the early 1990s. According to Roger van Boxtel, former Dutch Minister for Urban Policy and Integration of Ethnic Minorities, information and communication technology (ICT) 'enables the government to improve the efficiency and adequacy of some of the controlling tasks it performs'.[3] He additionally argued that in order to maintain a meaningful position in society, the government had to be fast and professional and respond to demands in the way the private sector would do.[4] Today, 46 per cent of individuals aged between 16 and 74 have at some point used the Internet to interact with governmental institutions in 2005 (57 per cent for businesses). This entailed obtaining information from public authorities' websites, downloading official documents and returning completed forms via email or submitting them online.[5] However, at the same time a declining trend in citizen satisfaction with government sites can be witnessed, as citizens rate these sites with an average of a mere 6.4 out of 10 in 2005 (6.6 in 2004). According to the government advice agency AdviesOverheid.nl this has to do with the fact that citizens' expectations grow faster and become more demanding, whereas the development of government sites is lagging behind these demands.[6]

In the ten years since the first policies were implemented, a variety of e-governance programmes and projects have been developed throughout the country. The earliest national ICT programme, the *National Action Programme on Electronic Highways*, was launched in 1994, making it one of the first e-government initiatives in Europe. With this action plan, the Ministry of Economic Affairs designed a set of six lines of action within a number of government proposals that were intended to lead to a dominant international position for the Netherlands in the area of ICT. Since then, many new policies have been developed and expanded at national, provincial and municipal levels. Extending the delivery of e-government services to the local level is of importance as the vast majority of all public services in the Netherlands are provided by municipalities. Since 2003, all Dutch municipalities have online portals where citizens can go to access a multitude of services.[7] This has resulted in the provision of fully-online services in a number of policy areas. Examples include: income tax submissions for citizens, the Sagitta system for customs declarations, and national databases for job searching and child benefits.

In the following section, an overview of the expansion of the use of e-governance in the Netherlands will be presented ahead of a more in-depth account of two government programmes in this field; the *ICT & Sectors Action Programme* (ISAP) and the *e-Citizen Charter*.

Overview of e-government policies: 1994–2006

As mentioned earlier, the first examples of e-government in the Netherlands date back to the mid-1990s. Their development since then can be observed along the lines of four stages, the first being the *information* phase during which Ministries, provinces, councils, a number of benefit agencies and various independent administrative bodies went online. During the *interaction* phase, citizens were able to start contacting their councils via e-mail. This phase was launched with the 'Innovative Policy Making Expertise Agency' (XPIN, in Dutch 'Expertisebureau Innovatieve Beleidsvorming'). Thirdly, the phase of *transaction* instigated a process of creating an online environment that would be safe to use for all parties involved. To facilitate this course of action a 'Public Key Infrastructure', a 'digital signature' and a 'Streamlining Key Data' programme were developed. The latter programme saw to the multiple use of information within the government by means of a series of authenticity registrations. However, in order for e-governance to work the government itself had to adjust. Therefore, during the final stage of *change*, emphasis was put on the creation of a 'new government' that stimulates citizen participation in the decision-making process and that, additionally, is capable of providing faster service.[8]

Throughout the stages of development and change, numerous government programmes were initiated. The first significant scheme to be launched after the

1994 National Action Programme was *OL2000* (Public Counter 2000 Project, in Dutch 'Overheidsloket 2000'),[9] which aimed to deliver an electronic 'one-stop counter' for citizens by providing a reference model for integrated public service delivery. At the end of 2002, this project was successfully brought to a close. Internationally this project was considered to be an 'advanced project with an ambitious aim: the creation of a nation-wide network of one-stop shops'. However, looking at the online services accomplishments of the project the results can arguably be claimed to have been moderate. The desired integration of services, in most cases, fell short of expectations and, at best, a municipal website with a significant amount of information on the diverse local services offered by the municipality was put into place.[10]

In 1998, two years after the OL2000 project, the *Electronic Government Action Programme*[11] was launched by the Ministry of Interior and Kingdom Relations. Three themes, each with their own aims, were to contribute to the overall aspiration of achieving a more efficient and effective electronic government. These themes were 'good electronic access to government', 'better service to the public' and 'improving the back-office of the national government'. Additionally, nine basic principles of e-government in the Netherlands were formulated by this programme. E-governance had to: be cost-effective, be multi-channel, be privacy respecting, allow collaboration with the private sector, be accountable in the long term, encourage the use of ICT, be compatible with existing structures, be interdepartmental and lastly have a system of delineated and integrated financial responsibilities.

With the publication of *Digital Delta – The Netherlands Online* (1999), the Dutch government sought to attain more uniformity of e-government initiatives and the further development of ICT in the country. The policy paper distinguished five pillars that collectively were of essential importance to the realisation of the aforesaid aim. The pillars identified issues such as the telecommunications infrastructure, knowledge and innovation, access and skills, legislation, and the use of ICT in the public sector.[12]

A vision of the electronic relationship between the government and citizens and the idea of a changed role for the administration in the information society were published in the *Contract with the Future* (2000). According to this document, the relationship between the two actors should be redefined and the new agreements should lead to a government that was more responsive to the needs of its citizens, accessible, transparent and communicative in an interactive process.[13] Within the main theme of 'freedom in solidarity' the government had to 'become an approachable government that is transparent, accessible and credible; a government that enables people to choose and become more involved'.[14] For the Dutch E-government Knowledge Centre this document signified 'the beginning of the practical realisation of electronic government in the Netherlands'.[15]

With the creation of the ICT Unit (ICTU) in 2001 an institution was set up for information and communication technology in the public sector. By attempting to improve the work processes of government organisations, their service to the community and the administration's interaction with citizens the ICTU is in charge of the co-ordination of ICT developments in government and aims to contribute to the structural development of e-government.[16] The first programme to be launched after the creation of this Unit was the *B4 Programme* (Beter Bestuur voor Burger en Bedrijf; in English: Better Governance for Citizens and Business, 2002).[17] B4's objective was to solve lingering social problems, reduce bureaucracy and decrease government spending. Moreover, e-government was no longer considered to be a purpose in itself, rather it had become a means to achieve a more efficient government that was capable of successfully dealing with economic and social challenges. In December 2005 the first ICTU evaluation took place and it was concluded that the unit was not only doing a good job, it was doing a qualitatively good job. According to the commission in charge of the evaluation the ICT Unit developed itself into an effective and efficient ICT-organisation, and carries out an important task for the central government, that is to say the realisation of the e-government.[18]

A year after the creation of the ICTU, in December 2003, the current Dutch e-government policy was introduced. The *Modernising Government Programme* continued the B4 programme and increased the government's commitment to implementing e-government. One of the targets set out in the new programme is to reduce the administrative burden on citizens by 25 per cent leading up to 2007 through the use of e-governance. In order to achieve this target a number of policies have been put in place, such as making 65 per cent of the public service provisions available via the Internet by the same year. To reach the objective of making the government and public services simpler, more effective and more efficient for the benefit of citizens and businesses the programme sets out four action lines:

- improve service provision to citizens;
- optimise regulation and lessen overhead;
- re-organise government to make it more efficient; and
- reform relations between central, regional and local governments.[19]

In addition, the *Digital Identification Service* (DigiD) was launched in January 2005 to enhance the use of online e-government services and achieve the aforementioned targets. The DigiD service provides citizens with a centralised online authentication system to facilitate the application of e-government services.[20] Once citizens are registered they can use their DigiD user ID and password to communicate with all levels of government and with regard to all online e-governance services. Over a million Dutch citizens now hold a digital signature and approximately 400,000 people used it in 2006 to sign their income tax submissions. However, the system has faced a number of criticisms. One year after the introduction of DigiD, voices were raised claiming that the digital signature was too weak to use with regard to a number of online services, such as income tax declarations. By merely using a username and password, the service was considered to be too vulnerable and identity theft too easy, as there are various ways to observe keystrokes online. As a consequence, even though no such cases of theft are known to have taken place safety measures are being developed. One method, for example, would entail combining the DigiD signature with a code that would be sent to the mobile phone of the signature holder via text message.[21]

Other e-government initiatives include the *ICT and Administrative Burden* (ICTAL) programme, the *eGovernment Knowledge Centre*, the *eGovernment Portal* overheid.nl, an *Open Source Software Exchange Platform*, an *e-Communes* project, the publication of the *ICT Agenda of The Netherlands: Better Performance with ICT*, the creation of a *Citizen Service Number*, a government sponsored *Mobile Alert System*, experiments with biometric passports and ID cards, Internet elections, the adoption of a metadata standard for public sector websites that is intended to facilitate finding and accessing information on the more than 1200 Dutch Governmental websites, and an 'Electronic Child File' for all children in the Netherlands, which was announced by the Dutch Government in September 2005.[22] With the creation of this digital file, each baby born in the country from 1 January 2007 will be assigned a unique identifying number and an electronic file. The file will initially contain information about the child's health and domestic situation, but as the child grows a number of institutions will be able to add information to the e-record, including schools, social services and the police. Once the system is in operation, all previously issued paper files relating to Dutch children will be digitised.[23]

The pursuit of high-volume, high-impact citizen e-services in the Netherlands

The overview provided above reflects the fact that the current Dutch national e-government strategy calls for a paradigm shift, 'moving beyond providing services online towards impact and benefits, progressing from modernisation to innovation, and towards a stronger contribution to jobs and economic and social growth – the revised Lisbon Agenda' (The 2005 online eGov Stakeholders consultation found at 'Your Voice').[24] This section, therefore, will focus on the theme that can be considered as the core issue of the new paradigm: 'the pursuit of high-volume, high-impact citizen e-services in the Netherlands'.

The Netherlands, like other countries, followed the path of bringing public services online benchmarked under the eEurope Action Plan (the Council of the EU in March 2001 established the common list of 20 basic public services – 12 for citizens, 8 for businesses – and endorsed the methodology used to assess their level of online availability and sophistication).[25] The 'Electronic Child File' initiative, however, demonstrates the fact that e-government is entering a new era. Availability of online services as such is no longer the key issue, but their impact on society is. The new emerging paradigm seems to be invoked by great concern about the slow take-up of the available online services, shared by the subgroup of leaders and representatives of national e-government initiatives of the eEurope Advisory Group. Take-up of a limited number of high-impact applications and services should demonstrate 'measurable significant benefits to businesses, citizens or administrations and provide a compelling case to combine efforts in resolving common and difficult challenges such as interoperability across the EU'.[26] The e-government subgroup seems less convinced about which services could be considered as 'high impact'. Although there is a consensus that public procurement could be one such service, further research is required to define other high-impact services.[27] Whether the Dutch 'ICT & Sectors Action Programme' (ISAP) could be considered as the proper means for identifying the right high-impact services to accelerate the take-up of e-government in the Netherlands will be discussed below. What can citizens expect when e-government is finally implemented? The e-Citizen Charter claims to provide the answers. Whether the charter really is an instrument to stimulate the further development of e-government from the citizen's perspective will be discussed later in this chapter (see Table 9.1).

ICT & sectors action programme (ISAP)

The ISAP programme seeks to force breakthroughs in developing and implementing innovative ICT solutions and services to help solve major issues in society. The programme focuses on education, mobility, security and healthcare, and is a collaborative effort between six ministries. Existing ICT applications and services are considered to be as-yet under-utilised. 'Many ICT-applications are deployed at a (too) small scale. Wider deployment or up-scaling should be achieved by means of collaboration between the partners involved.'[28] The programme is built around the principle that the numerous private and public stakeholders in the semi-public domain should each take up their own particular responsibilities. The overall rationale seems to be 'to tackle jointly major bottlenecks by means of result-driven projects and to boost economic growth & innovation at the same time'.[29] The ISAP programme is budgeted to spend 80 million euros in the period 2007 to 2008. This spending will be mainly financed by re-allocating and bundling budgets already devoted for ICT-uptake in the public sector, and therefore not all of the funding can be considered as 'new' money.[30]

The initial four-sectoral ISAP projects were published in early 2006.[31] The first one aims at providing a marketplace for vocational education and training (VET), and was scheduled to be online by mid-to-late 2006.[32] In the framework of a life-long learning action plan, providers of VET should make their offer transparent for all interested citizens. The lead partner is the ICT-network of universities (SURF-net). The second project should provide dynamic & actual travel information, allowing for door-to-door travel planning by citizens, preferably using public transport. This will turn existing static public transport travel information (online and mobile information about travel schemes and transport modalities[33]) into next generation added-value personalised mobility services (integrating actual route information, schedule modifications, real-time information concerning accidents & alterations, traffic jams, train delays, and so on). Small-scale pilots are already running at regional level, which should be up-scaled to national level as a result of the 2004 governmental mobility agenda, involving all public and private partners concerned.[34] This project is supposed to be based on the collaboration between public and other transport companies, regional authorities, other relevant service providers (Connekt/Transumo)[35] and fostered by the Ministries of Transport and

Table 9.1 e-Citizen Charter.

e-Citizen Charter (version 2.1)

1. Choice of channel
As a citizen I can choose for myself in which way to interact with government. Government ensures multi channel service delivery, i.e. the availability of all communication channels: counter, letter, phone, e-mail, internet.

2. Transparent public sector
As a citizen I know where to apply for official information and public services. Government guaranties one-stop-shop service delivery and acts as one seamless entity with no wrong doors.

3. Overview of rights and duties
As a citizen I know which services I am entitled to under which conditions. Government ensures that my rights and duties are at all times transparent.

4. Personalised information
As a citizen I am entitled to information that is complete, up-to-date and consistent. Government supplies appropriate information tailored to my needs.

5. Convenient services
As a citizen I can choose to provide personal data once and to be served in a proactive way.
Government makes clear what records it keeps about me and does not use data without my consent.

6. Comprehensive procedures
As a citizen I can easily get to know how government works and monitor progress. Government keeps me informed of procedures I am involved in by way of tracking and tracing.

7. Trust and reliability
As a citizen I presume government to be electronically competent.
Government guarantees secure identity management and reliable storage of electronic documents.

8. Considerate administration
As a citizen I can file ideas for improvement and lodge complaints.
Government compensates for mistakes and uses feedback information to improve its products and procedures.

9. Accountability and benchmarking
As a citizen I am able to compare, check and measure government outcome. Government actively supplies benchmark information about its performance.

10. Involvement and empowerment
As a citizen I am invited to participate in decision-making and to promote my interests. Government supports empowerment and ensures that the necessary information and instruments are available.

Economic Affairs. As of mid-2006, the project was still in an awareness-raising phase and not ready for broad implementation yet. The third project is targeted towards innovative surveillance of hot-spots known for their high rates of crime (business parks, shopping and leisure areas). Large-scale public–private collaboration should provide for cost-effective increased safety and security solutions, for example by pooling camera surveillance of business parks in different municipalities.

Fostered by the Ministries of Internal Affairs and Justice municipalities, police, chambers of commerce and regional crime-fighting initiatives are working to produce a safe and secure enterprising action plan that can then be rolled out on a regional level. The fourth project aims to improve management of care provision in the healthcare sector by introducing a comprehensive single electronic client dossier, accessible for all healthcare providers dealing with the same client. Client associations, healthcare providers, insurance companies, ICT companies, employers, banks, healthcare associations, housing corporations and applied science institutes should combine their efforts and expertise for a better quality of service by applying management techniques to the care provision processes in the health sector, like the Supply-Chain Operations Reference model (SCOR).[36]

The national law on privacy and data protection should safeguard individuals to be able to challenge the validity of the information generated by this integrated system. Regional public–private partnerships should take the lead. A first pilot project will run on 'chain-management focused on diabetes related care provision'. The NICTIZ (National IT Institute for Healthcare, Nationaal ICT Instituut in de Zorg)[37] is set to play the role of 'integrator' at national level.

When reviewing these four initial ISAP projects one might wonder why these four and not others? Obviously, these initial four are not representative of the whole picture of the Dutch e-government landscape. The sectoral approach is new though. Existing e-government programmes happen to be more geared towards the administrative tiers of Dutch government (municipal level, provincial level, national level), normally covering all governmental and administrative aspects but also a guarantee that the process will be slowed down. However, even then one might ask: why these four sectors? There are others, even more advanced, such as labour market services, geographical information systems, and so on. One could argue that some sectors are already taking care of themselves and/or are not really open for third-party co-operation (tax authority, justice, basic registrations of citizens and real estate, which all seem to have already developed robust ICT systems and are offering mature e-government applications and services; for example the Dutch tax authority provides a comprehensive set of tax collection facilities of which online application is mandatory for business companies).

As a consequence, sectors seem to have been selected that are lagging behind and desperately need more collaboration between involved stakeholders and/or are more open for public–private co-operation. In each of the four ISAP projects, some kind of existing collaboration between public and private partners has been put in place, although with quite different initial commitments it would seem. The safe and secure enterprising action plan is supposed to have more stakeholder commitment, although not necessarily at national level yet, whilst there is no such multi-stakeholder commitment for the life-long learning action plan aiming at the establishment of an online marketplace as first priority. The chain-management focused on diabetes-related care provision represents a strong case; one might wonder though whether the single electronic client dossier will automatically emerge from this. It does look very much that way if the sectoral initiatives are following the policy agenda priorities of the ministries involved and therefore not necessarily reflecting real demands of society at large, and that no overall comprehensive e-government roll-out masterplan is intended. However, to offer a more optimistic view, the innovative and interesting aspect of the defined portfolio is that the projects differ in their stages of 'maturity' (established partnerships, stage of implementation readiness) and ICT complexity, and will provide a sound comparative base for lessons to be learned.

Nevertheless it seems odd not to synergise with ongoing e-government practices, such as the Dutch examples that have been nominated (and in some case awarded) under the EU Good Practice Framework (for example, the 'Kadaster')[38] but are not included as a building block in the ISAP projects. In addition, the IST project eUSER 2004–5 identified another Dutch sectoral good practice case: 'Housing Benefits',[39] which could be up-scaled to financial support services for low-income citizens.[40] Also, the 'Mega ICT pilots' in large cities seem to have been ignored. Nor have the so-called 'Mega Broadband Pilots' ('Knowledge Districts')[41] been used as building-blocks for the ISAP projects, although the budgets from that existing Knowledge District programme will be re-allocated for ISAP. Finally, one might wonder why the ISAP is not embedded in ICTU-framework, or following the path of programmes under ICTU monitoring.[42] As mentioned earlier, the ICT Unit was created in 2001 by the Minister of Internal Affairs and Kingdom Relations and is in charge of co-ordinating ICT developments in government. Moreover, it executes programmes and projects that implement e-government policy.

Perhaps we should not take the initial sectoral themes as too serious provided they inspire others to bring forward other groundbreaking initiatives, as the prime analysis seems to be sound: 'Many ICT-applications are deployed at a (too) small scale. Wider deployment (up-scaling) should be reached by means of collaboration between partners involved.'[43] Challenging sectoral stakeholders to propose field-initiatives in one of the above four sectors seems to be the real purpose of the programme, as each project profile ends with the proposition: 'Inspired? Please check-out the rules for participating in the programme'. In that case, ISAP should be considered as a 'catalyst', not as a master plan. However, as the eUSER project already pointed out, the user orientation in Dutch e-government policies is rather weak.[44] The next section will explore whether the e-Citizen Charter is an instrument to stimulate the further development of e-government from the citizen's perspective.

The e-Citizen Charter

This charter consists of ten quality standards that define the digital relation between citizen and government (both in the field of information exchange, service delivery and political participation). These ten standards are formulated as rights citizens are entitled to, and matching obligations by government bodies (©burger@overheid, 2005).[45] They are conceived to be in the interest of both citizen and government. It allows citizens to call their government to account for the quality of online contacts. Government can use the charter to examine the external quality of e-government. 'At present the charter is not mandatory, but is based on the principle: Comply or Explain. In the foreseeable future, the charter might be turned into a benchmarking system or even quality mark.'[46]

Each standard is explained in more detail in the e-Citizen Charter document (an English version of the document can be obtained from the programme website).[47] The underlying philosophy is that 'by making eGovernment tangible in the front office, (this) would also give incentives to necessary reorganization in the back office.'[48] The citizens' perspective (as defined by the programme) is based upon research in which the four different relationships between citizens and government are used to define the different types of online contacts. 'Citizens can be customers of government services, commoners who vote or participate in political processes, subjects to rules and regulations and finally users of public services. In each capacity citizens meet another face of government: a provider of services, a political body, a law enforcer or a developer of public services.'[49]

The standards of the e-Citizen Charter will be applied to the functional requirements and interaction designs of several e-government applications and services at national level (the development and introduction of a unified public information infrastructure comprising all levels and sectors of government, consisting of four major components: portals; identity management; basic registers and information exchange).[50] The charter has been used as the basis for the National Web Awards 2005.[51] These annual prizes give publicity to successes and failures in e-government. The 2005 Web 'Wise' Award was given to the public organisation in the Netherlands which applied the e-Citizen Charter in the best way (for example, the National Student Grant Authority). The Web 'Sorry' Award was given to an organisation that did not meet the standards of the e-Citizen Charter and disappointed in using ICTs in bridging the gap between citizen and government (for example, the House of Representatives).[52]

A third area in which the charter claims to play a role is the quality of local e-government. As of 2002, the Mayor is legally obliged to deliver an annual report on local service delivery and political participation. At present, in most cases, this report is purely descriptive. The charter can be used by municipal councils and citizens as a series of standards that have to be met to increase performance. The National Union of Local Authorities (in Dutch: Vereniging van Nederlandse Gemeenten, VNG)[53] has recently decided to use the e-Citizen Charter as a reference model.[54] Another ICTU programme 'eGEM' (Electronic Municipalities)[55] promoted the e-Citizen Charter to play a role at the local council elections of March 2006 by asking councillors to make the e-government issues a major component of their platforms and use the Charter as an instrument to demonstrate the added value of ICT-based innovation in local government. As expectations of citizens' actions to enforce their digital rights personally seem rather naive, and although it seems unlikely that these rights will be taken-up by political parties as a 'hot election issue', the pro-active adoption of the Charter by municipal councils and their national association VNG might have a substantial effect on progressing e-government at local level, as the Charter will be used as a standard reference model for any further improvement of local government. Making government more transparent could be a real countervailing power when supported by means of ICT. Recently, the VNG started to provide all kinds of relevant policy information in more accessible formats, such as maps and charts (see the VNG-Net website for samples, like the chart of available e-services to citizens and business companies in pilot municipalities only – source: Ministry of Interiors, 2004; see the VNG-powered benchmark website 'watdoetjegemeente.nl').[56] The benchmark can be presented in several optional formats, of which the map-oriented format demonstrates that with an overall high availability of services, the business related service delivery is slightly lagging behind in most, but not all, cases. Municipal councils could use this information and that of the web-award rankings to benchmark their municipality when discussing their Mayor's Annual Report. For citizens, more content-oriented information is likely to be consulted, for example spatial and/or environmental policy-related matters, or when investigating crime figures as distributed between cities and city areas. One might doubt though whether this public access to information can compete with the private initiatives of free citizens, such as the initiative of journalists (www.misdaadkaart.nl). At this website, by using the Google Maps API[57] the citizen can search all records of criminal events, that have been gathered from local public sources, and render them down to any level of detail. Activities are registered in 17 different categories, including theft/robbery/burglary, public drugs and alcohol abuse, vandalism, murder/homicide, knifing, fights, indecency and sexual offence, traffic control, (road) accidents, and so on. This bottom-up tool is a powerful instrument for monitoring one's personal habitat, both for making choices as to where to live (or not) and to improve neighbourhood safety and security by means of civil society actions. One might expect that these civil initiatives may turn out to be more popular and better-utilised than official governmental web-based e-services.

If only used for more citizen-centred learning from benchmarking exercises (called 'benchlearning' in modernising government new-speak) within public administrations and their councils, the e-Citizen Charter could turn out to be a powerful tool to improve e-government practice in the Netherlands. It is therefore a pity that the connection between ISAP and the Charter has not yet been made. The impact of ISAP's role as a catalyst could increase dramatically when the e-Citizen Charter framework is adopted by all stakeholders concerned. Imagine what will happen when supply-chain management models in healthcare provision have to meet the 10 standards of the e-Citizen Charter right from the outset. Perhaps the Client Association and not the NICTIZ,[58] the supposed integrator at national level of this ISAP-project, should steer this development.

Conclusions

The e-government domain in the Netherlands can be characterised as an arena with many players that, to date, have not really synergised their initiatives into one comprehensive strategy. Given the Dutch governmental system that affords relative autonomy for different tiers of administration, the contrary would have been more surprising. Nevertheless, the overall climate for e-government initiatives since its early days in the mid-1990s has been very much dominated by the role central government has played at national level. It is always the Cabinet office that establishes agencies, programmes and budgets to promote e-government, and without it the policy would remain orphaned. In the brief period of political turmoil in 2002 when the government seemed to have temporarily forgotten the issue, the Netherlands immediately dropped some way down from top position in international e-government benchmarks. However, the administration ruling in the years 2003 to 2007 ('Cabinet Balkenende-II') seems to have used this time-out for launching a new political agenda of transfiguring government, which cannot be conceived without the uptake of ICT for modernising government services. The resulting mission statement can be summarised as follows: 'The government will regulate less over the coming years. By 2006 the administrative burden on citizens (and business) will have been reduced by 25 per cent.'[59] The latter part is mainly an ideological statement to announce 'dramatic changes in the relationship between government and civil society and the way in which government carries out its tasks' (as no-one can answer in quantitative terms the question '25 per cent of what?'). It is unclear which relationships might be redefined once more after the 2007 national elections. Meanwhile, there is a great continuity when looking at the implementation of e-government in practice. For the first time after a decade of fragmented e-government initiatives, the different tiers of government have joined forces to establish a common e-government 'directory room', called 'e-overheid' ('e-authorities').[60] In April 2006, all public authorities from national, provincial and municipal authorities, including the district water boards, signed an agreement to use the e-Citizen Charter as a framework 'to grease this eGovernment engine'.[61] It is therefore expected to survive any potential ideological changes that emerge from the 2007 to 2011 cabinet programme, as e-government will be driven by business logic of 'doing more with less' and not so much by the strong feelings of citizens. This is despite action plans, at national as well as at EU level, which keep talking about citizen-centred e-government implementation. But of course, better government will be widely appreciated.

Notes

1. IDC/World Times Information Society Index (ISI 2005) available at www.worldpaper.com/2005/june/index.html
2. Available at epp.eurostat.cec.eu.int/portal/page?_pageid = 1996,45323734&_dad = portal&_schema = PORTAL&screen = welcomeref&open = /&product = Yearlies_new_science_technology&depth = 3
3. van Boxtel, R. (2002) 'Rethinking Dutch Constitutional Democracy in the Information Society', *Information Polity* 7, 155–56.
4. van Boxtel, R. (2002) 'Rethinking Dutch Constitutional Democracy in the Information Society'.
5. Available at epp.eurostat.cec.eu.int/portal/page?_pageid = 1996,45323734&_dad = portal&_schema = PORTAL&screen = welcomeref&open = /&product = Yearlies_new_science_technology&depth = 3
6. Overheid.NL Monitor 2005: Prestaties van de e-Overheid gemeten, pp. 42–3, available at advies.overheid.nl/index.jsp

E-government in the Netherlands 131

7   eGovernment Observatory: *eGovernment in the Netherlands*, available at europa.eu.int/idabc/en/document/1376/406
8   van Boxtel, R. (2002) 'Rethinking Dutch Constitutional Democracy in the Information Society', 156–57.
9   Available at www.ol2000.nl
10 Leenes, R. (2004) *Local E-government in the Netherlands: From Ambitious Policy Goals to Harsh Reality*, p. 5. Available at www.oeaw.ac.at/ita/pdf/ita_04_04.pdf
11 Available at www.minbzk.nl/contents/pages/7597/electronicgovernmentaction-programme.pdf
12 Available at europa.eu.int/idabc/en/document/4855/5689 *and* europa.eu.int/idabc/servlets/Doc?id = 22652
13 Available at www.minbzk.nl/contents/pages/3925/contract_with_future_5-00.pdf
14 van Boxtel, R. (2002) 'Rethinking Dutch Constitutional Democracy in the Information Society', 157.
15 Kenniscentrum ELO (2005) *E-government in the Netherlands: A Brief History*, p. 8. Available at www.elo.nl/elo/Images/History_eGovernment-Netherlands_tcm70–46924.pdf
16 Available at www.ictu.nl/profile.html
17 www.minbzk.nl/contents/pages/3043/pva_beter_bestuur_12–02.pdf. See also Kenniscentrum ELO (2005) *E-government in the Netherlands: a brief history*, pp. 8–9.
18 www.ictu.nl/actueel_c.html#1. See also www.ictu.nl/download/Eindrapport%20Visitatie%20ICTU%20december%202005.pdf
19 Available at www.elo.nl/elo/Images/action-plan_transfiguring-government_tcm70–45796.pdf
20 europa.eu.int/idabc/en/document/4357/341
21 www.telegraaf.nl/binnenland/article37621821.ece
22 Available at europa.eu.int/idabc/en/document/1376/406
23 Chevallerau, F.-X. (2005) in *eGovernment in the Member States of the European Union*. IDABC eGovernment Observatory, pp. 394–415; available at europa.eu.int/idabc/egovo. See also 'Operation Young' (in Dutch, 'Operatie Jong'), available at www.regering.nl/actueel/nieuwsarchief/2005/09September/12/0-42-1_42–71006.jsp
24 europa.eu.int/yourvoice/. See also 'eGovernment Fact sheet – Netherlands – Strategy: Main strategic objectives and principles', available at europa.eu.int/idabc/en/document/1340/406. Last updated November 2005.
25 Chevallerau, F.-X. (2005) in *eGovernment in the Member States of the European Union*.
26 eGovernment Unit DG INFSO (2005) *Signposts Towards eGovernment 2010*. pp. 22–30; Report of eGovernment subgroup of leaders and representatives of national eGovernment initiatives of the eEurope Advisory Group (following Bloomsday and CoBrA recommendations).
27 eGovernment Unit DG INFSO (2005) *Signposts Towards eGovernment 2010*.
28 ISAP (2005) *ICT & Sectors Action Programme*.
29 ISAP (2005) *ICT & Sectors Action Programme*.
30 See www.maatschappelijkesectorenenict.nl for full report and background (under 'beleidsinformatie').
31 ISAP (2005) *ICT & Sectors Action Programme*.
32 See www.maatschappelijkesectorenenict.nl/index.php
33 As currently can be found at www.9292ov.nl
34 See www.vananaarbeter.nl/NotaMobiliteit/content/kortbestekUK.html
35 See www.transumo.nl/En/Organisation.aspx
36 See www.supply-chain.org/page.ww?section=SCOR+Model&name=SCOR+Model
37 See www.nictiz.nl, and for English version www.nictiz.nl/kr_nictiz/default.asp?datoom=2485
38 See www.kadaster.nl/international/default.html and also www.egov-goodpractice.org/gpd_details.php?&gpdid = 1805
39 See www.vrom.nl/huursubsidie

40 eUSER (2005) *Public Online Services and User Orientation.* Document 786.
41 See www.breedbandstad.nl/
42 Chevallerau, F.-X. (2005) in *eGovernment in the Member States of the European Union.*
43 ISAP (2005) *ICT & Sectors Action Programme.*
44 Dries, J. (2005) *eUSER Public Online Services and User Orientation.* Document 553.
45 © burger@overheid (2005) *e-Citizen Charter, Version 2.1* (November 2005). More information can be found on www.burger.overheid.nl; Burger@overheid is an initiative of the Ministry of the Interior. The bureau is part of ICTU, the Dutch implementation organization for ICT and government.
46 Poelmans, M. (2005a) *e-Citizen Charter, Version 2.1* (November 2005).
47 See www.burger.overheid.nl/actueel/?id = 712
48 Poelmans, M. (2005b) *The e-Citizen Charter, e-Quality promoting Equality between Citizens and their Government.* Paper for eChallenges conference, Ljubljana 2005.
49 Poelmans, M. (2005b) *The e-Citizen Charter.*
50 Poelmans, M. (2005b) *The e-Citizen Charter.*
51 See www.burger.overheid.nl/actueel/?id=712
52 See www.burger.overheid.nl/actueel/?id=712
53 See www.vng.nl/smartsite.dws?ID=41361
54 See www.vng.nl/smartsite.dws?ID=41361
55 See www.egem.nl
56 See www.watdoetjegemeente.nl/index.php?option=com_wrapper&Itemid= 64&cat_show=Publieke%20Dienstverlening&cat_open=Elektronishe%20dienstverlening&var=d13,d14&view=table
57 See www.google.com/apis/maps/
58 See www.nictiz.nl and for English version www.nictiz.nl/kr_nictiz/default.asp?datoom = 2485
59 Available at europa.eu.int/idabc/en/document/4859/5689
60 Available at www.e-overheid.nl/english/
61 Available at www.burger.overheid.nl/persberichten/?id = 802

Further reading

Van de Donk, W. and Van Dael, R. (2005) In *ICT en Openbaar Bestuur.* pp 161–96.

10 The reform and modernisation of Greek public administration via e-government[1]

Vassiliki N. Koutrakou

Introduction

This chapter charts the build-up of ventures towards establishing e-government and selected initiatives for e-democracy in Greece, a largely agricultural and public-sector-heavy country with a limited tradition in high technology and industrial innovation, and one of the poorest in Europe. It assesses how this late developer adjusts to the informatisation of its society in order to resolve long-standing problems relating to cumbersome bureaucracy, citizen-unfriendly administration, transparency deficit, and the centralisation of services.

The year 1981, the date of the country's entry into the then European Community marks, arguably, the starting point, with increased importation of hardware and technological know-how, primarily from its new European partner-countries. Widespread participation in basic research and application-oriented EC Information Technology programmes ensued, either under Regional Development policies such as the Integrated Mediterranean Programmes, or the Framework Programme of collaborative R&D ventures such as ESPRIT.[2]

A decade later Greece had jumped on the bandwagon of the technological revolution, with high growth rates and investment in education, a good sized and technologically highly-trained work force, international centres of excellence in R&D such as the University of Crete and its science park, and a booming consumer market for high tech products, particularly mobile telecommunications.

The potential to benefit from its large diaspora of scientists was also considerable; however, convincing opportunities domestically of planned, transparent and sustained conditions for growth to reverse the brain drain were scarce. Sophisticated levels of IT production and application were largely limited in that first decade, and the informatisation of society rather patchy. Businesses were often hesitant to invest in risky developments and long-term organisational planning, opting more for innovation consisting of readily applicable systems, developed and seen in use abroad, which can be relatively easily transplanted and require little training. Moreover, Greece is characterised by an ageing population which increases the resistance to new methods and the knowledge society. The public sector, plagued by anachronistic bureaucracy, has been even slower in re-organising to reap the benefits of IT. Private Internet use appears to limit itself almost exclusively to 15–45 year olds: Greece was still one of the lowest Internet users in the European Union by the end of the twentieth century, and is still playing catch-up today.

Nevertheless, despite starting from one of the lowest points in Europe, Greece depicts one of the fastest growth rates economically, and also technologically. Several classifications including the 'Technological Achievement Index',[3] the OECD and the United Nations' Human Development Report, place Greece among the 'potential leaders' and rank it at between 24th and 26th on the basis of countries' performance in technology diffusion and the building of a human skills base.[4] The end of the 1990s, which saw a spread of the e-government and even the e-democracy concepts internationally, captured the imagination of the Greeks, towards the recreation of a space reminiscent of the ancient Pnyx or the Agora, that is, a space for consultation, information exchange, conducting business, and democratic expression between citizens and between citizens and government. A range of ambitious initiatives ensued, aimed at transforming public administration and the citizen-government relationship, bringing about improved interconnectedness, transparency, efficiency, and accountability.

Strategy and action

The policy framework

The development of e-government in Greece has stemmed as much from political incentives to produce an agenda of modernisation, forward thinking, catching up with the country's forever aspired to 'bigger and better' European partners as from a genuine desire, and domestic as well as EU pressures, for administrative reform encompassing a whole range of strategies of which e-government is but one. The former is based on the political capital and enhanced electoral credentials successive governments expect to gain from an – almost ideological – endorsement of modernisation as being a de facto 'good thing'; the latter stems from practical imperatives for a holistic re-evaluation and overhaul of antiquated administrative mechanisms and procedures in the country. The two have combined happily to commit to a multi-pronged strategy that does not expect the development of e-government to solve all ills, but is seen nevertheless as a fundamental component of the process.

The strategy towards institutional and organisational changes in the Greek public sector comprises of a decentralisation of responsibilities from the centre to the periphery (regions and prefectures), the redefinition of the role of ministries as centres for the strategic planning and policy formulation, privatisation, suppression of state intervention and involvement of private enterprise in joint public/private ventures, the reorganisation of services, the listing of publicly-owned companies in the Athens Stock Exchange, changing drastically the functioning of government and public administration while implementing, at every step, modern information and communication technologies (ICTs).

As an integral part of this strategy, the development of e-government has involved a combination of public and private initiatives, with substantial financial facilitation by the EU. Actors engaged in the process include: the European Union (EU) through a number of initiatives such as TESTA (Trans-Services for Telematics between Administrations) and its IDA (Interchange of Data between Administrations) programme, funding from the European Regional Development Fund (ERDF), the Framework Programme and the Community Support Framework; the Greek government with projects relating to innovation in the co-ordination, handling and distribution of Public Administration services such as taxation, and even initiatives such as the 2003 Greek EU Presidency's e-Vote; private enterprises such as Archetypon S. A.; and finally, universities, which engage closely with government, EU authorities and business partners for the development of knowledge-based platforms for public sector online services such as the EU's SmartGov project. The central theme has been to explore ways in which government layers and civil society can come up with better connections with citizens, employees and business, employing ICTs to do so.

Already, since the mid-1990s a range of government policy statements have been backed up by the appointment of experts to drive forward the strategic use of IT for the development of e-government in the country. An IT counsellor to the Prime Minister has been appointed. The old General Secretariat for Research and Technology that operated under what up to the late 1980s was the Ministry for Industry, was revamped, and a new General Secretariat for Information Systems was created directly under the Ministry for Economy and Finance itself, to actively promote the implementation of Information Systems in what constitutes the primary nerve-centre for the Greek economy and one of the key components of the country's public administration network.

The operational programme 'KLISTHENIS', implemented in 1994 and spanning six years with a budget of 92 billion drachmas, marked the first real step towards the continuous functional and organisational modernisation of public administration in Greece, the development of integrated informative systems and the training of human resources, implying interventions of at once technical, organisational and educational character. It came into existence under the aegis of the 2nd EU Community Support Framework (CSF), which aimed to integrate sporadic actions into homogeneous sectoral operational programmes in fields such as public administration, telecommunications, education and training, and industry. Tangible results came with two important projects that emerged from it: the creation of the public administration network SYZEFXIS and the development of electronic taxation services through TAXIS.

The launch of KLISTHENIS was followed by the publication of the White Paper 'Greek Strategy for the Information Society: A Tool for Employment, Development and Quality of Life', a plan to reduce the technology gap between Greece and its partners and to reach international IS standards through preparing Greek firms to adopt ICTs, enabling more citizens to use them, and facilitating and promoting the use of electronic transactions with public administration agencies. Two years later, a 'Strategic Plan for Administrative Reform' fleshed out the policy in terms of innovation in the administrative system and activities, technologies and human resources. A manifestation of this was a network of Citizen Service Centres (KEPs), created in the five-year period that followed.

Another important policy milestone along this route was the publication of the White Book 'Greece in the Information Society; strategy and actions' in 1999, providing a comprehensive strategy and a framework for pilot, yet extendable, actions, for example the launch in 2000 of programmes such as ARIADNI for the dissemination and informatisation of local and regional administration services, and POLITEIA, for the reform and modernisation of the public sector.

The aims of the White Book were reiterated in an updated 'Greece in the Information Society; strategy and actions' White Paper in 2002[5] that, in tandem with the aims of the EU's 3rd Community Support Framework, offered further guidelines and specific means for the information society while again looking at the government's total policy framework, on open and effective public administration, labour and social welfare, health and environmental policies, economic development and competitiveness, justice and public order, cultural policy in a knowledge-based society, media, transport and regional development. These guidelines still run through a host of specific initiatives as well as the overarching Operational Programme for the Information Society (OPIS), in action today.

Alongside, the government initiated a scheme for the introduction of e-democracy mechanisms in Greek public life, starting with a pilot e-Vote on European and world affairs during the country's six-month presidency of the EU in 2003. The Greek Presidency also cultivated consultations between EU partners and neighbouring countries on co-ordination of action and sharing of best practice by holding a Ministerial Meeting on 'Tools of E-governance in the European Union and its South-Eastern European Neighbours'.

The change of government in 2004 saw a predictable slowing of activity in terms of policy-making in the field during the new conservative government's settling-in period, and the setting in motion of new priorities, especially ahead of the 2004 Athens Olympics which concentrated most of the government's attention. However, this proved temporary and renewed commitment has been apparent in 2005–2006 through the creation of a Central Procedure Simplification Committee to ensure the planning, implementation, monitoring and assessment of sufficient administrative reform as to enable the smooth and effective onset of the information society. As a later point will show, among a closer look at some of the programmes and projects mentioned above, the new government's e-government commitment was underpinned by new initiatives such as the launch of the e-Trikala digital city project in 2004 and the new three-year POLITEIA phase in 2005.

A public administration network based on e-government

As indicated in the introduction and in the sketching out of the policy framework above, the streamlining and informatisation of public administration in Greece is as imperative as it is complex. Policies, strategies and applications needed to consider the design and harmonisation of very disparate systems, as well as retraining and radical re-evaluation of processes, human skills and resources engaged. Any new coherent framework also needs to take into account severe lapses in technical infrastructure and operational support and lack of specification standardisation, as well as a lack of experienced specialist personnel. These shortcomings, however, facilitated the decision to adopt a 'clean slate' approach and to favour holistic strategies, enabled by national government backing and EU funding, and supplemented by private investment. Similarly the lack of 'best practice' which informed the judgement of more IT-experienced countries in the formulation of their own e-government policies, albeit a negative point for Greece at first glance, could also be seen as a time/trouble-saving advantage, in that many development and implementation problems to be expected had already been encountered and resolved by pioneering countries before the systems were transplanted and put into practice in Greece.[6]

The emphasis of the e-government agenda for public administration in Greece is on the need to develop flexible approaches to interconnectivity and interoperability, and one-stop integration[7] of accessible, user-friendly e-government services, enabling the simplification and transparency of hitherto painstaking bureaucratic procedures as well as growing interaction in terms of service to, and participation of, the citizen.

Some of the most interesting and ambitious projects that emerged in order to address the above agenda include:

The SYZEFXIS project

The pilot scheme SYZEFXIS (meaning joining together) – Informatics Development Agency[8] emerged in 1999 to provide a network for public administration in Greece, inter-linking the individual sites that central, regional, prefectural and local government administrations were responsible for and in the process of creating.

In late 2001, SYZEFXIS was becoming a kind of nation-wide intranet, involving 15 state organisations and expanding by inviting the participation of private telecommunications' suppliers and network manufacturers, such as Information Society S.A, for example. It became the gateway to the EU's TESTA, a 1996 initiative to promote a European inter-administrative network, across all EU, EFTA (European Free Trade Area) and EU accession-stage countries, building on the individual efforts of each in order to establish local and regional administrative networks linked together within a so-called Euro-Domain, and punctuated by Euro-Gates so as to ensure simultaneously the independence and inter-operability of local domains.

The SYZEFXIS network involved an investment of €90 million, aggregating public sector demand for telematic services, such as ease and speed in services for the citizen, one stop-shop services, interconnection of IT systems, capitalising on the liberalisation of telecommunications, achieving savings through telephony services, data and video transmission, and so on. It now provides for 1766 different actors and institutions including sectors as diverse as the public health system, army offices, and, of course, central and regional administrations and managing authorities. Each actor forms an end-point for the network, procuring SYZEFXIS services along a network of six geographical 'islands', some of which act as interchange points for the backbone network.

EURO-CITI and SMART-GOV

While linking different levels of government services in a coherent nation-wide (and euro-wide) electronic network, there is a need to address, ultimately, making these services better accessible to end-users, that is to say the public. The EC-funded EURO-CITI programme was financed by the Commission's 5th Framework Programme to design and test dynamically re-configurable architectures and platforms for citizen participation through services such as tele-voting, tele-consulting, and electronic submission of forms, petitions, and so on in order to improve direct democracy. Its testing grounds were the cities of Athens, Barcelona, and parts of London.[9] Meanwhile, the SmartGov project on a governmental knowledge-based platform for public sector online services[10] concentrates on elements still in great need of development in a variety of countries, but particularly in Greece, such as the processes behind the design and delivery of e-government services, internal/ external co-operation and public authorities, and the social acceptance of e-government services, looking at the adoption of a common ontology on e-government, the meeting of needs, the levels and modes of co-operation built, the shared purposes, the quality, trust, and monitoring, costs and benefits, affordability and sustainability of the government services provided. With three out of its seven partners from Greece, specifically, the government's General Secretariat for Information Systems, the University of Athens,[11] and the firm Archetypon S.A., the make-up of the project typifies the recent interest in this area by the Greek government, academia and business alike. Early evaluations of SmartGov identify the use of e-government ontology as the most important innovation of this platform as it 'enables the staff of the Public Authority to record and categorise expert knowledge that they have accrued about service provision so that it can be disseminated among staff, and where applicable selected knowledge can be made available to the users to assist in their completion of forms and use of the service'.[12]

The TAXIS system

A specific application of the above concepts, already in operation, is the online taxation system TAXIS (Taxation Information System). This system was first launched in 1995 by the Greek Ministry of Finance's (GMoF) General Secretariat for Information Systems (GSIS).[13] It cost €50 million and was co-financed by the Greek government and EU Structural Funds, primarily the European Regional Development Fund and the European Social Fund. It provided IT infrastructural support to central tax authorities in the capital, Athens, and a web of tax agencies all over Greece, eventually building mechanisms to cater for everything from the policy-making and monitoring aspects of taxation to full accessibility by taxpayers to information provision, as well as the electronic conduct of taxation transactions.

Initially criticised as being more introvert rather than end-user oriented,[14] the programme's strategy was reinforced in favour of making a wider range of services more easily available to citizens, and to that effect the TAXISnet website was introduced (www.taxisnet.gr). TAXISnet offers e-filing for VAT, income tax forms, tax payment facilities through links with banking services, call centres, and so on, ensuring 24-hour, 7-days a week real-time response on transactions, targeting individual citizens (extending the service especially to remote-region users), private businesses (encouraging use by SMEs) and private accountants.[15]

E-government initiatives are worth little unless there is evidence of substantial, or at least growing, take-up by citizens. According to figures by Gouzos et al,[16] with a total target-base of 800,000 VAT-liable Greeks, 82,000, that is to say approximately 10 per cent, appeared as registered users in the first year (May 2000 to June 2001) of the e-VAT service operation, displaying a registration rate of 300 per day. As no more than half of the total number of those liable areconsidered to be Internet users, this in fact represents 20 per cent of those having the ability to access the service. Similarly, on the basis of a total of 5 million income-tax-liable Greek taxpayers, the e-income tax service experienced a registration rate of 800 per day.

The operational cost of these services, many of which have been outsourced by industrial IT solution providers, amounts to approximately €600,000 for development, and €400,000 for yearly telecom, personnel, and other operational costs. The net balance however shows huge savings of the order of approximately €3.5 million in personnel salary costs, that offset operational costs as well as the initial €600,000 investment for the development of the system.

Ariadni

ARIADNI was a scheme devised to facilitate citizens requiring information and faster processing on any number of public administration matters, initially through telephone services, in order to make processes more efficient and eliminate perpetual long queues at government offices. The project started with the collection, organisation and processing of public information, together with the creation of Citizen Service Centres (KEP). Between the end of 2002 and beginning of 2005 the special telephone line (1564) had helped over six million callers. Nevertheless ARIADNI quickly transcended telephone services and migrated to the Internet providing, as of February 2003, the websites www.kep.gov.gr and www.polites.gr in order to achieve greater speed and volume of service to citizens.

ARIADNI also operates in public–private partnership. The company Newsphone-Hellas won a tender to provide the project with the necessary means for locating, organising, and updating public information in digital form.[17] The KEP centres that initially existed to provide information on, for example, what documents are necessary for the issuing of a birth or marriage certificate or a passport, are now increasingly actually processing citizen applications, thus providing, where possible, a more complete and effective service. Apart from the necessity for extensive cross-referencing, the project has also meant substantial specialised training and re-training of those public servants who operate it, in areas as diverse as the Social Insurance Institute or the Army Recruitment Service, through e-learning in virtual classrooms.

ARIADNI aims for, alongside providing practical help to citizens, better open government and monitoring the quality and speed of services to the citizen. It is estimated that the average time for processing citizen applications on various public administration matters was reduced from 15 to 7 days, the number of citizens who choose to re-use the system after first experimenting with it is increasing by 24 per cent per month, while first-time user numbers are steadily rising too.[18]

Politeia

The POLITEIA project emerged in 2001 due to the recognition that high technology applications alone were not enough to create a more effective public administration network without corresponding upgrading and reform of existing procedures. This state-funded project, managed by the Ministry of the Interior, therefore targeted modernisation in financial management models, brevity in administrative procedures, the recruitment of well-trained personnel, and the adoption of modern methods in administration and control so as to ensure more transparency and the elimination of corruption. In practice, POLITEIA brought together under a common umbrella all previous strategies and mechanisms for reform, requiring all ministries and regional authorities to take part – ensuring co-ordination and avoiding duplication. Interim assessment revealed that in its first two years, the objectives' convergence which POLITEIA heralded had ensured that all ministries and regions across the country had acquired the means to develop and implement operational programmes, and were already at different stages of putting these into effect according to local priorities. The central idea has been cohesion, so as to be able to address, aside from day-to-day requirements in the country's public administration network, the simplification and quality control of existing and new regulations, with regular quality control and regulatory impact assessment reports.[19]

Consolidating strategies – The OPIS umbrella

The Operational Programme for the Information Society, with a budget of €2,839 million, is regarded as the catalyst, and an aegis, for many initiatives such as those briefly outlined above. It is not just another programme. It is 75 per cent-funded by the 3rd EU CSF ending in 2006, and 25 per cent by national contributions. OPIS is a horizontal programme that encompasses the separate specialised operational programmes run by different central and regional administrations and their agencies. Each public administration concerned defines its goals, remit, structure, mission, planning, and field of activity of its own sub-programme, and these sub-programmes receive funding and are integrated within the OPIS regulatory environment with a view to encouraging the development of the information society.

In Greece, the overall co-ordination is taken up by the Ministries of Economy and Finance and the Ministry of Public Administration, as most sub-programmes concerned fall within their remit, but all other ministries are involved too[20] in a variety of programmes such as, for example, the regional development of knowledge management systems to handle problems faced by border regions, spearheaded by the Ministry of Macedonia and Thrace. Moreover, purpose-built instruments to organically manage the implementation and monitoring of OPIS include the Secretariat for the IS, a Managing Authority, the IS Observatory, and Information Society S.A.

OPIS comprises five main priority target areas under which all initiatives are grouped:

- education and culture (with approximately 14.8 per cent of the budget assigned to it);
- improvement to citizen-services and quality of life (31 per cent);
- the development of the digital economy and employment opportunities (31.8 per cent);
- communications (20 per cent); and
- technical assistance (2.4 per cent).[21]

The first area prioritises the improvement of IT infrastructure and networking facilities in the educational system, from schools to universities, teacher training, digitalisation and other ICT applications in education, but also in the documentation, management, and promotion of Greek cultural heritage. The second envisages a government online approach to public administration, as well as innovative ICT applications and corresponding training in matters of regional administration, health and welfare, and so-called 'intelligent transport'. The third area targets the digitalisation of the economic environment with support for business and sustained research and technological development, as well as skills and employment upgrading for the information society era. Area four's purpose is to support and consolidate the hitherto slow progress of telecommunications' liberalisation in the country while speeding up, in parallel, the development of local access infrastructure, advanced telecommunications, modernisation of postal services and associated training, so as to achieve a better service for the citizen.[22]

Syzefxis, Ariadni, and Taxisnet, discussed above, are but some of the better-established programmes being pooled under the OPIS umbrella. The impressively extensive website on the summer 2004 Athens Olympics is another example, combining information on event schedules, transport, weather, cultural promotion, as well as a degree of practical service and interactivity, souvenir and ticket-purchasing links, and so on.[23] Lesser known programmes concern, for example, the modernisation of procedures in the judicial sector and social security dispensation, the Foreign Office's immediate accessibility to citizens via telephone and website[24] on matters such as government-citizen co-ordinated action in international aid and development, aptly put to the test at the end of 2004 and early 2005 following the Asian earthquake/tsunami disaster, the 'police online' project for the improvement of policing through more effective information sharing and co-ordination and so on. Integration under OPIS aims ultimately at linking a variety of projects in such a way as to address internal processes and achieve interconnection between ministries, different actors, and end users.

An appraisal carried out by the United Nations Thessaloniki Centre for Public Service Professionalism identifies a range of problems in the implementation of this ambitious programme: occasionally inappropriate indicators in result measurement, lack of economies-of-scale and proper integration of technological infrastructures potentially hindering the delivery and prospect of increased added value of services, absence of adequate preparatory studies and pilot projects' feedback regarding the attempted organisational modernisation, as well as problems with management, project overlaps, and long-term financial planning. Recognising the strategy's potential but also the ambitious nature of the programme, they suggest solutions and conclude that it is 'preferable to move from a "perfect but not realised project" to one that is "imperfect, but [with] applicable projects and strategies"'.[25]

The goal, laboriously iterated by successive Greek governments in the pursuit of e-government, is a more open and effective government, and also one where the citizen is not just a customer in an one-way communication and servicing process but increasingly is a more directly active participant in the democratic process, using the advanced technologies and networking facilities that have come with globalisation to engage with his/her fellow citizens, civil society, and government.

Although e-government is not necessarily democratic, e-democracy presupposes some degree of e-government in place as e-democracy is dependent upon the existence of a sufficiently sophisticated electronic communication infrastructure.[26] Furthermore, the premise that, ultimately, the goal is to bring more immediacy in the web of relations between citizens and their representatives, is what links e-government and e-democracy; it is to this end that e-democracy was an area particularly championed by the former socialist (PASOK) government's Foreign Minister George Papandreou through the e-vote experiment conducted during the first half of 2003.

Dabbling in e-democracy

The e-democracy experiment was one of the most fascinating examples of diversifying e-government development in Greece. Launched by the Hellenic Ministry of Foreign Affairs on the occasion of Greece's 4th Presidency of the EU, January to June 2003, it invited citizens into an online polling booth to argue and vote on burning questions on European Union affairs, feeding issues raised into the regular programme of EU deliberations.

The website, evote.eu2003.gr/,[27] was a central part of the Greek Presidency, bringing the European Union closer to the European citizen and addressing problems of awareness, perceptions of democracy deficit, lack of consultation, and remoteness of EU institutions. According to the official statement issued by the Greek presidency, the site was to give Europeans 'the opportunity to actively participate in the democratic process and make their views heard at the highest level'[28] in a way similar to how vote.com functions in the United States.

The site ran a questionnaire gauging Europeans' views on important agenda-making issues and conducted monthly votes on topical matters. It also devoted a section on discussing the Greek Presidency's six main policy priorities: the future of Europe, enlargement, the EU's international role, asylum and immigration, the Lisbon process and sustainable development. This was all conducted via a number of tools including 'e-Vote', 'your question', 'your voice', and 'citizen forum'. Participants were able to log onto the e-Vote site, click on boxes and register their views, compare their posted opinions with those of others, and find out the results of e-votes, which were public and accessible in real-time. Parallel polls asked them for their views on a variety of broader current affairs and international developments, from taxation to the war on Iraq, the latter being one of the most visited topics throughout the whole period.[29] Most activities were hosted in 19 languages although, aside from Greek, English was widely used. The Foreign Minister, G. Papandreou, made a point of presenting the results of discussions and votes at certain European Council and other meetings, although it is arguable how influential they were upon decision-making. Nevertheless e-Vote can be credited with at least two benefits: encouraging people to use the Internet to have their voice heard on European affairs in a way much more interactive than that hitherto offered by the EU's standard EUROPA website, as well as introducing an element of immediacy and directness in communicating citizen response to policy-makers at the time of decision-making.

Created and co-ordinated by a team of independent scientists under the aegis of the Hellenic MFA, the e-vote initiative involved a variety of media partners and sponsors such as Deutsche Welle, the BBC, European Voice, Tiscali, Der Spiegel, and so on, and comprised several web-portals for local authority and government departments, universities, businesses, and so on. Although a slow starter in terms of wider media exposure, it eventually enjoyed considerable media coverage, even in the United States, as well as across the EU.

'Almost 20 per cent of the people who used e-Vote in its first two months identified themselves as Germans. The Greeks were the second-largest group, accounting for 14.75 per cent of the traffic, followed by the Belgians and the Italians, who each accounted for 12 per cent of the voting. The least frequent voters were the citizens of Ireland, Luxembourg and Sweden, each of those nationalities accounting for less than one per cent of the votes'.[30] Over 175,000 people had responded by the end of the six-month presidency period, nearly 60,000 e-voices had been submitted, and Greek, Belgian and Danish foreign ministers had been at times involved directly, responding online to EU citizens' questions. Apart from private individuals, participants represented EU and NGO organisations, political parties, local, regional and national authorities, interest groups, think-tanks, schools, universities, trade associations, and so on, acting as a further enabling tool for civil society engagement.'[31]

Taking momentarily the example of environmental issues: in her study of civil society mobilisation in several countries, including Greece, particularly in the area of the environment, Lisa Tsaliki[32] finds that the launch of an online survey by e-Vote on 21st May 2003 on the environment and sustainable development, breathed new life into the awareness campaigns and debates on environment and wildlife issues and the work of related Greek NGOs, revolutionising the, thus far rather static and limited to one-way information, provision of their separate websites.

The e-Vote initiative was deemed successful in triggering new ways for the EU to relate to its citizens. Its results cannot be scientifically analysed meaningfully as participation was evidently limited to those with Internet access, thus having no effect on those EU citizens without access, and even out of those involved whereas some were repeat-participants, others were much less so. For a European electronic demo to be meaningful and for a democracy to be successful, maximum public participation is required and this is some way off yet.[33] However, what transpired through this experiment was that the registering and quantifying of opinions eventually assumed less importance than the provision of a forum where one indeed had the opportunity to become aware of developments, and of different nuances in their interpretation, so as to then construct informed opinions.

Unfortunately the e-Vote was not taken up in any significant way by subsequent presidencies of the European Union, although the Europa website itself is increasingly adopting more interactive tools. In Greece, a similar, smaller-scale venture, called e-dialogue, was adopted by the PASOK party whose leadership had by then passed to Papandreou ahead of the 2004 elections, but it only became active one month before polling day and its take-up was limited. Although studies such as the one by Gibson, Nixon and Ward point to the potential gains by the use of the Internet by political parties,[34] it has yet to be taken up in anything that may be considered a major way in Greece at either a party or state government level. Nevertheless, a critical look at this type of venture reveals both shortcomings and encouraging insights. A mediated space for online consultation such as e-Vote needs to be of a large enough scale and to strike a balance between structure in discussion and effective moderation, demanding political and technical skills and significant man-hours by dedicated moderators, but it must also ensure a degree of freedom of expression. The striking of this balance is by default arbitrary, and e-Vote tried to achieve it by setting certain discussion topics and polls but also allowing discussion to ramble on; for example, the debate over the Iraq war which was at the time the most burning international issue. Balance is crucial to how meaningful such a consultation can be for national or European policy-making. Equally, the influence of the digital divide on the volume and nature of responses inevitably distorts, as is evident in many similar studies,[35] the representativeness of public opinion and this in turn diminishes the credibility and meaningfulness of the medium in terms of its potential to enhance the democratic process. Finally, although the communication of key-points expressed via e-Vote by the Greek presidency at certain EU meetings was an unprecedented initiative, for ventures such as this to have a future, the current reluctance by policy-makers to heed its outcomes needs to be overcome. Offsetting these shortcomings, critics agree[36] that the identification of sufficient issues emerging out of e-Vote as to warrant bringing to the EU Council discussions, and the enthusiastic response by EU citizens to the opportunities opened cannot be underestimated, and registers a definite demand for further such exploration in the evolution of democratic processes, particularly where a perception of remoteness of the governing institutions poses a question of democratic deficit.

The current state of affairs

Measurement approaches, with respect to the efficacy of e-government initiatives and their applicability, vary greatly according to models employed,[37] but a tentative picture can already be gained.

The Cyberspace Policy Research Group (CyPRG),[38] through their 'Webbing Governance' study (2000) and other studies, conducted surveys of nearly 3000 websites in 192 countries. Most were designed to serve government departments that are by their nature more technologically conversant, such as science and technology, trade and finance departments, then defence, justice, and so on, with areas such as labour, energy, and immigration, trailing. At the same time, the vast majority are top-down type public information sites rather than bottom-up or two-way consultative mechanisms. Based on studies such as this, researchers identify that, as one might expect, the more economically – and by extension technologically – advanced countries of North America and Western Europe, with sophisticatedly institutionalised democratic systems, are leaders in the provision of such facilities, with the poorest such as sub-Saharan Africa, for example, coming last. The pattern is emulated within Europe itself, with Germany and the UK ahead in e-governance, while Belgium and Greece are trailing.[39]

According to another study by Brown University on the take-up of e-government globally, out of 198 countries whose government websites were studied for overall e-government performance (including services, access to information, privacy, security, foreign language translation and disability access), and rated on a 100-point scale, Greece ranked seventy-first with a 30.9 per cent success rating.[40]

However, even if the take-up is still lagging, the technology push and the pro-active government strategies, combined with increased and diversified private enterprise involvement, are beginning to yield results. Desai et al[41] base their assessment on the technological achievement index, which takes into account the creation of technology, the diffusion of old and recent innovations, and human skills. Weighing these indicators produces an index that helps to classify the countries of the world as leaders, potential leaders, dynamic adopters and marginalised. A total of 72 make it into the top three categories, with 18 in the category of leaders; Greece ranks a promising 26th overall, and is among the potential leaders in the field.

At first glance, the series of programmes presented above might appear repetitive in terms of their stated goals, and unconvincing in terms of their successfulness. However, significant progress can be detected in the adoption of 'best practice' in the e-government operations of government departments and other authorities, no longer only through copying the ones tested abroad[42] but also now through accruing experience gained domestically in the context of the particular requirements of the Greek state and citizenry. Several of the programmes complement and build on each other, renewing and refocusing the strategy and commitment to the information society, the trend culminating in the OPIS Programme that serves to integrate these initiatives and prevent duplication of effort.

Greek expenditure on ICT stood at 2.4 per cent of GDP in 1990, visibly lower than the EU average of 3.6 per cent, but had by 2000 converged and hit the EU average at just over 6 per cent of GDP and has overtaken it since. Nevertheless, nearly 80 per cent of this has been devoted to telecommunications – particularly, mobile – with 20 per cent to IT proper, while Internet access in Greece remained the lowest in the EU (albeit rising rapidly) compared to its EU partners according to government estimates preceding the 2004 EU enlargement.[43]

In 2003, Greece's '1502' Telephone Application System, launched in 1998 and the precursor of the KEPs, which enabled citizens to apply for certificates and other administrative documents, received the first United Nations Public Service Award in the category of 'Improvement of Public Service Results' in the geographical area of North America and Europe. 'By the end of 2001 more than 870,000 applications for administrative forms and documents had been submitted, representing almost 608 applications per day. This figure shows the success of the service, which increases the responsiveness of public administration, promotes equal and user-friendly access to public services, helps to reduce red tape and administrative costs, and contributes to a better quality of life for citizens.'[44]

The year 2015 is the generally accepted interim milestone for evaluating the progress of the e-government drive and its initiatives in Greece. As this is some way off and availability of data on progress thus far are scarce, or at least project-specific, it is very tempting to resort to Delphi Oracle–type predictions. Nevertheless, some, general or more specific observations and projections can be made.

The RAND Europe project on 'Benchmarking E-government in Europe and the US'[45] conducts a survey of reactions to e-government initiatives. The survey reveals that next to the Danes, Greeks had, in 2002, the most enthusiastic attitude among all EU countries towards the developing electronic government services, coming near top in identifying particularly the elimination of mistakes made by public authorities and speed and convenience of location in dealing with public authorities as the most tangible advantages of e-government.[46] One might also argue that the psychological factor of aspiring to, at last, graduate to a more level playing field with the bigger partners and players in Europe is likely to play some role in Greek attitudes. At the same time there were misgivings relating to escalating amounts and cost of special equipment and software needed, and also a hesitation to use e-government services where issues of security and the Internet are perceived as a growing problem. Indicatively, in the graph below constructed on the basis of data gathered by RAND Europe, it becomes apparent that there is more readiness to actually or potentially use the Internet, not only for innocuous uses such as Library book searches, but also increasingly for e-government services

The reform and modernisation of Greek public administration 147

which include taxation, or the issuing of official documents, yet more reluctance to use it for publicising change of address details or for declarations to the police (see Figure 10.1).

It is evident that in terms of the Greek economy, news is positive. The streamlining of taxation in ways that ensure efficiency, transparency and facilitation are in the interests of both long-suffering tax-payers forever battling with bureaucracy, queues, and an ultra-complex system of multiple taxes but it is also yielding higher returns to government coffers, rendering tax evasion ever more difficult. Better networks of communications among business actors, as well as business and government, is improving Greek competitiveness and has already been transforming the country into the leading effective European business player in the Balkan region, and an increasingly more equitable partner for fellow EU member-states.

Developments in e-commerce and better education and training facilities, in tandem with the linking in of regional business, educational and administrative services with those in urban centres has the potential to improve employment opportunities and conditions, including for example, flexible or remote working,

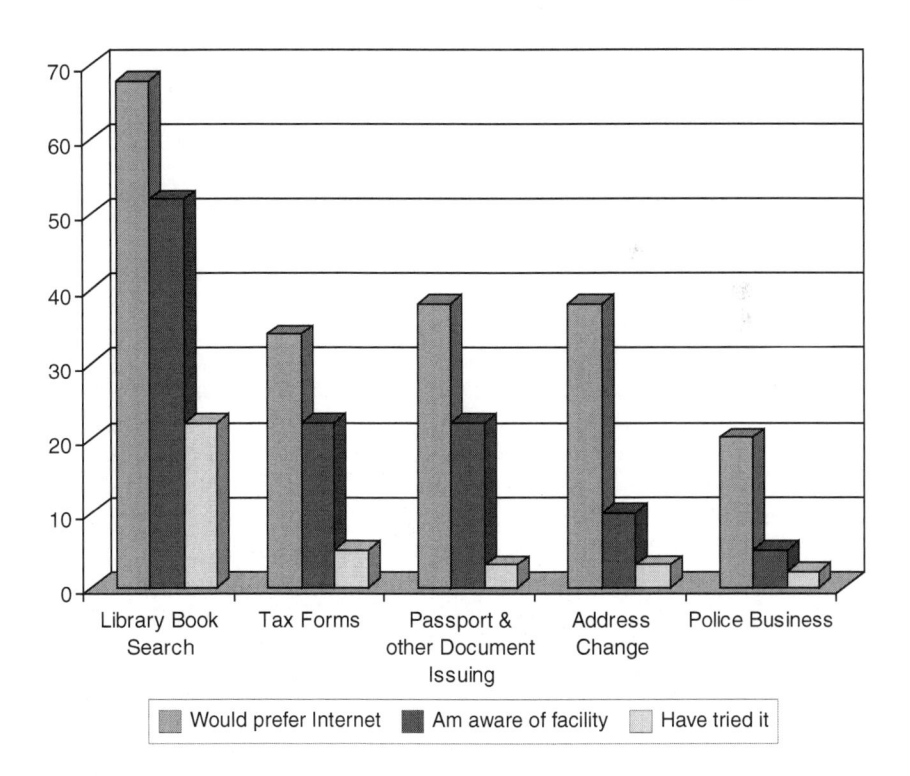

Figure 10.1 Greek attitudes towards the spread of e-government services.

Source: Data for this table originate in Rand Europe, 'Benchmarking E-government in Europe and the US' SIBIS 2002.

so as to rejuvenate different parts of Greece where the morphology of the country conspires in favour of considerable disparities in the provision of social and other services and in choice of work between big-city life and the countryside or the islands.

Certainly, the networked empowerment of local authorities as well as the provision of advanced, practical services such as tele-medicine are already improving matters in this direction. It would however be imprudent to expect spectacular results in the bridging of the gap between centre and periphery in the near future, or indeed the reversal of mass-migration to the main cities that took place over the last four decades and which, for the most part, appears here to stay.

Nevertheless, increased Internet access, an advanced knowledge society, and greater citizen participation via electronic means in public affairs is clearly empowering civil society and this can only be a plus for Greek society on a host of issues, such as a greater environmental consciousness, better integration of the significant numbers of refugees and economic migrants, better acceptance and provision with regard to multiculturalism, and in future, more effective dialogue between the citizens and their elected representatives at local, national, and European level. The electronic networking of public services across the country is significantly enabling the fundamental decentralisation strategy. There is still however substantial progress to be made in this area, and a sustained, pro-active campaign needs to be mounted. Learning from domestic practice as well as foreign studies[47] seems imperative, given the ageing population and the resistance of both older people and administrators with guaranteed life-long employment, to change. Currently only approximately 10 per cent of the country's almost 11 million inhabitants are Internet users.

It was unclear for a period whether the 2004 national elections would bring about a sustained momentum, or a change in pace in the e-government programme in the country. Although in practice some of the initiatives did experience a period of relative freezing until the new administration was up and running, the conservative Nea Dimokratia government elected in the spring of 2004 vowed to embrace the e-government mission with the same enthusiasm as their predecessors. The Minister of the Interior, Public Administration and Decentralisation, Prokopis Pavlopoulos, stated specifically that 'reforming the state through e-government is a key goal priority' announcing a legislative framework (such as the 3242/2004 law) specifically designed to combat red tape and improve the transparency, simplification, and citizen-focus of public affairs, the creation of a data and voice network connecting approximately 2000 public bodies via the National Public Administration Network and renewing attention upon the continued development of the Citizen Service Centres (KEΠ).[48]

Rhetoric seems for the time being to be backed by action, with taxpayers being offered, for example, tax discounts for opting to use the TAXIS website for their tax returns, in a renewed wave of incentives aimed at increasing take-up of the new e-government services by citizens. E-government services are becoming easier to deploy with time, and indeed cheaper.

A new three-year state-funded 'POLITEIA 2005–7' Programme was launched in March 2005, revealing the endorsement by the conservative government of the targets met thus far and the re-establishment of the state's commitment to increased transparency in public administration, better service to citizens, restructuring agencies and processes, and the implementation of e-government at all levels of administration.

Meanwhile the EC supported a new initiative, OntoGov, with pilots in municipalities of Greece, Spain, and Switzerland for 2005 and 2006, to strengthen back-office operations that might have been hitherto eclipsed by most programmes' emphasis upon 'front-office'.

Previous to that, an interesting new project was launched in late 2004; the e-Trikala Digital City Project,[49] under the direction of the municipality of the northwestern Greek city of Trikala, with funding from the Greek Information Society Strategy group. This project, designed to act as a model for the future development of every city across the country, aims to simplify transactions in public services, reduce telecommunications costs, provide electronic services, and empower citizens so as to involve them more directly in policy-making. It envisages infrastructural hardware and software development and applications to render the digital city operational. Straightforward applications take the form of electronic services and linkage of: firstly the back-office type, so as to enable public authorities and organisations to gather, organise and deliver information, and secondly, the end-user type, engaging citizens, interest groups, and businesses in a global environment for public transactions.[50] This means promotion of broadband use and linkages using the SYZEFXIS network, e-government provision of services to citizens by municipalities, intelligent transport with real-time information for users and tele-care centres for the support of vulnerable individuals or groups requiring on-going social and/or health care. User-friendliness, security and privacy are three of the ingredients stressed in this project, aside from the obvious goal to create an integrated electronic environment for the use of citizens and businesses in a city. The programme has reportedly been taken up with enthusiasm by all components and is running ahead of schedule, opening up the possibility for emulation by other cities in the very near future.

With goodwill and sustained commitment offsetting teething problems in the first decade of Greece's e-government experiment, the signs for e-government development policy as an end within itself and as an enabling strategy for the reform and modernisation of Greek public administration appear promising.

Notes

1. See also: Koutrakou, V. N. (2006) 'The Greek E-government Experiment: Reflections and Directions', in *Journal of E-government*, Haworth Press JEG, Vol. 3, Issue 2.
2. Koutrakou, V. N. (1995) *Technological Collaboration for Europe's Survival*. Avebury.
3. European Foundation for the Improvement of Living and Working Conditions, (2004) 'The Knowledge Society in Greece'.
4. See for example: CountryWatch.com (2002); See also: United Nations Development Program, Human Development Report, various years.

5. Greek government (2002) 'Greece in the Information Society; Strategy and Actions'. Greek government White Paper.
6. Boufeas, G., Halaris, I. and Kokkinou, A. (2004) 'Business Plans for the Development of E-government in Greece; An Appraisal', *UNTC Occasional Papers*, No.5.
7. Verginadis, G., Gouscos, D., Legal, M. Mentzas, G. (2003) 'An Architecture for Integrating Heterogeneous Administrative Services'. eChallenges Conference 2003, Bologna.
8. See www.syzefxis.gov.gr/en/
9. Tambouris, E., Gorilas, S. Boukis, G. (2001) 'Investigation of Electronic Government', Archetypon S.A, Greece, Proceedings of the 8th Panhellenic Conference on Informatics, vol. 2, pp. 367–376. See also: www.euro-citi.org
10. IST Project 2001–35399 funded by the European Community under the Information Society Technologies Programme (1998–2002).
11. Innovations Report, IST Results (2004), 'Easier On-line Transactions for E-government'. See comments made by project manager George Lepouras, University of Athens.
12. Adams, N. J., Haston, S., Macintosh, A., Fraser, J., McKay-Hubbard, A. and Unsworth, A. (2003) 'SmartGov: A Knowledge-Based Design Approach to On-line Social Services Creation', in Bramer, M., Ellis, R., Macintosh, A. (eds) *Applications and Innovations in Knowledge-Based Systems and Applied Artificial Intelligence, XI Proceedings of AI-2003*, the 23rd Annual International Conference of the British Computer Society's Group on Artificial Intelligence, Peterhouse College, Cambridge, UK, 16–17 December 2003.
13. See www.gsis.gov.gr
14. Gouscos, D., Mentzas, G. and Georgiadis, P. (2001) 'Planning and Implementing E-government Service Delivery: Achievements and Learnings from On-Line Taxation in Greece', Paper presented at the Workshop on E-government, 8th Panhellenic Conference on Informatics, Nicosia, Cyprus, 8–10 Nov. 2001.
15. Tsiavos, P., Smithson, S. and Kotyvos, S. (2002) 'A Path of Discontinuity: The TAXIS Case as a Transition from E-government to e-Regulation' in Bench-Capon, T.J.M., Daskalopulu, A., Winkels, R.G.F. (eds) *Legal Knowledge and Information Systems*, Jurix 2002: The Fifteenth Annual Conference. Amsterdam: IOS Press, pp. 53–62.
16. Gouscos, D., Mentzas, G. and Georgiadis, P. (2001) 'Planning and Implementing E-government Service Delivery'.
17. Newsphone Hellas – 2003 development at: www.newsphone.gr/eng/main.asp?C=12&S=182
18. TO BHMA (The Podium) Newspaper (2005) 'Case Studies: The Example of Citizen Facilitation Centres', Monday 7th March edn, Athens.
19. OECD Focus (2002) Public Management Newsletter, No.23 (March).
20. Other ministries involved are (in no particular order): The Ministry of Press and Mass Communication Media, the Ministry of Culture, the Ministry of Spatial Planning and Public Works, the Ministry of Education and Religious Affairs, the Ministry of the Aegean, the Ministry of Labour and Social Security, the Ministry of Transport, the Ministry of the Commercial Navy, the Ministry of Justice, the Ministry of Development, the Ministry of Agriculture, the Ministry of Public Order, the Ministry of Defence, the Ministry of Foreign Affairs, and the Ministry of Health and Social Welfare.
21. Priftis, A.(2002) 'From Administration to E-government for all in Greece', Bucharest. A. Priftis is adviser to the Greek Minister of Economy and Finance.
22. Priftis, A. (2002) 'From Administration to E-government for all in Greece'.
23. www.athens2004.com/
24. Hellenic Ministry of Foreign Affairs website: www.mfa.gr/
25. Boufeas, G., Halaris, I. and Kokkinou, A. (2004) 'Business Plans for the Development of E-government in Greece', p. 23.

26 Chadwick, A. (2003) 'Bringing e-Democracy Back In', *Social Science Computer Review*, Vol.21, Issue 4.
27 Although this site is no longer active, the results of forum consultations are archived and accessible at www.eu2003.gr/en/cat/214/index.asp?
28 Greek Presidency website: www.eu2003.gr/en/cat/0/index.asp?
29 www.presstext.com/pte.mc?pte=030211014&phrase=evote
30 www.greece.gr/index.htm
31 Access2Democracy NGO website available at www.access2democracy.org
32 Tsaliki, L. (2003) 'Electronic Citizenship and Global Social Movements' available at: firstmonday.org/issues/issue8_2/tsaliki/index.html
33 Howard, R. and Patelis, K. (2003) 'e-Vote: An Experiment in E-democracy for the European Union', *International Journal of Communications Law and Policy*, Issue 8.
34 Gibson, R., Nixon, P. and Ward, S. (eds) (2003) *Political Parties and the Internet: Net Gain?*. Routledge, London and New York.
35 Netchaeva, I. (2002) 'E-government and E-democracy', *Gazette: International Journal of Communication Studies*, Vol. 64, Issue 5.
36 Howard, R. and Patelis, K. (2003) 'e-vote'.
37 Janssen, D. (2004) 'If you Measure it They Will Score: An Assessment of International eGovernment Benchmarking', *Information Polity: The International Journal of Government & Democracy in the Information Age*, Vol. 9, Issue 3/4, p. 121.
38 See www.cyprg.arizona.edu
39 See for example, Norris, P. (2002) *Digital Divide*. Cambridge University Press, Chapter 6.
40 Third Annual Global E-government Study, Brown University, 29 September 2003.
41 Desai, M., Fukuda-Parr, S., Johansson, C. and Sagasti, F. (2002) 'Measuring the Technology Achievement and the Capacity to Participate in the Network Age', *Journal of Human Development*, Vol. 3, No. 1.
42 See for example: Brueckner, A. (2005) 'E-government: Best Practices for Digital Government', *Bulletin of the American Society for Information Science & Technology*, Vol. 31, Issue 3, p. 16.
43 Priftis, A. (2002) 'From Administration to E-government for all in Greece'.
44 EUROPA – IDABC – eGovernment Factsheet – Greece
45 Graafland-Essers I. and Ettedgui E. (2002) *Benchmarking E-government in Europe and the US*, SIBIS (Statistical Indicators Benchmarking the Information Society), IST-2000-26276, Project funded by the European Community under the 'Information Society Technology' Programme (1998–2002).
46 Graafland-Essers I. and Ettedgui E. (2002) *Benchmarking E-government in Europe and the US*, p. 35, 59, 61, 62.
47 Leith, P. (2004) 'Communication and Dialogue: What Government Websites Might Tell us about Citizenship and Governance', *International Review of Law, Computers and Technology*, Vol. 18, Issue 1.
48 EUROPA-IDABC (2004) 'E-government a Priority for Greece, says Minister of the Interior', eGovernment News, 22 October.
49 Anthopoulos, L. G. and Tsoukalas, I.A. (2006) 'The Implementation Model of a Digital City: The Case Study of the Digital City of Trikala, Greece: e-Trikala', *Journal of E-government* Vol. 2, Issue 2.

Further reading

Hahamis, P., Iles, J. and Healy, M. (2005) 'E-government in Greece: Bridging the Gap Between Need and Reality', *Electronic Journal of E-government*, Vol.3, Issue 4.

11 'Alt-Tab'

From ICTs to organisational innovation in Portugal

Gustavo Cardoso and Tiago Lapa

Introduction

Alt-Tab is the set of keystrokes that are used in the Windows operating system to change between applications. Using this expression as the opening title for this chapter is a way to remind us that when analysing the relation between ICTs and state, we should not only focus on the implementation of new services and routines but ask ourselves up to what point are we also dealing with organisational change. We need to change our focus of attention from technology to organisational innovation in order to fully understand the changes that ICTs might bring to the state. This is the perspective that we tried to follow connecting the analysis of the appropriation of ICTs in Portugal by the state, at the same time contributing to a better knowledge of organisational innovation through technology.

In the following pages we will clarify what has been the scope of the e-governance initiatives in Portugal, identifying the limitations and opportunities of Portuguese society in the global context of network societies, and the difficulties that the state in a society in transition, such as the Portuguese society, faces.

The first part deals with the possibility of the emergence of new trends in governance in Portugal. We will argue that there are still few initiatives that are transversal and that can be identified as new trends in governance caused by the technological innovation of the Portuguese public administration. Nevertheless, we have identified three different trends promoted by e-governance within the Portuguese public administration. The first is 'Administrative Network Swarming', occurring when one department under hierarchical dependence from a given ministry becomes, in fact, temporarily networked to another hierarchal dependency due to the implementation of ICTs. An example might be found in the programme to connect all Portuguese schools to the Internet; a programme led by the Ministry of Science and Technology in schools that are hierarchically dependent on the Ministry of Education. Under network swarming some level of agreement between the entities is needed, but in reality what occurs is the formal substitution of one entity by another for a short period, implying in the end structural changes in both administrative entities involved.

The second identifiable trend is what we have called 'Networked Archipelagos', found when, through the implementation of ICTs, a set of services are networked to the public but that at the same time are not connected between themselves within the public administration organisational matrix. This trend tends to use the citizen as a hub or node of interaction between departments. The third identifiable trend is what we have entitled 'Networked Administration' that is when, through the horizontal sharing of processes and accountability, entities within the administration reach a level of networking that changes the organisational matrix. Such a process cannot yet be identified in Portugal with specific examples – nevertheless, initiatives put forward during 2006, such as the merger of several identification cards into one smart card of individual identification containing several services (drivers licence, national identity card, NHS number, social security number, tax revenue card, and so on), might be a first step into inducing such changes.

We will also discuss here the heuristic utility of the ideal-typical dichotomy between traditional and digital political and government models. What seems to be notorious is that the technological innovation and the organisational innovation of the public administration has been at the centre of political discourse in recent years, but very little organisational change has been identified.

In the second part, we will discuss ICT-supported forms of interaction between citizens and the Portuguese government, and try to identify new capacities and patterns of interaction. Then, in the third part, we will take a closer view and overall assessment of the adoption of e-government practices and future developments.

New trends in governance in Portugal?

From 1995 onwards, the 'information society' started to become a national priority in the programme of the XIIIth Constitutional Government (1995–2000), substantiated in the publication of the Green Paper for the Information Society.[1] This document presented strategic reflections and proposals for structured action concerning firstly, the democratisation of the Information Society, guaranteeing free access to all citizens; secondly, the introduction of ICTs into the public administration; and thirdly the widespread development of ICT competencies in society, counteracting the phenomenon of 'cyber-exclusion'.

Later, in 2000, the national initiative for the information society was approved, including the guidelines for the central and local public administration ('the open state') and its relationship with citizens, refusing *a priori* a new modality of electronic bureaucracy: free-service electronic systems and electronic forms for contact between the administration, enterprises and citizens, the diffusion of office systems based on e-mail and e-commerce across the public administration, the training of public servants with the certification of the acquired competences and so on.

Effectively, the concept of e-government, defined as an offer of better and faster services, closer to the end user and with less costs, took the central role in the international discussion about new forms of political power in the era of information, an orientation that has been developed in Portugal through the creation in 2002 of a new special unit called UMIC (Unidade de Missão, Inovação e Conhecimento), set up to plan, coordinate and develop projects in the areas of information society and e-government, following an integrated and transversal vision that aggregates all governmental organisations. The creation of UMIC had as its main objective the conversion of Internet access into new opportunities for enterprises and other measures, such as the implementation of e-business, broadband investments and public access to the Internet at competitive prices.

With the programme of the XVth Constitutional Government (2002–5), the policies concerning information society underwent strategic modifications that clearly gave special attention to the concept of e-government by the state. This programme centred mainly on the measures concerning online provision of all public services in the term of one year, with regard to functions responding to the citizens' and enterprises' needs and not the internal structure of the public administration – namely launching of information portals to citizens and businesses.[2]

Table 11.1 below presents the range of e-government programmes launched in Portugal over the past decade.

Having as a philosophy the improvement of the representative democratic system, the political conception of the XVth Constitutional Government defined the citizen as the main actor, but ideally as 'a *citizen-client* that accesses the services of the public administration at any time and at any place; a *citizen-consumer* linked by broadband connections; and a *competent citizen* that possesses basic competences in information technologies'.[3]

More recently, the Socialist Government, elected in 2005, set as a national priority the implementation of a technological plan. The programme of the technological plan (www.planotecnologico.pt) focuses on policies concerning the growth of the Portuguese economy, setting incentives (fiscal, infrastructural, and so on) for technological and organisational innovation of enterprises, for the promotion of investment in research and development necessary for the creation of new knowledge. In this context, the bulk of e-government measures are set to meet the purposes of the government's growth agenda, reducing the bureaucratic wall between the public administration and citizens and enterprises.

In the sphere of the relationship between state and citizen, the policies for the information society were essentially designed for the communication between citizens and the public administration. However, none of the political actors had used ICT for the promotion of participation in the legislative process or the communication between citizens and elected politicians as a priority.

In terms of the modernisation of the public administration, Mulgan[4] proposes delineation between radical, systemic and incremental innovation in e-government. The nature of innovation in Portugal has been distinctly incremental and cautious, despite ambitious rhetoric, and the impact on underlying state structures has been very limited. It remains the case that there is not an example in the entire public service sector that has been radically reengineered to make full use of new technology. There are some good reasons for caution, such as risk, uncertainty and the likelihood that significant citizen-customer groups would not be able to use new technologies. However, vested interests are also a crucial factor, as a result of which the new measures are added as layers on top of the old ones, thus making it unfeasible to obtain maximum efficiency gains.

Table 11.1 Portuguese e-government initiatives: brief descriptions

Program	Description
Government to Citizen	
The Citizen's Portal (www.portaldocidadao.pt)	The Citizen's Portal is the central digital channel for public services, complementing with total convenience and availability the physical Citizen's Shops. Since it was released in the first quarter of 2004, the Citizen's Portal has offered more than 700 citizen-oriented 24/7 services (56% informational, 26% interactive, 18% transactional), provided by 118 public administration bodies. It is already a well-known brand, recognised by 30% of the Portuguese population. More than half a million users access it on a regular basis, with 2.5 million page views per month, mainly for such services as information on the public administration, income tax declaration, change of address notifications to public services, official certifications requests from public bodies. The Citizen's Portal is regularly classified among the ten best Portuguese sites (KPBI30, Internet performance Portuguese index, January 2005). The development of the Citizen's Portal has been continuous. Besides improvements on the user interface, since February 2005 it has offered services supported by sms, and access through wap protocol by mobile phones and PDAs. The services provided to citizens will be further enhanced by the adoption of the electronic Citizen's Card to be launched at the end of 2006.
Public employment offers (www.bep.gov.pt)	Online search of public jobs for citizens of the UE who would like to work in the Portuguese Public administration. Civil servants who want to exchange to other department or workplace can also use this online service and can post their mobility requests.
Electronic delivery of tax declarations (www.e-financas.gov.pt/de/jsp-dgci/main.jsp)	This service was created to facilitate the relationship between the taxpayers and the General-Direction of Taxes (DGCI).
e-Accessibility (www.acesso.umic.pt/)	A special unit promotes, since 1999, the adoption of good practices for accessibility of the public administration websites to citizens with special needs. This unit also promotes the availability of digital libraries and audiobooks in high schools, the adoption of assistive technologies in hospitals, and the infrastructuring of (re)habilitation centres (53 projects led by consortiums involving NGOs and people with special needs).
Solidarity Network (redesolidaria.org.pt/)	In 2001, a Solidarity Network connected NGOs concerned with people with special needs (elderly and impaired) to the Internet. Presently, this network involves 240 broadband access points, maintains 650 email boxes for use of the target groups, as well as specific content of interest, and includes 13 videoconference connections between schools and hospitals allowing bed-ridden students to remotely attend classes and to keep in touch with family and friends.

Program	Description
e-Democracy (www.votoelectronico.pt/index.php?lang=EN)	The main goal of the Portuguese Electronic Vote Project is to allow, in the future, citizens who are far away from their normal polling stations to be able to vote from wherever they are on election day. In this context, an initial pilot project of Electronic Voting was held in the 2004 European Elections. Three different technologies were tested, with 150,000 voters in nine municipalities. The second pilot project, in the 2005 Legislative Elections, improved voting platforms, with technology for citizens with special needs and a paper trail. It also tested internet voting for Portuguese citizens living abroad (with 4,500 participants from 38 countries). Both non-binding pilot projects were audited and evaluated by a multidisciplinary task force of university specialists, and the results were very positive. At the same time, the Electronic Democracy Project is developing initiatives to enable, in a near future, citizen participation in the discussion of public policy issues, in order to contribute to a modern and participative society.
All schools connected to the Internet since 2001 (www.infosociety.gov.pt/projects.htm)	'Providing all the schools with a broadband DSL connection to the Internet through the Science Technology and Society Network'
Public Internet Spaces (www.espacosinternet.pt/)	'More than 260 public spaces for free access to the Internet operating, since 2001, all over the country'
Science Alive ('Ciencia Viva'): a program for the promotion of science and technology within society (www.cienciaviva.pt)	Created in 1997, the Science Alive ('Ciencia Viva') program has been a highly successful initiative for promoting science and technology within society through a variety of schemes that involve a wide network of research centres and institutes, special education projects in schools for the experimental teaching of sciences, and a network of Ciencia Viva Centres throughout the country which operate as hands-on science museums for all ages. Many activities are based upon electronic communications and include educational projects using collaborative computational tools and the Internet, including projects performed in partnership with schools in other countries.
b-on: Online Knowledge Library (www.b-on.pt)	Through b-on, full texts of the main academic and scientific journals published internationally are accessible to individuals in all research and higher education institutions in Portugal.
Basic ICT Skills Diploma (www.posc.mctes.pt/)	The process of recognition of basic competencies in ICT and the associated awarding of is assured since 2001, based on a network of accredited entities of varied nature, most of which can also provide training in ICT, namely schools, Science Alive ('Ciencia Viva') Centres, centres for promoting the diffusion of ICT, professional training centres, and others. So far more than 100,000 people have obtained the diploma. The ICT competencies recognition system is being expanded to include intermediate and higher levels of competencies and e-learning.

Program	Description
e-U: Electronic University/ Virtual Campus (www.e-u.pt)	The e-U initiative is targeted at students and professors of higher education institutions and includes the extensive wireless networking of campuses with more than 5,000 access points, as well as higher education electronic services, contents and applications.
Health Portal (www.portaldasaude.pt/)	This initiative aims to improve the efficiency of rendered health services and guide the user of the National Health System. The citizen can have a simple and more direct access to information and services via the system, with better knowledge of the Ministry of Health and of health policies, access to health related news, information on the support services for citizens, and they can raise questions and submit suggestions as well as learn more about health conditions and healthier lifestyles.

Government to Business

Neotec: New Technological Enterprises (www.neotec.gov.pt/)	The Neotec initiative promotes the creation of new technological enterprises based on ICT and with high potential growth by providing financial support different phases of the enterprise creation process, from idea development to business plan and beginning of operations. The initiative is designed for the particular needs of students of higher education institutions and researchers of these or other scientific institutions. Neotec is implemented through the Innovation Agency, a company owned by the Portuguese State through FCT – Foundation for Science and Technology of the Ministry of Science, Technology and Higher Education, IAPMEI – Institute for Small and Medium Enterprises and Investment, and PME Investimentos – Small and Medium Enterprises Investments, both of the Ministry of Economy and Innovation.
Public e-Procurement (www.compras.gov.pt)	The main objectives of the National e-Procurement Program are: to increase efficiency and transparency, to generate savings, and promote the adoption of e-commerce. During the last year, the focus was on the characterisation of the expense and the reformulation of procedures, whereby new processes were adopted, such as sourcing, aggregation and negotiation. In the pilot phase the project involved eight ministries and a few public bodies and product categories. One of the objectives of the e-Procurement Program is to enable the access of small and medium enterprises to the public market. While the program was still only in its first year, the achieved savings for the public administration largely surpassed the investment. Presently, the process is at a generalisation and enlargement phase to all public bodies/ministries, and other product categories.

Program	Description
	The program directly involved 8 ministries, 132 public bodies, 907 users, and 27 aggregation and negotiation processes, with 12 million euros negotiated and 30% estimated savings. Total savings expected from the ongoing expansion of this initiative to all ministries amount to 250 million euros per year (source: AT Kearney).
Government to Government	
Digital Cities and Digital Regions (www.cidadesdigitais.pt)	The Digital Cities initiative was launched in the beginning of 1998 with pilot projects in a few cities in Portugal. Each Digital City project included several lines of activity that cover the main lines thought relevant to increase the use of information and communication technologies (ICT) to improve the quality of life and developed the economy. More than 25 projects for the development of Digital Cities and Digital Regions are being publicly supported, with a total investment over 200 million euros. The projects involve electronic government solutions for local public administrations, conditions for reinforcing the competitiveness of small and medium enterprises, and a wide variety of citizen centred services (e.g, information, health, education, safety).
Benchmarking	
Information and Knowledge Society Observatory (www.osic.umic.pt/)	The Information and Knowledge Society Observatory is the part of UMIC – Knowledge Society Agency in charge statistical indicators and studies on the Information Society and the use of Information and Communication Technologies (ICT) in Portugal. It assures regular surveys and studies on the use of ICT by families, enterprises, hotels, hospitals, schools, public administration, and other sectors, as well as on the employment in the ICT sector, the quality of public administration websites and other matters of interest to monitor the development of the Information Society in Portugal and compare it with the development observed in other countries. This part of UMIC assures the representation of Portugal in international organisations that deal with indicators and statistics related to the information society or TIC, such as EUROSTAT, OECD and the DG Information Society of the European Commission.
Web@x (www.acesso.umic.pt/webax/index.php)	Benchmarking of the web accessibility of the Portuguese Public Administration

According to Mulgan, each wave of technology has changed the options available for governmental organisation, determining how much can be managed, delegated, commanded or coordinated. There has been a co-evolution of techniques of governance through times (professional know-how, methods of increasing taxes, quantification and monitoring) and of communications technology, such as scripts, roads, telegraphs, satellites and more recently the web and the network grid.

As Fountain[5] points out, the effects of ICT on governance are still playing out slowly, perhaps in the order of a generation rather than changes occurring at 'Internet speed', not only due to lack of market mechanisms but also due to the complexities of government bureaucracies and their tasks as well as to the importance of related governance questions – such as accountability, jurisdiction, distributions of power, and equity – that must be debated, contested and resolved democratically.

In fact, Portuguese government still follows a Weberian hierarchical, vertically-organised model and, therefore, remains traditionally organised into what Mulgan designates as functional silos. On one hand, it is true that the bureaucratic state is not outmoded as Fountain points out,[6] remaining critical to standard setting, integrity of processes, accountability and rule by systemic trust.[7] On the other hand, the rigidity of the vertical model of organisation might be a huge setback when transversal policies and measures are being implemented. One critical example has been the definition of the priorities of the technological plan by the Portuguese Government, which hasn't been uncontested. The heads of two ministries, Economy and Science and Technology, seem to come out in public with two, if not totally different, at least somewhat divergent strategies.

Another identifiable trend is the emergence of organisations and agencies that work as isolated islands – although networked to the Internet – within the public administration, what we have called 'Networked Archipelagos' that reflect the governmental organisation by functional silos. With these examples, we stress the usefulness of Fountain's technology enactment framework that takes into account structural and institutional realities. This framework emphasises the influences of organisational and 'soft' normative structures on the design, development, implementation and use of technology. In many cases, organisations use ICT to reinforce the political status quo. ICT enactment expects the tendency of certain actors to implement new technologies in ways that reproduce and strengthen, institutionalised socio-structural mechanisms even when such employment may lead to apparently irrational and sub-optimal use of technology. For example, websites might mirror the (dis)organisation of the departments causing the navigation to be a mystery. Indeed, the same information system in different organisational contexts leads to different results or, in other words, the same system might produce beneficial effects in one organisational context and negative effects in a different context. Therefore, embeddedness and cultures have to be taken into account in the employment of ICT. Embeddedness refers to the fact that information systems are situated in the context of complex organisational histories, social and political relationships, regulations and rules, and operational procedures.

Policy makers have to bear in mind that it is not a straightforward process to change an information system when it is embedded in a complex organisational and institutional system.

In fact, the implementation of ICT within the public administration faces a series of challenges. First of all, public executives may face 'perverse' incentives for networked governance, as the efficiency of new information systems might enact a situation in which their budget and resources are decreased, redundancies across agencies and programmes threaten public servants' positions, and inter-agency systems challenge the autonomy of departments. Furthermore, there is the issue of misuse of capital and labour substitution when introducing ICT in organisations.

ICT-supported forms of interaction between citizens and the Portuguese government

The widespread public access to ICTs within the development of a global era of information has contributed to the awareness of the difficulties and inadequacies of traditional actors, procedures and institutions to face daily problems. Indeed, technology can potentially change the character of the dialogue between state and citizen, making it more reciprocal, open and nuanced,[8] and provide the chance for them to intervene more regularly and directly in the policy process.

Many support the idea that democracies are undergoing a crisis of representation characterised by the emergence of new non-governmental actors and pressure groups in the political sphere,[9] the breakdown of trust in traditional institutions, the weakening of procedures and a profound change in the values underpinning democracy.[10] These strained conditions in democratic governance and representation need to be balanced with a capacity to respond to the emerging challenges, and new ICTs are expected to play an important role in their reform and reinvention.

In the new client-oriented model of public administration, ICTs were conceived as a doubled-edged solution to the growing representative deficit of modern democracies. At first, the diverse 'cyberoptimist' views[11] expected ICTs to bridge the distance between public decisions and processes and citizens' needs, promoting their direct involvement and support for democracy and thus strengthening the overall performance of representative institutions. In addition, they were sought to boost bureaucratic efficiency and effectiveness and to have an impact on parliamentary actors, institutions and processes in the perspective of upcoming institutional reforms.

One of the main constraints on the development of ICT-supported forms of interaction between citizens and the Portuguese government are the low qualification levels of the Portuguese population and hence of the public servants themselves. This is the real core of the digital divide in Portugal, a deep-rooted structural problem that constitutes a factor of inertia to social programmes such as *ConnectingPortugal*, aimed at stimulating the perception of the Portuguese citizens regarding the relevance of ICTs and to provide training programmes and incentives of affordable or free computers and free access to the Internet.

But citizens are only part of the equation. The other part is, of course, formed by the various organisations of the public administration and politicians. Table 11.2 shows the synthesis of the main indicators of the Survey of the Central Public Administration's Usage of ICTs applied by UMIC's Information and Knowledge Society Observatory.[12]

The introduction of ICTs in the Portuguese public administration had the highest impact in frequent or regular digital communications within the administration itself. 84 per cent of the public organisations surveyed kept frequent or regular internal communications between the departments of the same ministry, and 83 per cent showed Internet activity between, and external communications with, other organisations of the public administration. The percentage of organisations that maintained frequent or regular external communications with businesses and citizens was 67 and 58 per cent, respectively.

The services provided on the website by public organisations are largely based around the availability of information that can, in some cases, be a substitute for face-to-face interaction. Ninety-six per cent of the central administration's organisations have institutional information on their websites, 91 per cent information of the services in place, 84 per cent information about their internal organisation and 79 per cent about legislation.

But there is still much work to do on the provision of other online services. Fifty-eight per cent of public organisations' websites provide forms to download, but

Table 11.2 Synthesis of the main indicators

	2000 (%)	2002 (%)	2003 (%)	2004 (%)	Average rate of annual growth (%)
Departments that have Internet access	98	98	99	100	1
Departments that have an internet connection superior to 512 kbps	–	–	42	53	26
Departments that have e-mail	90	92	95	93	1
Departments with websites	71	81	87	86	5
Departments that have a policy of free access to internet to all the workers	50	–	72	76	11
Departments that buy goods and/or services through the Internet	–	–	–	19	–
Departments with personnel placed exclusively to ICT's	–	–	72	75	4

Sources: OCT, Instituto de Informática do Ministério das Finanças, "Inquérito à Utilização das TIC na Administração Pública Central, 2000"; OCT, "Inquérito à Utilização das TIC na Administração Pública Central, 2002"; OSIC/UMIC, Instituto de Informática do Ministério das finanças, "Inquérito à Utilização das TIC na Administração Pública Central, 2003–2004".

only 29 per cent permit the completion and submission of forms online. Also, payments online and the sale of services or products in a digital format is far from being an alternative to paper based interactions as only 8 per cent of organisations have those services available via their websites.

Other possibilities of online interaction that can be improved are the access to databases (available on 47 per cent of public websites), provision of free online services or products (46 per cent of websites) and recruitment opportunities (20 per cent of websites). Measurement of user satisfaction only happens totally on 14 per cent of websites and partially on 25 per cent. Other usual forms of interaction such as support to the user (helpdesks, FAQs) are only fully available on 28 per cent of websites.

As for local administration, 91 per cent of city halls have a website. Of those that have no Internet presence, 96 per cent state that a website is under construction. 97 per cent state that the reason behind the decision to construct a website is the promotion of tourism and local culture, 96 per cent the straightforward diffusion of institutional information and 78 per cent the ability to strengthen relationships with citizens. Sixty-seven per cent of city halls answered they had a specific strategy on the development of ICTs. Eighty-four per cent give priority to online services aimed to serve the citizen, 80 per cent to the implementation of security policy in the use of ICTs and 46 per cent to training in ICTs. e-Commerce was far behind with only 18 per cent of organisations citing it as a reason to introduce a web presence.

As usual, in Portugal, local administration is behind central administration in terms of innovation, as shown in the provision of online services with only 49 per cent of city hall websites providing them and only 9 per cent allowing citizens to fill in and submit online forms, although 49 per cent provide the option to download the forms. In terms of interactivity 74 per cent provide an e-mail address for the submission of suggestions and complaints, but only 6 per cent allow voting online.

Portugal has been registering a fall in ranking concerning ICT indicators, such as the provision of basic public services, in terms of quantity as well of quality of the services provided. But the supply of the services isn't the only important thing. Policies that stimulate the demand of those services by citizens are also needed.

In addition, there is the fact that five million Portuguese citizens don't have academic qualifications correspondent to compulsory education. Thus, the provision of public services needs to be segmented according to the specific needs and demands of different users, especially of the under-qualified segments of the population. Only 20 per cent of Portuguese citizens have completed secondary school, a number that is far surpassed by the new EU members from Eastern Europe. Coupled with the lack of ICT competencies of a significant portion of the Portuguese population, what we are witnessing is the creation of conditions that will lead to a new gap, this time an electronic one.

Adoption of e-government practices in Portugal and future developments

The United Nations Global E-government Readiness Report 2005 provides an assessment of the countries according to their state of e-government readiness and the extent of e-participation. The assessment is made taking into account a quantitative composite index of e-readiness based on website assessment, telecommunication infrastructure and human resource endowment.

According to the Report, Portugal is in 30th place in the e-government readiness index. In the European context, Portugal is in 21st place while Denmark is in the lead. In terms of the offer of online payment facilities for any public service, Portugal ranks in 40th while the lead belongs to the United States followed by the UK. The Report suggests that resource availability appears to be a critical factor inhibiting e-government initiatives, and part of the reason for the high e-readiness in the leading European countries is past investment in, and development of, infrastructure, which might explain the setbacks of Portugal in the European context.

Portugal is in the middle ranking on the provision of online services.[13] Nevertheless, according to an annual report from Cap Gemini on the use of electronic public services in Europe, despite the recent evolution of sophisticated online services in Portugal, the gap as measured against the European average has been growing. Services destined for citizens and businesses have had the greatest development, permitting consultation and printing of forms, but still not covering total procedures. Still, Portugal marked its presence in the eGovernment Good Practice Framework,[14] created by the European Commission with several initiatives, including the Virtual Campus programme (e-U), the electronic Vote, the Citizens' Portal or the Public e-Procurement.

The Portuguese government continues to provide public services through multiple channels: face-to-face, telephone, mail, and Internet, which means it has to tackle the strategic and operational complexities of employing multiple channels for services. But, it seems necessary to avoid the elimination of paper-based channels and a radical move to e-government because of the demographic differences in Internet use. Despite the technological possibilities for e-government, the social decision to take into account the information excluded such as the elderly and other groups within the population prevails.

The policy of implementation of e-government measures in Portugal needs the revision of the model of interaction with citizens and enterprises, and a client-oriented view of citizens in the public administration. That entails the development of a system of quality management in public services, producing measurement indicators from the citizens' expectations that are accessible to aid the comparability of the quality of the various public services. This transversal logic of comparability is being set in the Common Network of Knowledge, with the aim of gathering the knowledge produced by public administration in terms of modernisation, innovation and administrative simplification in a single a database available to all public institutions and to citizens and economic agents. Through this network it will possible to re-utilise knowledge and avoid unnecessary duplication of information.

The implementation of a transversal and networking logic is also present in the interesting initiative so-called Digital Cities Programme, a major programme to extend the use of ICT applications at the local level aimed at improving the quality of life of citizens, using ICTs in a whole range of policy areas, such as healthcare, education, employment, e-commerce, administrative reform and leisure/culture. At an initial stage the Digital Cities Programme developed along four major action lines: firstly, improving life in cities; secondly, developing peripheral areas by enabling easier and more efficient access to the Local Administration (that is to say, reduce 'red tape' and simplify administrative processes for citizens and companies); thirdly improving the competitiveness of local economy and employment (that is to say, access to new markets, improve productivity of companies, create incentives to e-commerce and tele-work); and fourthly, the implementation of measures aimed at fighting cyber-exclusion and helping citizens with special needs (for example, the handicapped, elderly citizens, people in hospitals, and social minorities). In 2000, the programme entered a second stage aimed at reinforcing partnership programmes and initiatives between local public and private entities (mainly Small and Medium Enterprises – SMEs). Nevertheless, there has been reluctance from the candidate projects to include sub-projects in providing online services of the administration due to the 'complexity of doing it'.

Another interesting initiative bridging and networking various departments is one of the most emblematic e-government projects promoted by the UMIC: the website *Citizen's Portal*. This portal is an online interface of the most requested public administration services available to citizens and enterprises (50 services at the outset). Through a single website, citizens have access to several administrative services and are able to pay online avoiding the long queues at administration desks.

The prevalent philosophy of initiatives such as the *Solidarity Network* and the *Health Portal* might be the seed of an e-government that functions as an infrastructure enabling citizens or social agents. The *Solidarity Network* encourages connected NGOs concerned with people with special needs (elderly and impaired) to use an infrastructure of e-government to proceed with their own initiatives. In the *Health Portal*, information related to health issues and some services are centralised on a single website. The integration of an encyclopaedia of health that covers useful information about nutrition, ageing, diseases, oral and mental health or the prevention of illnesses might enable the citizens to follow healthier habits or to, for example, carry out a self-diagnosis in the case of simple flu and avoid the unnecessary use of healthcare facilities.

Other initiatives are aimed at promoting the diffusion of the Internet for educational purposes and scientific and technological production. One such initiative, as suggested by the Green Paper for the Information Society, was the exploration of the Internet as a teaching/learning medium which led to the consequent creation of the Science, Technology and Society Network (RCTS). This network was designed to disseminate information across all centres for scientific investigation, universities, polytechnics, elementary and secondary schools, municipal libraries, museums and archives. A new *Virtual Campus* programme (e-U) has also been adopted to promote the expansion of wireless connections within higher-level education institutions and to make portable computers more affordable to students and academic staff.[15] An additional project is *b-On*, a digital library with an online databank including almost 2200 international scientific publications available for consultation.

Another issue is the trust of citizens on the reliance of the system. The failure of the Ministry of Education in 2004 to develop an efficient ICT based system to allocate teachers to the schools is a significant example of how an inadequate response results in a greater public distrust of the new systems being implemented, threatening the rule by systemic trust of the bureaucratic system supported by ICT. In effect this systemic trust is essential to governance activities such as raising taxes, changing procedures, electoral success and the daily functioning of government.

Another issue in terms of trust is confidence in government's commitment to confidentiality. According to the UMIC's Information and Knowledge Society Observatory, in 2004 only 13 per cent of public organs and 6 per cent of city halls were fully capable of guaranteeing safe transactions via their websites. It may require stronger principles or mechanisms to support the use of personal data in Portugal. Those mechanisms could be the control of the identifiable personal data by the individual concerned or guarantees of total anonymity to organisations and citizens providing data to governments and the regulation of sanctions for misuse of data.

An important obstacle arises from the complexity of the legal framework, which presents the administration with a very complex and resource-consuming decision process due to the intricate complexity needed to cope with all possible situations.[16] Central and municipal government bodies tend to generate a significant amount of legislative and regulatory work, burdening the bureaucratic administration with an added complexity that is difficult to deal with. The constant changes in the legal framework from year-to-year entail ongoing upgrades to the information systems, adding costs and the potential inclusion of errors. This system also leads to a less transparent and democratic framework with potentially less transparent decisions. In some cases, creating an opaque wall for less-favoured citizens and for small and medium enterprises that do not have the resources to deal with its complexity.

A worrying indicator is that in a country where there is lack of qualified human resources, only 9 per cent of the central administration's organisations carry out frequent or regular human resources training programmes or e-learning initiatives.[17] Indeed, 39 per cent of city halls consider that the lack of dedicated ICT personnel has negatively constrained the development of their activities.[18]

A greater interaction with other organisations of the central administration is also needed. Only 11 per cent of them are involved in frequent or regular interdepartmental initiatives that promote a centralised online attendance and a transversal logic throughout the administration. Just 13 per cent of organisations provide online services and information relating to databases of other public organisations, and only 16 per cent carry out research and development activities, co-operating and sharing resources with other bodies on a regular basis.

Portals, websites, formularies and tax declarations through the Internet don't translate immediately into a new culture within public administration. Indeed, the tendency to 'put a web interface on top of what exists' might reflect the department's bureaucratic intricacy or inefficiency and even add to the complexity of the public service. Organisational innovation through the reengineering of the administration or of administrative processes is also necessary to allow a form of co-evolution between technology and organisation.

Conclusions

During the last ten years, several identifiable steps towards new forms of governance enhanced by ICTs in the domain of public administration have occurred. However, a significant amount of work still has to be done and many obstacles have to be faced. We have argued that there is a lack of culture of collaboration and networking within the public administration and that a true transversal policy that could establish a new trend in governance promoted by the ICTs has yet to be enacted.

Indeed, there are few initiatives that are transversal in terms of their application in the public administration. One of the main problems arises from the extremely complex organisation of the public administration and from the very rigid structure of the Portuguese administration and its tradition of working as an 'archipelagos of isolated islands', even inside the same ministry.

Another obstacle to the implementation of transversal e-governance is the lack of standardisation between departments, that is, each department uses its own vocabulary, policies and rules. The public administration utilises many different logics from department to department, even sometimes within the same ministry. The existence of a 'legislative shell' resulting from the accumulation of rules and laws that have been altered through the years constitutes another obstacle. Policies applied to the whole public administration are sometimes disconnected or uncoordinated, resulting in many incremental reforms, each of them adding further complexity on top of the previous ones. The inability, until 2006, to bring into public administration a model of evaluation of performance that might trigger a culture of responsibility within the civil service constitutes another level of complexity that has not helped the introduction of ICTs have any visible impact of transformation of organisational routines. Finally, we have to take into account that administration is, in the end, the provision of services by people, and that when those people have low qualifications and digital illiteracy the obstacles to success increase.

The *raison d'être* of the 'Alt-Tab' metaphor that gives title to this analysis is that without organisational innovation, the introduction of ICTs in public administration can only mean, at best, an upgrade in a system with many logics and differentiated realities.

Many instances of the implementation of ICTs in public administration reflect the traditional bureaucratic organisations already in existence. More services online might guarantee their inter-connectivity but they should also be accompanied by a change in methods of organisation, such as the capacity to work in a network or the capacity of a department to be autonomous but to co-operate with other departments. To face the challenges such as the diversification, complexity and global nature of policy issues[19] and the crisis of the Welfare State,[20] it is necessary to create a public administration with a transversal networking logic.

In addition, the traditional sovereignty of national governments is faced today by a more complex system of regional co-decision and shared-responsibility – that is to say, the so-called multi-level and polycentric governance[21] or Network State.[22] For the implementation of these changes the public administration should breed a culture of benchmarking, where successes and difficulties are jointly discussed and information, resources and services are shared.

The Portuguese government still follows the ideal of an hierarchical model organised vertically, following the Weberian bureaucracy. A digital policy and government model should follow the constitution of an open state that reshapes itself to be less a structure that provides services or achieves outcomes directly and more an infrastructure,[23] managing complex systems with capacities for self-organisation, working together with citizens and civil society at large in the co-creation of outcomes. This certainly entails agreements over common protocols, supporting user-friendly public systems with clear underlying rules and simpler interfaces, albeit with the complexity of the underlying processes.

A digital governance model might make the government less visible, more modular and customisable, enabling more variation and personalisation within the system. However, this undoubtedly comprises a great challenge for the state to re-conceptualise fundamental aspects of governance such as accountability and oversight into a new digital model of 'open-source' governance based on networked relationships.

On the basis of all that has been said on the characteristics of Portugal, our difficulties in the transition to an e-government system seems to need a response other than a voluntaristic approach centred on the restricted aspects directly represented by the conventional figures and indicators. But that doesn't mean that as long as all other structural obstacles to development remain we are condemned to be stuck in terms of implementing e-government initiatives. The clear formulation of strategic guidelines and, above all, making decisions at the right time and on the basis of knowledge of the current economic and social trends, are absolutely crucial for stimulating and monitoring the necessary changes.

In other words, full exploitation of the ICTs with a view to modernising the public administration and the state itself can only be achieved if, before this, in each one of the principal fields of economic and social life, the main barriers associated with the conventional organisational models and modes of operation are examined.

Portugal, a society in transition to a network society, is a fine example of the limitations of the technological innovations standing by themselves. On the contrary, it will always be the organisational innovation and the emergence of new institutional models that will lead to the development of the potential of the new technologies. Without organisational innovation, technological innovation will never constitute an effective development factor and a source of competitiveness.

Notes

1. www.acesso.mct.pt/docs/lverde.htm
2. www.portugal.gov.pt/pt/Programa+do+Governo/programa_p023.htm
3. Vasconcelos, D. (2002) 'O *e-government* e a construção da cidadania num mundo globalizado', communication to the *VII Reunion of Presidency Ministers of the Ibero-American Community of Nations*, Lisbon, 9 September.
4. Mulgan, G. (2006) 'Reshaping the State and its Relationship with Citizens: the Short, Medium and Long-term Potential of ICTs and E-government', in Castells, M. and Cardoso, G. (eds) *The Network Society – From Knowledge to Policy*. Washington, DC: Johns Hopkins Center for Transatlantic Relations.
5. Fountain, J. (2006) 'Central Issues in the Political Development of the Virtual State', in Castells, M. and Cardoso, G. (eds) *The Network Society – From Knowledge to Policy*. Washington, DC: Johns Hopkins Center for Transatlantic Relations.
6. Fountain, J. (2006) 'Central Issues in the Political Development of the Virtual State'.
7. Luhmann, N. (1979) *Trust and Power*. New York, John Wiley; Giddens, A. (1991) *The Consequences of Modernity*. Cambridge: Polity Press.
8. Mulgan, G. (2006) 'Reshaping the State and its Relationship with Citizens'.
9. Burns, T. (2000) 'The Future of Parliamentary Democracy', Green Paper prepared for the *Conference of the Speakers of EU Parliaments*, Rome, 22–24 September 2000. Available at www.camera.it/_cppueg/ing/conferenza_odg_Conclusioni_gruppoesperti.as
10. Johnston, M. (1991) 'Political Corruption: Historical Conflict and the Rise of Standards', in *Journal of Democracy* 2: 48–60; Mény, Y. (1996) 'Corruption «Fin de Siècle»: Changement, Crise et Transformation des Valeurs' in *Revue Internationale des Sciences Sociales*, vol.149 (September), United Nations in collaboration with éditions Erès, pp. 359–70; Putnam, R. and Pharr, S. (eds) (2000) *Disaffected Democracies: What's Troubling the Trilateral Countries?* Princeton, NJ: Princeton University Press.
11. Norris, P. (2000) 'Democratic Divide? TheImpact of the Internet on Parliaments Worldwide', paper for presentation at the *Political Communications Panel* 'Media Virtue and Disdain', American Political Association annual meeting, Washington, DC, August 31. Available at ksghome.harvard.edu/~.pnorris.shorenstein.ksg/acrobat/apsa2000demdiv.pdf
12. This survey was carried out between September and December 2004 and its focus was all Central Administration organizations in Continental Portugal. The survey was sent by surface mail and online and the response rate was 74%.
13. *Jornal de Negócios*, 11 March 2005.
14. This purports to be a database that has the support of every member-State as a locale for the exchange of experiences between coordinating teams of e-government in the various countries.
15. Fifty-four higher-level education institutions have already applied to this programme.
16. Veiga, P. (2006) 'A Reforma Organizacional e Modernização Tecnológica no Sector Público em Portugal' in Castells, M. and Cardoso, G. (eds) *A Sociedade em Rede – Do Conhecimento à Acção Política*. Lisboa: INCM.
17. UMIC's Information and Knowledge Society Observatory (2005).
18. *Semana Informática*, 'Autarquias estão todas ligadas à Web', Week No. 725, 14–20 January 2005.
19. Burns, T. (2000) 'The Future of Parliamentary Democracy'.
20. Rhodes, M. (1997) 'Southern European Welfare States, Identity, Problems and Prospects for Reform', in Rhodes, M. (ed.) *Southern European Welfare States, between crisis and reform*. London: Frank Cass, pp. 1–22.

21 Schmitter, P. (2001) 'What is There toLegitimize in the European Union, and How Might this be Accomplished?', in *Europe 2004 – Le Grand Debate. Setting the Agenda and Outlining the Options*, symposium proceedings 16 October 2001. Brussels: European Commission.
22 Castells, M. (2001) *The Internet Galaxy: Reflections on the Internet, Business and Society*. Oxford: Oxford University Press.
23 Mulgan, G. (2006) 'Reshaping the State and its Relationship with Citizens'.

Further reading

Cardoso, G. and Neto, P. (2003) 'Mass Media Driven Mobilization and On-line Protest: ICTs and the Pro East-Timor Movement in Portugal', in Van De Donk, W., Loader, B., Nixon P. and Rucht, D. (eds) *CYBERPROTEST. New Media, Citizens and Social Movements*. London: Routledge.

Cardoso, G., Cunha, C. and Nascimento, S. (2003) 'O Parlamento Português Na Construção de Uma Democracia Digital', in *Sociologia Problemas e Práticas* 42, Oeiras: Celta.

Cardoso, G., Hespanha R., Morgado, A. and Nascimento, S. (2005) *Democracia Digital – Eleitos e Eleitores na Era da Informação*. Oeiras: Celta.

Castells, M. (1997) *The Information Age: Economy, Society and Culture: The Power of Identity* (volume 2). Massachusetts: Blackwell.

Cheta, R. (2004) 'Disembodied Citizenship? Re-@ccessing Disabled People's Voices in Portugal', in Van De Donk, W., Loader, B., Nixon P. and Rucht, D. (eds) *CYBERPROTEST. New Media, Citizens and Social Movements*. London: Routledge.

Costa, A.F., Cardoso, G., Gomes, M. do C. and Conceiçao, C.P. (2003) *A Sociedade em Rede em Portugal*. Lisboa, Centro de Investigação e Estudos de Sociologia (CIES) – Instituto Superior de Ciências do Trabalho e da Empresa (ISCTE).

Cunha, C. (2002) 'Political Campaigning with New Information Communication Technologies in Portugal', *Information and Communication Technology (ICTs) and Political Organizations Research Meeting*, May 30/June 1, Sweden, University of Malmo.

De Sousa, L. and Cardoso G. (2003) 'Country report: Portugal', in Trechsel A., Kies, R., Mendez, F., and Schmitter, P. (eds) *Evaluation of the Use of New Technologies in Order to Facilitate Democracy in Europe: E-democratizing the Parliaments and Parties of Europe*. Publication for STOA (Scientific and Technological Option Assessment), European Parliament, Directorate-General for Research (research report).

Hacker, K. L. and van Dijk, J. (eds) (2000) *Digital Democracy: Issues of Theory and Practice*. London: Sage.

GUIA/PASIG *(Portuguese Accessibility Special Interest Group)*. Available at www.acessibilidade.net

Inquérito à Utilização das Tecnologias da Informação e da Comunicação pela População Portuguesa (2001) Ministério da Ciência e da Tecnologia, available at www.si.mct.pt/file?src=1&mid=1137&bid=868

Livro Verde para a Sociedade da Informação, Ministério da Ciência e da Tecnologia, available at www.acesso.mct.pt/docs/lverde.htm

OSIC/UMIC (2005) Administração Pública Central 2004 – Inquérito à Utilização das Tecnologias da Informação e da Comunicação, UMIC, Observatory of the Information and Knowledge Society. Available at compras.gov.pt/NR/rdonlyres/0C99CAC9-DD9F-4786-BD44-C86E6772447A/3941/APCentral2004.pdf

Semana Informática 'Autarquias estão todas ligadas à Web', Week No. 725 from 14–20 January 2005, available at www.semanainformatica.xl.pt/725/act/100.shtml

UMIC Knowledge Society Agency, Portugal (2004) 'e-Health'. Retrieved January 26, 2005. Available at www.infosociety.gov.pt/egov/ehealth.aspx
UN Global E-government Readiness Report 2005 – From E-government to E-inclusion, United Nations. Available at unpan1.un.org/intradoc/groups/public/documents/un/unpan021888.pdf

12 Estonia

The short road to e-government and e-democracy

Marc Ernsdorff and Adriana Berbec

Introduction

Estonia has managed to gain global attention through its advanced information and technology infrastructure, especially through its efforts to implement e-government and further the application of information technology in banking, education, health, transport and public administration. Estonian membership of the European Union (EU) has accelerated the improvement of Estonian public administration, which encompasses the main goals of the promotion of democracy, transparency and accountability. Today, Estonia stands as the e-government leader in Central and Eastern Europe[1] and as 3rd in the world in e-government systems.[2] At the same time, it is setting an example in terms of e-democracy throughout the European Union, being the first country in the world to enable all its citizens to vote over the Internet in political elections. But it was not just the EU membership that expanded the use of Information and Communication Technologies (ICT) in Estonian society; it was mainly the strategic thinking within the government to implement e-democracy, good attention to detail and a positive attitude towards ICT policy, innovative thinking and the development of a legal framework, and the economic growth and the macroeconomic stability of the country. The progress made by Estonia in the field of information technology has led to the development of some of the most dynamic ICT companies in the world, placing Estonia on the world map with three major technological innovations: Kazaa (software that allows file sharing), Skype (Internet-based free phone service) and Hotmail (free web-based e-mail) – all three originating from Estonia.

In order to understand the contemporary status of e-government in Estonia, this chapter will provide a retrospective view of the different steps of the Estonian public administration reform, along with the factors that contributed to the development of ICT in the public sector. In this context, attention is drawn to citizens' opportunities to get involved in the political decision-making process via Internet participatory platforms such as *TOM* or *Themis*, which will be described later in the chapter. Furthermore, the results of the government efforts to increase e-democracy are analysed through the case study of the nationwide introduction of e-voting in 2005.

General overview of Estonian public administration

Estonia started its public administration modernisation at the beginning of the 1990s, shortly after it regained its independence in 1991. Although resources were scarce, Estonia made considerable efforts to eliminate the old Soviet public administration system and to implement a new one. As the private sector was reluctant to invest in the development of IT projects and communication networks, the Estonian government relied heavily on intellectual capital and local entrepreneurship, leading the way towards the creation of new major companies such as Microlink, the largest information technology (IT) company in the Baltic States, Elcoteq Tallinn, and Estonian Mobile Telephone. The progress of ICT in a small country with less than 1.4 million inhabitants proved successful and that is why the Harvard University Global Information Report ranked the development of ICT in Estonia in 23rd place in the world among the 75 countries surveyed, surpassing countries such as France, Italy and Spain.[3]

The deregulation and privatisation process (including that of Estonian Telecom) has also contributed to the reform in public administration, as this has made Estonia an attractive destination for foreign investments. Bound up with this was the influence from Estonia's Nordic neighbours,[4] well known for their high level of IT development, who provided advice and assistance in modernising Estonian public administration. Thus, Estonia managed to become part of the Scandinavian IT supply chain, establishing partnerships with Swedish and Finnish telecommunication operators and forging connections with the international markets. In addition, the society's openness towards the use of IT also played a key role, as Estonians spend 3%[5] of their income on IT every month, which is significant for a country with a GDP per capita of EUR 7,923.[6]

An education system to increase digital literacy was also created, placing a great emphasis on providing students in universities with the practical skills required for the growing ICT sector. EENet, a non-profit organisation established by the Ministry of Education, played an important role in providing a high-quality national computer network infrastructure. However, the driving force beyond the modernisation of the public sector was the political will that made the implementation of public administration projects and of a comprehensive financing system, for which the state allocated a modest one per cent of the budget to the development of the IT sector, possible. It is admirable that the IT financing budget grew almost four times from 7.66 million EUR in 1997 to almost 29 million EUR in 2003.[7] All these factors have contributed to the development of the technology infrastructure in Estonia and boosted the modernisation of the public sector.

The reform in public administration was mainly focused on the decentralisation of its functions, its delegation to the private sector and civil society and on the increasing usage of ICT in the public sector. Today, Estonian Public Administration includes a central government and a one-tier local government, with decentralised public service management with the main responsibilities divided between the State Chancellery, the Ministry of Finance, Ministry of Interior, Ministry of Justice and Ministry of Economic Affairs and Communications. An important step towards the modernisation of the Estonian public administration through the use of ICT was the drafting of the Personal Data Protection Act that came into force in 1996, and had as its main purpose the protection of fundamental rights of individuals in accordance with public interests with regard to processing of personal data.[8]

In April 1998, an information policy was published with the aim to increase co-operation in developing the information society. It is completed by an action plan that sets up annual priorities and details of different projects. The action plan is generally renewed every year while the policy is revised every four to five years. In October 1998, the government also launched a wide backbone network, EEBone, which connected all government offices across the country, and in 1999, the government adopted a new reform strategy called Public Administration Development Concept (PADC) that called for better coordination and transparency in the public sector and more flexible and competitive management of it.

On the 8th of March 2000 the Digital Signature Act was approved, which places electronic signatures on equal footing with physical signatures. Shortly after, the government launched e-Tax Board, which enables taxpayers to file, view and correct their income tax returns online. In 2004, 76 per cent of all tax declarations were filled in online.[9]

The Public Information Act became part of the legislature on the 1st of January 2001, establishing the freedom of information in Estonia. In the summer of the same year a new e-democracy project was launched – TOM ('*Täna Otsustan Mina*', which literally means 'Today I decide') enhancing citizens' participation in the legislative process.

The *X-Road* project was implemented in December 2001 allowing government databases to communicate. This enables every Estonian to search data from the national database over the Internet, within the limits of their warrant.

Electronic ID cards were issued in January 2002, fulfilling the requirements of the Digital Signature Act. Those cards are mandatory for Estonian citizens and are meant to be the primary document for identification in any (governmental, business or private) form of communication. According to Government information, every Estonian citizen will have an ID card by the end of 2006.

IT policy in Estonia and its role in enhancing e-government and e-democracy

The Estonian Informatics Centre, subordinated to the Ministry of Economic Affairs and Communications, is responsible for the implementation of IT policy in public administration, with a special focus on e-government and the promotion of the digital signature. The strategic and efficient implementation of e-governance and e-democracy is coordinated by a non-profit organisation called the E-governance Academy, which has as its main objective the improvement of the democratic process in Estonia and the development of civil society. The government saw a great opportunity in using IT to promote democracy and make the public administration more transparent and accountable to Estonian citizens. The *Principles of Estonian Information Policy* are approved both by *Riigikogu* (the Estonian Parliament) and the

EU information society policies, and it has developed the following priorities for the building up of the information society from 2004 to 2006:[10]

- development of e-services for citizens, business sector and public administration, with a special focus on eHealth and eLearning;
- analysis and provision of IT-solutions promoting the development of e-Democracy (e-Voting system);
- increase of the effectiveness of the public sector (integration of state registers, new finance and statistical information systems);
- increase of the computer literacy of the population, e-Education;
- development of the Information Technology Security Policy, e-Security; and
- increasing opportunities for the society to use IT and digital solutions.

The development of ICT in public administration has led to the implementation of e-government and e-democracy with the creation of an Internet-based voting system. In order to avoid a digital divide and to ensure Internet penetration at all levels in Estonia, as well as improving participatory democracy, the ICT strategy has been developed through three important projects, discussed below.

The first project is focused on the development of technology infrastructure, giving access to the Internet to all Estonian citizens. Two important networks have been created: *Pea Tee* (Main Road), which was launched in 1998 and connects Estonian country centres and several nodes in the capital Tallinn, and *Küla Tee* (Village Road), launched at the end of 1998 to promote Internet access in rural areas and also provide fixed Internet access to schools and libraries. There are 726 public Internet access points throughout the country.[11] The inclusion of IT in the citizens' public life has proved to be a success, as nowadays 52 per cent of the Estonian population uses the Internet, 35 per cent have their own computer at home and all public employees have Internet access at their workplace.[12] The government is continuously making efforts to diminish the digital divide and has launched another project called Village Road 3, which aims at providing almost 90 per cent of Estonian citizens with Internet access by the end of 2006. Moreover, in 1998, during the project *Vahetu Riik* (translation: Direct Government) a common web portal named '*riik.ee*' (translation: gov.ee) for Estonian government agencies was created, and it became widely known as 'an inseparable part of Estonian e-government and the symbol of Estonia in the Internet.'[13] It is worth mentioning that Estonia has another IT development programme called *Tiger Leap*, which was launched in 1996 and was aimed at the computerisation of schools (Estonian IT Foundation). The programme soon became a positive brand characterising Estonia.

The second project is the *X-Road* project, as mentioned earlier. It is a programme that enables each civil servant, legal entity and natural citizen to search data from national databases over the Internet within their warrant. The system can be used through a public service portal called *e-Citizen*, and requires authentication through ID cards or Internet banking codes. In spring 2003, the *X-Road* program entered the competition 'eEurope awards for E-government' and was among the 20 finalists in the category 'A better life for European Citizens'. It was also awarded an Honorary Mention for original architecture and security solutions for its e-services.[14] The success of the *X-Road* project is guaranteed by the use of Internet banking (there were 1,125,454 debit payment cards as of September 2005 and more than 740,000 Internet-banking clients) – Estonia being the 2nd-ranked country in the world in Internet Banking – and by the use of ID cards – 867,484 ID cards in November 2005.[15] The ID cards are used for personal identification, and replace a manual signature with the digital one. Estonian Internet banking is at the same level as its developed Nordic neighbour countries and over 90 per cent of bank transactions are made via electronic means.[16] The Nordic countries, especially Finland, have always been an example and stimulator for the development of Estonian ICT and following the success of its implementation in the public sector, the Finish government has become more interested in learning more about the e-government system in Estonia.

The third project is the *e-Citizen* portal (also known as citizens' IT environment), a nationwide project designed to develop citizen-oriented e-Services by stimulating co-operation between Estonian citizens and the public sector using the Internet. Hence, Estonians can interact with the state via a 24 hours a day 7 days a week virtual operating one-stop-shop. The system also requires authentication through ID cards or Internet banking codes. The *e-Citizen* portal (www.eesti.ee) is a tool for e-Services that delivers a comprehensible database about the citizens' rights and obligations in relation to their local government, acting as the main link to related e-Services websites.

To increase productivity and competitiveness the government has also developed online public services for enterprises through the use of eBusiness. The main task of the eBusiness portal is to improve communication between enterprises and state agencies through online services. The development of eBusiness is mainly the responsibility of the private sector, while the government's role is to create a favourable IT environment for enterprises and to raise awareness of the benefits of eBusiness.

Reforms for transparency and accountability in the Estonian public administration were accomplished hand-in-hand with the development of ICT. The intelligent use of these technologies resulted in a closer co-operation between the citizens and the state and various services were offered via the Internet. In a second stage, Estonia took further advantage of this expansion and launched Internet-based forums, linking its users to policy-makers, thus promoting e-democracy on the basis of empowering citizens in the democratic process.

Examples of participatory democracy: Tom and Themis

On the 25th July 2001, the Estonian government launched yet another e-democracy tool. As the political will to initiate e-democracy existed and the IT framework was available, Estonia was prepared and ready to launch *TOM* ('Today I Decide'), an online portal. The aim of this participatory tool is to ameliorate the relationship between the state and society and to bring closer the decision-making process to the citizen.[17]

The concept of the *TOM* portal was defined in three words: 'Quick, robust and simple'.[18] On one hand *TOM* publishes drafts submitted by Ministers on which amendments can be suggested and, on the other, Estonian citizens can write their own proposals to be implemented. In practice, the different sequences in this process are as follows:[19]

- *Idea*: many people have potentially useful ideas on how to change and improve their environment. *TOM* offers the possibility to submit new proposals or to amend incoming Minister's drafts.
- *Comment*: as soon as a proposal is submitted, other subscribers of the portal have the possibility to comment or criticise the proposal over the next 14 days. Of course the author of the text can also defend his or her suggestion.
- *Editing*: taking all arguments into consideration, it is now up to the author to make amendments if necessary.
- *Vote*: the proposal is now voted on and a simple majority is sufficient for it to be endorsed.
- *Signature*: after the text is voted on, all supporters should sign for its validity.
- *Implementation/Answer*: once a proposal has been signed, it is directed to the administration concerned. This public agency has one month's time to either start implementation or to submit a well-founded explanation of why the proposal has been rejected. All answers are published on the portal.

The *TOM* program has often been cited as a pioneer instrument to increase public participation in the policy-making process. Thus, *TOM* offers the chance to combine citizens' deliberation on actual affairs with the sending of their suggestions to the government.

Most innovative about *TOM*, however, is the idea to disrupt the top-down approach. Not all legislation is decided on by only political elites, ordinary citizens are heard and their ideas are eventually taken into consideration. Interaction between the government and citizen appears real.

After almost five years of experience, many problems exist despite an elaborate approach. As a result of TOM, 5 per cent of the submitted drafts by ministers were amended,[20] however no new proposal from a citizen, in no relation to any ministerial draft, has so far become an official act.[21] The *TOM* portal was a success at its launch in July 2001 when 359 proposals were forwarded up to the end of that year; this enthusiasm was however not maintained and this is reflected by only 49 proposals being submitted in 2005.

There is interaction between different actors in the political decision-making process, but a real dialogue between citizens and politicians is missing. Discussions are carried out by a small number of users, compared to a population of 1.4 million. The potential mass participation via the portal, despite 52 per cent of the population being Internet users, has not occurred. User numbers have fallen and activity on the portal has dropped with the introduction of registration by digital signature via the electronic ID card in spring 2005.

In order to avoid most proposals being rejected as non-constructive, clear and understandable rules should be established to facilitate the management of discussions. On the other side, users have to be aware of the extent to which their input is considered in the policy-shaping process. Disproportionate emotions and sentiments of impunity, have to be avoided and a basic netiquette of Internet forums and chats observed. Anonymity is the reason that people undermine their responsibility, consequently leading to the introduction of the registration, which moreover had the negative effect of attracting even fewer users to the *TOM* portal.[22]

Opinions on *TOM* vary: the political élite consider *TOM* to be a successful initiative as it is an important channel of communication between the state and its citizens.[23] Academics tend to judge it as part of a learning process in using the Internet to augment democratic participation. Seen in this light, *TOM* has the framework to potentially establish itself as an Internet-based procedure that will be part of the policy-making process in the near future. Thus, participatory democracy will become part of the Internet and grow to be as important as information, consultation, discussions and petitions. Therefore a high level of participation is considered less essential at the moment than citizens' awareness of the existence of ICT-tools.[24]

Finally, *TOM* has also been a PR project.[25] Being internationally recognised – *TOM* won a European Commission award at the e-government conference in 2001 – *TOM* helps to promote the image of Estonia as a fast-growing modern state. Here, one can see parallels with Purcell's account of Slovenia elsewhere in this book.

Simultaneously to *TOM*, a private legislative platform was launched in March 2001. *Themis*,[26] established by the Estonian Law Center Foundation, is a similar Internet portal but it serves as an independent intermediary between the state and civil society, and mainly attracts non-profit organisations.[27]

The operation mode of *Themis* is further developed and more informative than that of *TOM*: Ministers' drafts are published on *Themis* at an early stage and changes of the drafts are closely monitored up until the implementation of the final act. Occasional roundtables are organised and phone surveys are conducted. Forum users are asked to comment on those drafts which then are resumed by *Themis* and submitted to the policy-makers. Although authorities are not committed to *Themis* and feedback is not mandatory, approximately 10 per cent of ideas from *Themis* have been considered in the decision-making process.

Themis has proven successful in the way it delivers information, but it faces an uncertain future in that it is merely a private platform lacking in official support. Moreover, there are problems of management, finance and a lack of awareness among the public.

Both *TOM* and *Themis* are discussion forums rather than real participatory tools.[28] The fact that both forums are short of participants raises the question of their legitimacy: should one really allow a minority of two, 10 or even 100 unelected people amend laws that will then be applied to more than 1.4 million people?[29]

TOM and *Themis* are also two examples offering unequalled opportunities. In relation to the application of modern ICT, Estonia is a precursor in what concerns participatory democracy. Nevertheless, these are not the only Estonian efforts to augment participation and interest in politics among the population. A case study of the 2005 Local Elections reflects this intention.

e-Voting

e-Voting is another project that was launched at the beginning of the twenty-first century. The then Prime Minister, Maart Laar, was a strong promoter of the idea and it was he who had already suggested the possibility of testing e-voting in the 2001 elections, even before any analysis was undertaken or any law was enforced.[30]

Ultimately, the resulting legislation became a sort of a pilot project of its own – common to other laws in Estonia – as no experience on technical and organisational aspects was available. The legal basis to carry out e-voting was subsequently laid out in the Local Communities Election Act, the Referendum Act, the Riigikogu Election Act (national election) and the European Parliament Election Act, which, between March 2002 and January 2003, were all adopted and entered into force. It should be mentioned here that e-voting only became an alternative platform to vote and not an exclusive one.

It would be wrong to argue that e-voting in Estonia is seen as another public service that has been adapted to respond to people's wish to exercise their political rights electronically. e-voting has never been the result of a popular demand but rather a result of the imposition of yet another initiative by a young Estonian political élite.[31]

A major purpose of introducing voting over the Internet is to augment the turnout. As a higher turnout is generally attributed to a higher level of democracy, e-voting is considered an option to diminish the democratic deficit. Today, e-voting attracts mostly young voters as a new computer- and Internet-literate generation is emerging – 91 per cent of the Estonian population aged between 10 and 24 are regular Internet users. It is assumed that this most-evolving part of the population can be attracted to elections in the long term via the means of online voting. Therefore, the aim is to create an essential convenience in an information society.[32]

Another aspect is party competition, which will be carried out more and more on the Internet, thus becoming another means to attract the electorate.[33]

It was thought that Estonia would become the world leader in regular e-voting in the 2002 local elections. This was, however, not achieved as technical problems could not be fixed in time and scepticism among certain politicians was too apparent. As part of a political compromise, e-voting was only introduced three years later. The Estonian local elections of 2005 were the first worldwide where a whole nation had the possibility to post their ballot via the Internet.[34]

The introduction of different acts, as mentioned above, had been forgone by debates between all major parties. Some political parties considered e-voting an opportunity to increase their support, while others conceived it a threat.[35] A major issue was the anonymity and the secrecy of voting in elections over the Internet: secrecy is understood as a means, and not as an aim itself anymore, to protect an individual from any pressure or influence on their freedom to express their views.[36]

In order to avoid vote-buying and/or coercion, possible instruments to misuse one's freedom of expression, the concept of e-voting suggests two measures:[37]

- The possibility to re-vote: during the advance voting period an e-voter has the opportunity to cast his or her vote more than once. Only the final vote will be counted.
- The priority of traditional voting: a citizen who has voted via the Internet has the possibility to replace his or her electronically recorded vote by a paper ballot at the polling station. Thereafter, the e-vote is cancelled. Hereby we should note that e-voting takes place in advance of the designated natural polling day (six to four days before Election Day).

One person who did not agree with these changes was Estonian President Arnold Rüütel, who opposed these proposals on the grounds of violating the constitutional principles of uniformity and equality among voters. Voters using paper ballots do not have the opportunity to change their choice. Managing to veto the Internet voting legislation earlier in 2005, he was eventually overruled a month prior to the elections by the Supreme Court on the claim that each citizen still has only one vote.[38]

Besides the legislative perspective, principles of behaviour for political parties were laid down in order to achieve successful and fair e-voting.[39]

On the eve of Election Day, the authorities expected to achieve a higher turnout due to the introduction of e-voting. Madise[40] highlighted a positive attitude towards e-voting: 84 per cent of Internet users supported the initiative, while even 56 per cent of non-users found it to be a valuable idea. The government's aim to increase participation among the young part of the population was also about to be accomplished as two out of three (65 per cent) young Estonians' (aged 18–34) preferred voting means was the Internet. Another key aspect of the Internet vote is the mandatory ID card required for the identification when logging onto a computer and casting the vote. At the moment of the elections, 80 per cent of the voting population was in possession of such an ID card.[41]

Hence, trust in new technologies was more widespread in Estonia and a fiasco such as the US presidential elections of 2000 in Florida, where thousands of votes were lost due to problems with electronic voting machines, was not feared. The final result of the election was nonetheless disappointing.

Experts' predictions of an increase in the general turnout due to e-voting were incorrect.[42] As the number of submitted votes via the Internet was surprisingly low, a higher turnout was not about to occur. Only 9,287 out of 1.06 million registered voters cast their vote online, resulting in a marginal e-vote turnout of only 0.88 per cent or 7 per cent of the advance voting. With this insignificant number of e-voters, the overall turnout of 47 per cent was a sharp fall of 5.5 per cent compared to the previous local elections.[43]

Before exploring the possible explanations of this poor and rather unexpected outcome, two positive points about the Estonian experience need highlighting: firstly, no glitches or attempts of hacking were reported. From a technical viewpoint the process of the advance e-voting flowed smoothly. One can, however, argue that a country such as Estonia, due to its small size, is less at risk of such an attack than, for example, the USA would be. Secondly, as mentioned above, the Estonian election was a world premiere that resulted in Estonia being under the spotlight of the international press for a few days. This helped to promote the modern face of a society that celebrated only its 15th year of independence in 2006. Reporting was, however, biased, as more attention was paid to the so called sensational 'world premiere' rather than to the real purposes of e-voting or to the outcome.

So what is to blame for the poor outcome? One prerequisite for popular e-voting had certainly not been satisfied, namely that of the spreading of specific electronic ID card readers. Dull as it might sound, the fact that no citizen had such a device at home made Internet voting less possible in the end. ID card readers are located almost exclusively in banks, telecommunication companies or state and municipal offices, but they are not common for personal use and furthermore, they are expensive. Estonians have no need to possess a card reader as it would only be useful for e-voting and for the use of a digital signature; two procedures that can easily be carried out in the above-mentioned locations, thus creating an inbuilt disincentive to use Internet voting in this case.

This raises the question of the principal purpose of e-voting. How is it possible to create convenience in an information society when the most popular places of use are public buildings and not private homes?[44] Where is the promised comfort and ease of operation?

As for a rising turnout, the Estonian case confirms in fact what some ICT specialists such as Darin Barney have long been trying to put forward; 'that network technologies tend to reinforce existing patterns of democratic behaviour rather than mobilise new actors and practices.' It seems that those people who vote online are already gifted Internet users, equally being already politically educated.[45]

A cost-benefit analysis is negative too: A small number of users and the right to re-vote at the polling station are expensive procedures. In economic terms, e-voting is an unprofitable e-tool, at least at the moment.

Conclusions

An early investment in ICT, accompanied by the necessary reforms has made of Estonia one of the most developed states in e-government in Europe, even in the world. Its proximity to the Scandinavian technology sector, and the fact that Estonia is a relatively small country, have further accelerated this progress.

Hence, initiatives to create interaction between the state and its citizens were enhanced by the launch of *TOM* and *Themis*. Both portals give citizens the opportunity to engage in the decision-making process of the state. This engagement is proof of e-democracy in the way that it provides a forum where citizens can submit proposals on legislation or comment to amend a Minister's draft proposals. Even though there is interaction, a real debate is missing or only taking place between *TOM* or *Themis* users rather than between the general public and policy-makers, that in the end makes the portals more of a discussion forum than an elaborate channel of participation. This resulted in lower participation in these forums and reasons for this are two fold: firstly, citizens lack not only interest but often also the required political knowledge to get their voice taken into consideration. Secondly, the determination among civil servants to be involved in such procedures and to respond suitably to proposals is not always present. For such participatory tools to become a success, one has to 'break down bureaucratic firewalls' according to Ivan Tallo, Director of the E-governance Academy in Estonia.[46]

The analysis of the e-voting case-study has shown us that electronic voting is not the solution to increasing electoral turnout, even though the diffusion of only a few card readers has to be taken into consideration. One can only speculate on the consequences if everything had been smoothly prepared. But experts' opinions differ on whether it is possible to take advantage of the Internet to raise voter numbers or if those citizens who cast their ballot online are an electorate that would vote in any case. While only the coming elections – hopefully with better possibilities to vote online – can prove or disprove this, the 2005 elections have shown us that e-voting cannot be dismissed from Estonians' thoughts. Internet voting was supported by a majority of Estonians.

Estonia is the uncontested e-government leader of the Central and Eastern European countries, and the government's efforts to further develop ICT will consolidate Estonia's position Europe-wide. With regards to the co-ordination of this development, attention must be focused so older projects are not neglected in favour of recently-launched programmes. Nonetheless, with regard to the example of e-voting, Western European countries started to look up to this Baltic country. Considering Estonians' e-democracy tools a failure is sometimes more a jealous and hypocritical critique than anything else; numerous are the countries that have never experienced e-government and e-democracy to such an extent, in spite of having the potential resources to put it into practice.

Notes

1 Economist Intelligence Unit (2004) *E-government in Central Europe – Rethinking Public Administration.* Available from www.investinestonia.com/pdf/Central_Europe_egov.pdf (Accessed 23 January 2006), p. 1.
2 IPR Helpdesk Bulletin (2006) *EE:-government, E-voting and Digital Signing-Benefits for IPR and Every Citizen.* Available from www.ipr-helpdesk.org/newsletter/25/html/EN/IPRTDarticleN11621.html (Accessed 19 February 2006).
3 Kerem, K. (2003) *Internet Banking in Estonia.* PRAXIS Centre for Policy Studies, p. 9. Available from unpan1.un.org/intradoc/groups/public/documents/UNTC/UNPAN018529.pdf (Accessed 21 January 2006).
4 Berg, E. (2002) 'Local Resistance, National Identity and Global Swings in Post-Soviet Estonia', *Europe-Asia Studies*, vol. 54, no. 1, pp. 109–22.
5 Krull, A. (2002) *ICT Infrastructure and e-Readiness Assessment Report: Estonia.* PRAXIS Centre for Policy Studies, p. 14. Available from results.eforesee.info/Final%20Deliverables/D08%20Annexes/Pilot%201%20-%20Annex%20-%20PRAXIS%20-%20e-readiness%20report.pdf (Accessed 6 February 2006).

6   Federation of International Trade Association (2005) available from www.fita.org/countries/estonia.html (Accessed 22 February 2006).
7   Krull, A. (2002) *ICT Infrastructure and e-Readiness Assessment Report*, p. 7.
8   Estonian Information Society in Facts and Figures (ESIS), *Personal Data Protection Act*. Available from www.esis.ee/ist2004/103.html (Accessed 17 February 2006).
9   Tallo, I. (2005a) *The Case of Estonia: When Committed Actors Make a Difference*. Available from egov.epfl.ch/open_event/Downloads/ivar_tallo.pdf (Accessed 20 February 2006), p. 3.
10 State Chancellor of Republic of Estonia (2004) *Public Administration in Estonia*. Available from www.riigikantselei.ee/failid/Public_administration_in_Estonia.pdf (Accessed 15 February 2006), p. 20.
11 Tallo, I. (2005b) *e-Estonia: Is the Success Story Continuing?* Baltic IT&T Review, No. 38(3). Available from eganews.blogspot.com/2005/11/e-estonia-is-success-story-continuing.html (Accessed 3 March 2006).
12 Information Management Journal (2003) *Estonia Embraces Cyberspace*, vol. 37(4), p. 12.
13 Estonian Ministry of Foreign Affairs (2005) *Estonia Today – e-Estonia*. Press and Information Department, Tallinn. Available from web-static.vm.ee/static/failid/286/e-Estonia_uus.pdf (Accessed 26 January 2006).
14 *IT in Public Administration in Estonia Yearbook 2003*. RISO (State Information System). Available from www.riso.ee/en/pub/2003it/p34.htm (Accessed 17 February 2006).
15 IPR Helpdesk Bulletin (2006) *EE*.
16 Siil, I. (2001), *Estonia: Preparing for the Information Age*, No. 74. Available from www.ica-it.org/docs/issue74/issue74-siil.pdf (Accessed 16 February 2006).
17 Organization for Economic Co-operation and Development (2003) *Open Government Fostering Dialogue with Civil Society: Consultation and Participation*. Available from www1.oecd.org/publications/e-book/4203011E.PDF (Accessed 15 March 2006), p. 115.
18 Vertmann, T. (2004) *Speech on Electronic Participation of Citizens*. Available from www.riigikantselei.ee/3qc/ docs/tom/Tex_kone_hiina_eng_1009.doc(Accessed 6 February 2006).
19 United Nations (2003) *UN World Public Sector Report 2003*, UN Department of Economic and Social Affairs, New York, p. 49.
20 Estonian Ministry of Foreign Affairs (2005) *Estonia Today – e-Estonia*.
21 Lepa, R., Illimg, E., Kasemets, A., Lepp, Ü. and Kallaste, E. (2004) *Engaging Interest Groups in Decision-Making Processes*, Praxis Center for Policy Studies, Tallin, p.12. Available from www.praxis.ee/data/kaasamine_eng_9_03.pdf (Accessed 10 February 2006).
22 Due to the cover of anonymity, many user submitted proposals or comments by expressing their dislikes vulgarly, which is no longer the case as users now have to reveal their true identity; see Rainu, R. (2002) *e-Democracy: A Case of Estonia*, BA Thesis, Tartu University, Tartu, pp. 47–49. Secondly, anonymity has lead in a few cases to manipulation. A person can possess multiple user accounts and thus control the outcome of a vote; see Rainu, R. (2002) *e-Democracy*, pp. 54–55.
23 Vertmann, T. (2004) *Speech on Electronic Participation of Citizens*.
24 Vertmann, T. (2004) *Speech on Electronic Participation of Citizens*.
25 Rainu, R. (2002) *e-Democracy*, p. 50.
26 Rainu, R. (2002) *e-Democracy*, pp. 37–58; see also: Lepa et al (2004) *Engaging Interest Groups in Decision-Making Processes*, pp. 13–4.
27 While *Themis* is completely independent from the state as a whole, *TOM* is also independent from the different Ministries concerned but is nevertheless maintained by the State Chancellery.
28 Rainu, R. (2002) *e-Democracy*, p. 41.
29 Rainu, R. (2002) *e-Democracy*, p. 52.

30 Drechsler, W. *The Estonian e-Voting Laws Discourse: Paradigmatic Benchmarking for Central and Eastern Europe*, UNPAN, p. 2. Available from unpan1.un.org/intradoc/groups/public/documents/nispacee/unpan 009212.pdf (Accessed 19 February 2006).
31 Drechsler, W. *The Estonian e-Voting Laws Discourse*, p. 6.
32 Madise, Ü. (2005) *e-Voting in Estonia*. Estonian National Electoral Committee (presentation), p. 3. Available from www.vvk.ee/english/ylle.ppt (Accessed 5 February 2006).
33 Madise, Ü. (2005) *e-Voting in Estonia*.
34 The very first ballot posted via the Internet was that of US astronaut David Wolf, who was allowed to vote by e-mail from the space station Mir in the 1997 Texas election.
35 Drechsler, W. *The Estonian e-Voting Laws Discourse*, p. 3.
36 Drechsler, W. *The Estonian e-Voting Laws Discourse*, pp. 4–5.
37 Maaten, E. (2005) *Internet Voting System*. Estonian National Electoral Committee (presentation), p. 4. Available from www.vvk.ee/english/epp.ppt (Accessed 13 February 2006).
38 EurActiv website. Available from www.euractiv.com/Article?tcmuri=tcm:29-145735-16&type=News (Accessed 18 February 2006).
39 Madise, Ü. (2005) *e-Voting in Estonia*, p. 16.
40 Madise, Ü. (2005) *e-Voting in Estonia*, pp. 6–11.
41 Estonian Ministry of Foreign Affairs (2005) *Estonia Today – e-Estonia*.
42 EurActiv website. Available from www.euractiv.com; Lemke, J. (2005) *Internet Democracy – e-Voting Comes to Estonia*. Financial Mirror. Available from www.financialmirror.com/more_news.php?id = 2133 (Accessed 7 February 2006).
43 Estonian National Electoral Committee. Available from www.vvk.ee/engindex.html (Accessed 19/02/2006).
44 Maaten, E. (2005) *Internet Voting System*, p. 13.
45 Barney, D. (2001) *Prometheus Wired: The Hope for Democracy in the Age of Network Technology*. University of Chicago Press, Chicago, USA, p. 264.
46 Tallo, I. (2005a) *The Case of Estonia*.; Tallo, I. (2005b) *e-Estonia*.

Further reading

E-government (2005) Available from www.vm.ee/estonia/kat_175/pea_175/2972.html
Estonian National Electoral Committee (2005, *Statistics of e-Voting*. Available from www.vvk.ee/english/results.pdf
Täna Otsustan Mina. Available from www.eesti.ee/tom

13 This revolution will be digitised!

E-government in Hungary

Katalin Szalóki and Paul G. Nixon

Introduction

Hungary has a rich history as a transformational state within Europe. Recently, it has experienced the latest in a sequence of paradigm shifts that has seen it emerge from its communist heritage to become a modern, independent, democratic state. Its evolution as such, in common with many other former communist states, has witnessed major restructuring in almost every field since the change of regime in 1989, not least in the field of public administration and governance. The process of European integration, and later the requirements under which Hungary could become a Member State of the EU, brought about challenges in society, the economy, and in all levels of politics and the administration itself. As the EU, meanwhile, experienced an information explosion with the moves towards an information society, Hungary was struggling to come to terms with its new freedoms and to adapt to its new situation.

The role of the EU

Before 1989, the economic strategy of Hungary was largely based upon heavy industry and as a nation it was slow to see the potentialities of ICT development, and thus was in a weak position to benefit having a heritage that had left it with an ageing infrastructure and educational un-preparedness for the coming digital revolution. As Schneider notes, the economic strategy '… had severe consequences on the ecological balance, employment structures, skills development etc., and in effect cut the region off from the first decade of the "e-revolution"'.[2] The new state had other, more pressing, priorities than a long-term development of e-government services at that time. However, the requirements for EU membership, to which the Hungarian government aspired, acted as a galvanising force for the restructuring of government in Hungary to enable it to meet the accession criteria and to adopt the 'acquis communautaire'. Funding support was available via the Structural Funds grant system for pre-accession countries, such as Hungary, to enable the transition to be made. Through the Instrument for Structural Policies for Pre-Accession (ISPA), Hungary's administration was prepared to meet the challenges of EU membership. Such funds are still being paid to Romania and

Bulgaria in order to help them have a smooth transition to membership. Hungary was, in a sense, fortunate that it could gain from not having to blindly undergo the sometimes painful transformation towards e-government in an incremental mode where a nation had to learn by its mistakes, but could gain some advantage by learning from the successes and failures of the EU-15 who had already moved some way along the road to e-government implementation.

Following on from the Bangemann Report,[3] the EU sought to include central and eastern European countries in discussions relating to the information society. Commissioner Bangemann hosted a conference in Brussels in 1995 that led to the creation of the EU-CEEC Information Society Forum. This Forum stipulated largely voluntary measures, although its importance in demonstrating the values of co-operation should not be understated. It led to the creation of a Joint High Level Committee on the Information Society that underpinned the subsequent efforts to include, at least to some degree, the aspirations and ideas of the CEEC countries in the Lisbon Strategy and subsequent developments as outlined earlier in this volume.

Historical overview

To review, in short, the history of the Internet in Hungary, the very first date that needs to be mentioned is 1991, which was when the first Hungarian domain name was registered. By 1999, the number of people who had Internet access had already grown to exceed 1 million[4] and this number is increasing rapidly. Between 2000 and 2004, the proportion of Internet users increased by 124 per cent, with 27 per cent of the population having Internet access in 2004. At the time of writing the most recent figures from the end of December 2005 show some discrepancy between sources, with 'emarketer' reporting the number of everyday Internet users to be approximately 3,200,000 (32 per cent of the adult population),[5] whilst another source, Internet World Stats, reports a figure of slightly more than 3,050,000 (30.3 per cent) having Internet access.[6] It is also worth remembering that the spatial inequalities between different parts of Hungary are vast. Much of the concentration of access is centred around Budapest and other major conurbations, with rural access rates being much lower.[7] More than 1.4 million households in Hungary have a computer, although only 48 per cent of all households with a computer actually have access to the Internet, leaving approximately 52 per cent, or 720,000 households, having a computer terminal without Internet access.[8] There is also a gender imbalance, with 30 per cent of men having access compared to 26 per cent of women.[9]

These numbers do not look too promising when we compare them to other European countries. According to a research project that was undertaken at the end of 2005, out of 37 European countries, Hungary is ranked in twenty-ninth position.[10] The average percentage of Internet users per country in the European Union is 41.8 per cent, which leads us to realise that the Hungarian government and its agencies have some way to go to meet their own stated targets in bringing Hungary up to EU average standards. The government needs to make continuous and strenuous efforts to spread access opportunities, but also to build up the use of the Internet in the daily life of the Hungarian people on a systematic basis that ensures the seamless adoption of the technology across their life experiences. We can see varying reasons for the comparatively slow adoption of the Internet by Hungarians. Firstly, the late investment in information society infrastructure due to the previous focus of the commanding economy in Hungary and its reliance on old fashioned, heavy industries, as noted above, meant that many Hungarians were not exposed to information culture through their workplace tasks as was becoming the case in many of the other EU countries. Secondly, the low level of personal ownership of PCs (although this is increasing). Thirdly, Hungarians face relatively high subscription fees for Internet services due somewhat paradoxically to a 'vicious circle' effect of the first two reasons noted above, in that the lack of awareness or experience of the benefits of Internet use, coupled with a low level of personal ownership, means that Internet Service Providers cannot pass on the benefits of economies of scale to the consumer at present. Currently, broadband access in Hungary is relatively low, with the Hungarian Statistics Office (KSH) recording that in the third quarter of 2005 there were 327,500 xDSL lines – an increase of more than 75 per cent on the previous year.[11] Additionally, the lack of knowledge of – or perceived competency in – other foreign languages, particularly English, the dominant language of the Internet, can cause an uncertainty that can act as a barrier to Internet usage. The Hungarian language, being unique and spoken only by one nation, limits the content available in that language and therefore may act as an inhibitor to wider usage.

So in a sense we have a conundrum of the state wishing to increase ICT usage at a much wider level and to integrate Hungarians into the wider information society, but the population being put off by the barriers mentioned above. How could the government stimulate or act as a catalyst for such usage? One model of course is to lead by example and to create the demand for ICT usage by providing, in the first instance, online government services that offer specific benefits to users, which encourage citizens to engage in the online world in one facet that would hopefully lead them to engage in other subsequent online activities on a wider basis. Thus, both the progress in the rise of IT facilities for citizens and the advancing use of IT solutions by both the government authorities and public administrative services are interlinked.

Place and role of e-government in the public administration of Hungary

One can see that public administrations in Hungary are charged with a leading role in the promotion of an e-society. Not only are they expected to create e-government services and to deliver them to the Hungarian public, but also to act as champions for the information society and to promote and stimulate the uptake of ICTs in wider society. Despite the relatively low proportion of Internet users and the uneven progress in IT development and Internet use in Hungary, e-government has emerged and has continued to evolve over the past few years. This is perhaps unsurprising when one considers the time savings that e-government implementation potentially affords both to the administration and to the citizen. Csuhaj-Varjú estimates that Hungarian citizens spend more than 18,000,000 hours each year on performing administrative tasks,[12] many of which could easily be achieved using ICTs.

The early history of the moves to e-government in Hungary largely stem from the Prime Minister's Office. In July 1991, the Prime Minister established the Inter-Departmental Committee of Informatics to oversee Hungary's transition towards an information society.[13] In 1999 the government published a document on how Hungary could respond to the challenges of the Information Society.[14] The most visible commitment in this direction was shown when setting up the Ministry of Informatics (Informatikai és Hírközlési Minisztérium – IHM) in 2002 that took over the tasks that previously had been the responsibility of the Office of the Government Commissioner for Information and Communication Technology (IKB) attached to the Prime Minister's office. The IHM is still responsible for the vast majority of the tasks of e-government, although some other tasks concerning the informatisation of the central government are taken care of by the Prime Minister's Office (Miniszterelnöki Hivatal – MeH).

The duties and the sphere of authority of the Minister heading the Ministry of Informatics are regulated by the Government Decree 141/2002 (VI. 28.), according to which the Minister's authority includes the planning, realisation and operation of the related projects in a social, administrative, cultural, educational and economic context, though his responsibility does not include programmes of informatics involving the central government.

The Hungarian Information Society Strategy or Magyar Információs Társadalom Stratégia (MITS) of 2003 recognised that successful e-government service provision to the public could act as a catalyst to encourage uptake of ICTs in other areas of life, and thus convince Hungarians to embrace the notion of the information society. The ministry has identified five strategic goals, outlined below:

- to establish widespread and cheap Internet access (to increase Internet penetration to EU average levels and beyond);
- to make available all public information online on a compulsory basis;
- to provide incentives for the development and publication of quality online content;
- to bring government services online (e-government); and
- to provide equal access to information for all citizens and protect personal, human, social and community rights.[15]

The elaboration of the national strategy on the information society is primarily executed by the Ministry of Informatics, which is obliged to reconcile with the Prime Minister's Office and to co-operate with other relevant ministries that may be concerned. The Ministry of Informatics is a co-submitter of proposals of laws in the field of information policy, the spreading of electronic democracy, and the formation of media in the information society. The Government Decree 1214/

2002 (XII. 28.) contained regulations concerning the creation of an Inter-Departmental Committee on Information Society Coordination, which supports the Minister of Informatics in his relevant work. This Committee is being coordinated within the Ministry of Informatics.

The Government Decree 148/2002 (VII. 1.) on the Prime Minister's Office defines tasks regarding informatics of central government, which concerns information systems applied by ministries and other subordinated institutions, and nationwide authorities. This decree concerns those tasks that do not fall under the competence of the Ministry of Informatics. In the Prime Minister's Office, the so-called Electronic Government Centre (Elektronikus Kormányzat Központja – EKK), created in 2003, is responsible for tasks involving informatics of the central government, under the direction of a government commissioner (in the position of a state secretary). According to the decree, the EGC's duties include overseeing the facilitation of the informatics infrastructure of the central government, supporting the establishment and spreading of electronic public administration, the development of the procedural order of central government informatics, and the definition of the professional and quality requirements of the applied solutions. It also ensures the openness and transparency of usage and accessibility of any data that may be of public interest within the scope of governmental informatics, and the survey and inventory of the public administration datasets. It also performs duties connected to informatics in the process of the European Union integration and other international liabilities or contracts, and directs Hungarian interconnection with other international systems of informatics, or the application of foreign information systems in Hungary. The most important tasks of the Electronic Government Centre are included in the official government strategy 'E-government 2005', which was incorporated in Government Decision 1126/2003 (XII. 12.) to elevate it to legal status. In the execution of the strategy, the Electronic Government Centre is supported by the Inter-Departmental Coordinating Government Committee on Informatics (Kormányzati Informatikai Egyeztető Tárcaközi Bizottság – KIETB).[16] The Inter-Departmental Coordinating Government Committee on Informatics has the IDA Professional Committee, which carries out the coordination of the IDA and IDAbc programmes in Hungary.

Although coordination is handled by the Ministry of Informatics and the Electronic Government Centre of the Prime Minister's Office, e-government services are not only offered by them but also by several other ministries and also government institutions whose scope of competences cover the whole country, such as the Tax Office (APEH) or the Central Statistical Office (KSH). The e-government services in Hungary are meant to be developed in a top-down method, starting from the central government moving downwards to the local level, although in reality there is a degree of cross-fertilisation with local government also innovating in its relations with citizens and enterprises. This also means that e-government services are mainly available at the level of central government and less at local level, although this is changing.

Legal background of e-government in Hungary

The very first initiative in legal rulings related to public administration informatics happened in 1993, when the modernisation of public administration informatics appeared via the aim of IT development in the central government and its institutions. The Act 1039/1993 (V. 21.) on the development of the information coordination of central government and, two years later, Government Decision 1106/1995 (IX. 9.) were embryonic attempts, but in 1999 with Government Decision 1066/1999 (VI. 11.) concerning the further development of informatics in public administration, a corner was turned as then human and financial resources that were previously lacking were finally both guaranteed so the stated aims could be met.

The year 2000 brought about the next significant batch of legislation on ICT. In 2000, a government strategy was published outlining that this field was to be supervised by the Prime Minister's Office, where the Government Committee on Informatics was situated. This Committee aimed to shape the central model of strategic planning and control, such as the preparation of the legislation to engender ICT use. In the EU accession period, the legal approximation and harmonisation of this field was also influenced by the European Union as further and deeper legal underpinnings needed to be created and put into action in fields such as data protection, electronic commerce and payment, customer protection and copyright. Meanwhile, Hungary also joined many international agreements related to ICT. It was also part of the European Union Commission's 2001 eEurope+ Action Plan, which had as its goal the fostering and continued development of the information society in the then-applicant countries.

In 2001, a raft of IT-related legal acts were adopted, such as the Act on Electronic Signature (2001. XXXV), Act on Communication (2001. XL), and Act on Electronic Commerce Services and other Services in the Information Society (2001. CVIII). Though these developments were very promising, some problems still occurred caused by underdeveloped electronic data management, filing and workflow issues, by the lack of precise procedures and legal rulings and in part by the inertia of relevant government decision-making authorities. This constrained and delayed the introduction of e-government in administration, in spite of the laws being passed that were supposed to enable just such a scenario. The year 2001 also saw the launch of the first Hungarian e-government portal, which is discussed below.

Therefore, it was decided that in order to counter such inhibitors the next step on the way forward in the drive for modernisation and digitisation of Hungarian public services would be the establishment of a separate Ministry of Informatics, empowered to manage the relevant legislative process as well (with those exceptions that still remained at the Prime Minister's Office, as noted above).

The year 2003 was another important period in the ICT field of the Hungarian public administration, where one can see concerted action by the central authorities in creating legislation to facilitate the conditions necessary to meet the missed targets of the decrees. A new Act on communication was passed by Parliament; this Act covered (tele)communication and postal rights. Act 2003. C came into effect on 1 January 2004, and was accompanied by other acts; one on the modification of the protection of industrial innovation and copyrights (2003 CII) and also a further Act 2003 XCVII that modified and improved upon the earlier act on electronic commercial services and other services in information society (2001. CVIII). Act 2003. LXXXI was a very important piece of legislation, as it was the first act to ensure the opportunity of full electronic procedures in company incorporation and electronic publication of company data. A further act, Act 2003. CXXIX concerning procurement, provided the necessary legal rulings relating to electronic procurement, although at the time of writing there is still no central e-procurement infrastructure in Hungary. Thus, e-procurement is somewhat in its infancy, with the E-government Observatory's report on Hungary showing that in 2004 only 16 per cent of Hungarian enterprises had made purchase orders using the Internet and only 1 per cent had received orders via the Internet.[17]

In 2004, Act 2004. CCCVII on the National Digital Data Assets including the National Audiovisual Archives, which represent a significant part of national cultural heritage, was adopted. A further law, Act 2004. CXL on the General Rules of Administrative Procedures and Services came into effect on 1 November 2005 and replaced Act 1957. IV on State Administrative Procedures. The new act on administrative procedures gives prominence to electronic government services, and facilitates their creation depending on the ability of government institutions and local governments. The most recent act, at the time of writing, is Act 2005 XC, which further defines the rules relating to the freedom of electronic information within Hungarian administrations.

Strategy

As one might expect, the strategy of the Hungarian government related to e-government has evolved over time from its initial strategy for Informatics in 1995. A series of programmes has culminated in the 2005 E-government Strategy and Programme (eKormanyzat Strategia) that, following on from MITS in 2003, has recognised the role that e-government can play in stimulating the information society in Hungary. It seeks to create a more citizen-centred notion of public administration in Hungary.

The Hungarian strategy for electronic government's objectives for the medium and long term are summarised thus in the EU's E-government Observatory's report on Hungary:

- Electronic government should help to make public administration and the working of the state more efficient, transparent and – in the longer term – cheaper.
- A more efficient central public administration providing better services should permit a broadening of participatory democracy, an increase in the confidence of citizens and business actors, and greater participation by people in political life. Efforts should be made to develop more open and substantial relationships between representatives of public authority and citizens.

- By providing new public forums and easier access to public services oriented towards the needs of citizens, an environment can be created in which public administrative bodies and communities can share their experiences and influence the realization of the local and national e-government programmes. The relationship between the state, citizens and their communities will be laid on new foundations that meet the requirements of citizens and businesses.
- Increasingly, the state as service provider and creator of opportunities will only be able to accomplish its tasks by ensuring the free flow of information. The system of public administration must lead the process of consultation and of creating opportunities, and it must be able to assume an initiating role in every respect.
- The opportunities provided by electronic government are some of the most important means (but not the only means) at the disposal of the service-provider state and for the construction of such a state. Exploiting these means, Hungary could catch up with the countries that are currently at the forefront of the development and use of electronic government services (irrespective of whether these countries are Hungary's neighbours or lie elsewhere in the EU).
- If the state can play a leading role in the application, use and dissemination of the modern means of information and communication technology (ICT), it will be able, in addition to the success of government activities, to support the process of constructing and developing a knowledge-based society and increase the competitiveness of society and the economy.[18]

The strategy seeks to achieve its goals through six key action programmes encompassing 19 different action plans. There can be no doubt that the strategy is an optimistic statement that reflects the burgeoning self-confidence of a state emerging from a difficult past into a potentially bright future. If one was to be slightly critical, it is that the strategy so closely mirrors that of other EU nations – which is, perhaps, no surprise given the role that the EU plays as a focus for knowledge and experience sharing as described earlier in this volume. It mirrors it in the way that it seeks to give a prominence to the thought of cheaper government rather than better government. Efficiency rather than effectiveness seems to be the watchword, which is disappointing to see in a recently-developing democracy that one might have hoped would champion other values.

When one looks at the performance of Hungary in the benchmarking of public services as set out by the Council of the EU,[19] we can see that Hungary has some way to go to achieve its goal of catching up.[20] In general, Hungary is trailing behind some of the other new member states and is also below the EU average. Hungary falls short of full case-handling in all its citizen categories, although with the eight services to businesses it does fare somewhat better.

From portal to gateway

The history of the development of e-government portals in Hungary dates back to December 2001, when the Prime Minister's Office launched www.kormanyzat.hu,[21] which sought to provide a user-friendly interface between citizens, enterprises and government and to provide access to information and services. In September 2003, kormanyzat was replaced by a new portal Magyarorszag,[22] which offered a more complete interaction between citizen and government. It offered the citizen an institutional portal and an embryonic service platform.

One of the problems noted by Csuhaj-Varjú (2002) was that although the central administration was virtually fully computerised, local administrations were not necessarily so far advanced. Even where local authorities had followed a similar route towards computerisation, they had often done so in an independent manner that left them with isolated systems that were difficult to incorporate into a national strategy.[23] In November 2004, the portal was once more revamped to ensure compatibility with the new Electronic Government Backbone (Elektronikus Kormányzati Gerincháló́zat. EKG), which it was hoped would help alleviate the problem by providing the Hungarian public administration sector with a single IP network backed up by a secure broadband infrastructure. EKG is connected to the EU's TESTA network.

The most recent achievement in the field of e-government in Hungary is the new government portal and the so-called 'Client Gateway', or Ügyfélkapu[24] in Hungarian. The general objective of this new government portal is to serve as a basis of e-democracy and e-administration in the country, bringing the average citizen closer to the administration by giving them the chance to arrange more and more of their official procedures online, offering them considerable time savings as noted above. A user can fill in a temporary personal registration, after which they can benefit from various basic electronic services that can ease their life by saving time that would otherwise be spent queuing at a physical office when it is not absolutely necessary. Other more intricate and complex transactions require an authenticated registration to access services, such as the completion of tax returns. The services provided in electronic form include secure and single identification of the citizen, and linking him/her to the services of the relevant institution; the citizens can reach the relevant system of the institution providing e-services, enabling them, for example, to download application forms or receive electronic documents authenticated by standard electronic signatures. The Gateway also provides a link to the virtual document office, where certain procedures can be undertaken and appointments can also be made in relation to certain procedures.[25] This Gateway is also already designed for future change that may allow citizens to make use of m-government services via mobile phones, and thus overcome the problems associated with low levels of PC ownership and Internet access in Hungary and other similar states. As new technological advances enable us to do more and more via our phones it is envisaged that many e-government services may platform-share between PCs and mobiles.

Use of m-government services

When one considers the fact that the Hungarian people have 93 per cent[26] levels of of mobile phone ownership, and compare this to the aforementioned levels of

Internet access, it is clear that Hungary has an opportunity – and indeed one could argue has a pressing need – to benefit from the idea and practical innovations of the use of m-government. It is vital to avoid e-exclusion so that all Hungarians feel a part of the changes that are sweeping through the country, particularly in the fields of public administration. The potential for Hungarians to use mobile phones for managing at least some of their public administrative procedures without the need to sit behind a computer terminal offers a splendid opportunity to involve more and more citizens in e-government through the use of familiar technology without the need to learn new complex procedures on other platforms. Though m-government implementation is at an early stage, some important measures can already be seen.

Hungary had the honour to organise the first European Conference on Mobile Government in Budapest on 28–29 October 2004. At the event, an m-Government Declaration establishing an international m-Government Study Group (MGSG) was approved. The aim of this group is to disseminate information on m-government issues and best practices, and undertake research and development projects focused on the delivery of public services over mobile devices and on the political and social impact of m-government. The MGSG consists of members from public administration, professors and the representatives of industry.

On a practical level, the first initiative in making use of m-government in Hungary was introduced by the Ministry of Interior in 2003 in the form of a special vehicle history report available via mobile phone (SMS message). After the success of this first attempt, other mobile phone-based services have been launched such as payment of parking fees, notification of school results, notification of processed forms, or applications to make use of public premises.

Conclusions

Clearly, Hungary has some way to go to catch up with other EU member states in the field of e-government. However we can see the seeds of a new digital revolution spreading through the country's public administration as well as other sectors of society. The dual share of responsibilities in the field of e-government is considered a problematic situation in the view of many experts, which explains the attempts to bring it under one roof in the future. However, the situation of exactly how 'government of e-government' is organised in Hungary is in the process of changing, particularly since the elections of April 2006.

The possibilities will likely expand further within 'The Gateway' system in the future, with further developments and/or refinements of the legal and technical underpinnings. Moreover, there is a high probability that, for the reasons noted above, there will be an expansion in the use of m-government services – particularly as 3G phone adoption is increasing rapidly, enabling a morphing of the technologies to engender new opportunities for mobile usage in the world of public administration.

We can clearly see that Hungarian public administration is undergoing a paradigm shift as it attempts to follow the lead of advanced e-governance whilst retaining a specific Hungarian character to its administrative activities. The examination of the progress in the field of e-government in Hungary is by necessity fairly positive, although much remains to be done. Great progress has been made to provide the legal and strategic underpinnings necessary for the flourishing of e-government in Hungary within the context of a wider move to an information society. Both the governmental actors, and the researchers engaged in the field have helped the Hungarian public administration to witness a great advancement. The future is bright for e-government and m-government in Hungary. One can be sure that Hungary will continue along the path of modernisation, quietly revolutionising the way its businesses and citizens interact with the state at all levels. It is hoped that partnerships can be developed to move Hungarian public administration forward in the interests of all its citizens.

Notes

1 We would like to thank Mr Balázs Benjámin Budai and Mr István Tózsa for their support in the writing of this paper. In addition, since the time of writing (March 2006), there have been elections resulting in changes of personnel, structures and policy related to e-government in Hungary. The Prime Minister's office is now directly responsible for e-government issues as the former Ministry responsible was abolished. There will also be a new Centre for Electronic Public Services that will begin operations in January 2007. Further, the projected adoption of the Euro has lead to budgetary constraints and proposals to trim the public sector. It is envisaged that technology will allow significant personnel savings. It remains to be seen whether those savings will be achieved.
2 Schneider, M. (2002) 'Implementing an Information Society in Central and Eastern Europe', *Forschungsstelle Osteuropa Bremen* Arbietspapiere No 38; July 2002.
3 European Commission (1994) 'Europe and the Global Information Society', Bangemann Report accessed online at europa.eu.int/ISPO/docs/basics/docs/bangemann.pdf
4 Compared to the population of the country, which is 10,000,025.
5 http//www.etcnewmedia.com/review/default.asp?SectionID=11&CountryID=60
6 http//www.etcnewmedia.com/review/default.asp?SectionID=11&CountryID=60
7 For further information on this, see Jakobi, A. (2005) 'Revaluating Regional Influences of ICT factors in Hungary'. Paper presented at 45th European Congress of the Regional Science Association, Amsterdam, Netherlands.
8 http//www.etcnewmedia.com/review/default.asp?SectionID=11&CountryID=60
9 http//www.etcnewmedia.com/review/default.asp?SectionID=11&CountryID=60
10 The research was undertaken by the Fessel Gfk Market Research company.
11 http//www.etcnewmedia.com/review/default.asp?SectionID=11&CountryID=60
12 Csuhaj-Varjú, E. (2002) *E-government Programme in Hungary*. Published online at www.ercim.org/publication/Ercim_News/enw48/varju.html
13 For a thorough historical overview see the E-government Observatory's report on Hungary, available online at europa.eu.int/idabc/servlets/Doc?id=21012
14 www.iif.hu/%7Elengyel/valasz/MV.doc
15 en.ihm.gov.hu/
16 This body is the successor of the Inter-Departmental Committee on Informatics, which was created in 1991. The new Committee was designated by Government Decision 1054/2004 (VI. 3.).
17 Available online at europa.eu.int/idabc/servlets/Doc?id=21012
18 europa.eu.int/idabc/servlets/Doc?id=21012

19 europa.eu.int/idabc/servlets/Doc?id=18402
20 Reis, F. (2005) *Statistics in Focus* 35/2005, available online at epp.eurostat.cec.eu.int/cache/ITY_OFFPUB/KS-NP-05-035/EN/KS-NP-05-035-EN.PDF
21 www.kormanyzat.hu
22 www.magyarorszag.hu/
23 www.ercim.org/publication/Ercim_News/enw48/varju.html
24 www.magyarorszag.hu/ugyfelkapu
25 These procedures are the following: change of address registration and address card administration, issuing entrepreneur licences, registry of marriage, birth, death, driving license administration, parking licences for the disabled, car registry administration.
26 http//www.etcnewmedia.com/review/default.asp?SectionID=11&CountryID=60

Further reading

Budai, B.B., Sükösd, M. (2005) *M-kormányzat – M-demokrácia* (M-governance, M-democracy). Akadémiai Kiadó, Budapest, April, 2005.

Budai, B.B., Sükösd, M. (2005a) 'M-kormányzat – M-demokrácia', *e-világ folyóirat* (e-World bulletin).

Budai, B.B., Szakolyi, A. (2005) *Interaktív Önkormányzat* (Interactive Local Government), Magyar Mediprint Szakkiadó, May, 2005.

Budai, B.B., Tózsa, I. (2005) 'M-government in Hungary', in *EURO mGOV 2005*.

Budai, B.B., Szentkirályi-Holota, S. (2005) 'Az elektronikus közigazgatás jogi környezete (Legal Environment of E-government)', *e-kormányzati Tanulmányok; e-government Alapítvány*, Budapest, ISSN 1785-6108.

www.apeh.hu
www.e-government.hu
www.ihm.hu
www.infotars.hu
www.itarsadalom.hu
www.itkht.hu
www.ittk.hu
www.meh.hu/ekk
www.mgsg.org

14 E-government and Slovenia's multiple transitions

Darren Purcell and Aaron Champion

Introduction

The status of e-governance in East-Central Europe reflects the expansion and increasingly hegemonic status of neo-liberal ideology vis-à-vis the role of government in the region's societies. Experiencing a unique and detrimental version of state ownership of property, the region has seen multiple governments embrace neo-liberal ideologies as a cleansing mechanism, ridding themselves of the vestiges of communist governance. This ideology has facilitated a reworking of societal expectations of government in the minds of various stakeholders, including the populace as a whole, businesses, and political parties. The common theme is greater emphasis on efficiency and service to customers, the people that governments formerly conceived of as just mere citizens of the nation-state. What is of interest is how this neo-liberal idea has permeated all parties in politics. Governments from Estonia and Slovenia have swung from left to right politically, two countries that are touted as examples of successful transitions to free market societies. Others such as Hungary and Poland have also experienced similar political shifts. The unifying factor is that all of them, as new members of the European Union, openly embrace the idea of e-governance to varying degrees and are concerned about being left behind as the European Union governance structures move toward a greater reliance on e-government.

As the above makes clear, the transitions to forms of free market economies have been steady in movement toward the goal of free-market development, but uneven in results. Likewise, the adoption of e-government and the diffusion of attendant assumptions implicit in a move toward e-government services are uneven within Europe, just as the infrastructure to support societal embrace of information and communication technologies (ICTs) is uneven and concentrated in certain segments of European societies. Particular states in the transition region of East-Central Europe possessing specific advantages, based on historical levels of technological innovation and the specific experiences under communism, have become regional leaders in the e-government trend.

The nation-state examined here, Slovenia, is an example of the particular contexts that set the stage for e-governance efforts. A republic within the former Yugoslavia, Slovenia was considered more developed economically than the rest of former Yugoslavia (and indeed, ahead of many former Soviet satellites), and in possession of a more western outlook toward the free market and technological change. This chapter examines the understandings and claims of Slovenia's government in regards to e-government, specifically the opportunities and the barriers to adoption. Based on this background, this chapter engages Slovenia's e-government in terms of symbolic value for a new member of the European Union, which must still deal with the legacy of communist rule, and signal to the rest of Europe and the globe that it is a modern state. The chapter also addresses what tangible benefits are generated by e-government implementation, and the actual utility to the populace. The second part of the chapter examines the current state of e-government as reported by secondary sources, and considers trends in e-government in the larger effort to integrate within the European Union.

The Slovenian context

The combination of an Austro-Hungarian legacy, a Western orientation and physical proximity which facilitated what Bebler[1] terms the 'demonstration effect', Slovenia became the most economically-developed region of the former Yugoslavia and stands as an example of a reasonably peaceful transformation from a single-party authoritarian state to a progressive, multi-party democratic state. The western-most republic of the Former Yugoslavia, the country was the benefactor of proximity to, and comparatively open borders with, Italy and Austria, vis-à-vis other transition states. This allowed greater exposure to western media, ideals, and standards of living, fostering an atmosphere necessary for the social and political movements that led to the dissolution of Yugoslavia. Today, Slovenia stands as an independent nation-state for the first time in the history of the Slovene nation. The country is a member of the EU (admitted in 2004) and NATO (also admitted in 2004), and aims to play a larger role in European and global affairs. This is exemplified through an aggressive pursuit of opportunities to demonstrate the country's utility in larger international organisations. Slovenia's foreign minister completed a term as OSCE chairman-in-office at the end of 2005. The country is preparing to assume the European Union presidency in January of 2008, and stands as the first of the newest European Union members to serve in this capacity.[2] The symbolism of these leadership posts is not lost on the Slovenian government, as it leverages an image of being the West's darling of the ten new European Union members.[3] Support for the EU presidency bid was unanimous across the political spectrum, as the country seeks to enhance its image as a modern, globally integrated nation, in order to better position itself in the global economy.

With just over 2 million citizens, the country is one of the smallest in Europe. When compared on a global level Slovenia ranks 84th in purchasing power parity, but 45th in GDP per capita at $19,597.[4] This relative affluence places it in proximity with other countries that are rapidly adopting Internet technologies into daily life such as New Zealand and South Korea.

E-government – we need this because?

One of the great myths of the Internet age is that the development of the information society is inevitable. The Government Center of the Republic of Slovenia for Informatics (CVI) unabashedly proclaims this:

> Slovenia, being a part of Europe, cannot avoid the processes that are going on in its surroundings. A transition into an information society is thus inevitable. For a federal transition into an information society it is necessary to join forces of all the citizens and provide an extended social consensus, which also brings along changes of current life patterns and search of new ones.[5]

Of interest by itself, the quote above is from a document placing CVI front and centre in the effort to plan, develop, and implement e-government. The role of government proposed is interesting because, in many ways, it runs counter to the neo-liberal ideologies of how ICTs will transform government structures, decentralisation of power and democratising access. In the CVI vision of e-government, the government will be leading the way by effectively responding to societal needs and demands for changes in the way interaction between the citizenry and state structures occurs. Neo-liberal approaches usually emphasise privatisation of these processes together with an emphasis on the reduction of the size of government. The CVI's efforts to be proactive in shaping the strategic plan for informatisation of Slovenian e-government are an effort to insure that the CVI remains central to the effort, in part due to its strategic role within the state and the fact that much of Slovenia's expertise in the field is concentrated in the CVI.

A variety of social forces have shaped the CVI's understanding of the move toward e-government. A particularly strong one is the feeling that Slovenia is playing 'catch up' to the rest of Europe. When the CVI document was created, Slovenia was on the cusp of European Union membership. The need to stay with Europe in terms of standards is made clear in the following quote:

> Slovenia is aware of the fact that transition into information society is the only possible way to the future and to improve its position in Europe. As a young country that wishes to join the EU, Slovenia will implement the transition into an information society only with a full understanding of what is happening in EU and by taking into account its own possibilities and wishes.[6]

The paragraph demonstrates a clear understanding of the situation the country faces. Fostering a clear, unequivocal European identity necessitates greater integration into European structures. Successful integration depends on the smooth interface between Slovenian government and society and the expectations and norms of governance existing within the EU. An undercurrent of wanting to pursue this path in a Slovenian manner is encapsulated in the last line. Slovenia is a relatively young country, only achieving independence in 1991, with a desire to shape the processes that are transforming the country to dovetail with national needs, such as the fostering of Slovenian identity and forms of governance that respond to distinctly Slovenian needs and sensibilities. The use of the Internet to facilitate e-government is part of this, but clearly the desire to use technology for greater integration into the EU is important for Slovenia's future.

The Slovenian state's use of the Internet has been ongoing since the mid-1990s. The use has changed with time, as the needs of the state have changed given the various contexts it existed within. Early use of ICTs such as the Internet focused on proclaiming the existence of the state and achieving strategic goals such as EU and NATO accession, attracting tourism, and encouraging foreign direct investment via a billboard model of Internet usage.[7] Little interactivity was seen on early versions of ministry websites, with offers of email addresses being the predominant form of encouraging interaction. This has changed today, with the diffusion of software programs that enable sophisticated web design and allow complex pages to be developed with little or no programming experience.

The well-chronicled reasons of greater levels of service for the citizens implicit in neo-liberal ideology and the idea that greater EU integration requires it, all support the embrace of e-government. There are deeper questions to consider, however. One question involves the rationale for Internet use by the state. The push for greater levels of e-government activity by the EU requires that new members and those states aspiring to membership (Romania, Bulgaria and Turkey are prime examples) also embrace the ideals of e-governance, because there is little room for resistance.

One can conceive of the European Union operations facilitating the spread of e-government in cyberspace as a space of colonisation, where territory must be staked out and the virtual high-ground taken for strategic reasons. The colonisation metaphor is appropriate if we consider the idea of a noosphere,[8] a realm of ideas and knowledge, a rising global consciousness which Catholic theologian Teilhard des Jardin foreshadowed decades ago. If we accept the existence of a noosphere, then we need to consider how a consensus develops in this space. Arquilla and Ronfeldt describe *noopolitik*, their modern day version of *geopolitik*, as the effort to shape the emerging terrain of cyberspace. Noopolitik serves as the state-centered efforts to shape cyberspace, to extend control over it. While Arquilla and Ronfeldt emphasise the possibilities of this form of soft power exercise for military purposes, the use of the noosphere for propagating specific attitudes toward governance are very closely related.

The terrain of the noosphere is important to control, and it is vital for Slovenia to establish its own parcel via e-government and a strong Internet presence. This begs the question of whether the establishment of e-government merely serves a symbolic role for government officials desperate to demonstrate modernity and technological competency as part of an overarching strategy of economic development. Again, the claims to inevitability would indicate that the use of e-government is an expectation foisted upon Slovenia, and thus as the expectations of the wider world must be met, Slovenia must join in this race to modernise. It is irrelevant whether the promises of e-government are delivered upon; the appearance of e-government and technical competence are vital to put forth.

European Union rules and regulations structure patterns of governance within its borders, and thus must be adopted by new members and those aspiring members seeking to ease the accession and transition process in the future. Slovenia has little choice in the face of hegemonic rules of how e-governance is to be structured. Despite the quote above, there is little Slovenia can do save implement EU rules and standards in a manner that does not alienate the domestic population, and foster a society that is accustomed to using the tools e-government supporters aspire to provide. To think that Slovenia's public administration can shape e-government to its own liking is perhaps optimistic. If used as a domestic development programme, the government fails to interact with the very companies and regional interests that support e-government through consulting, hardware sales, and software sales. In combination with technocrats that have embraced the neo-liberal ideology of less government equals good government, those that stand to profit from greater levels of e-governance are part and parcel of the colonisation of the noosphere.

If we take the colonisation of the noosphere metaphor further, we should consider the use of force in establishing a colony. The taking or marking of territory in the material realm requires specific strategies to be in play, including the inculcation of a new culture, which serves to supplant the prevailing culture. It is this cultural violence that is resisted at first, until it becomes assimilated and creates an odd mixture of cultures. The 'natives' are civilised through a variety of means, including education and inducements to switch to e-government substitutes. The foisting of e-government rules on a reticent population necessitates specific strategies, just like colonisation. Carter and Belanger in 2004 openly invoke marketing concepts to foster transition to e-government. A telling quote paints a picture for us:

> Specifically, state government agencies should capitalize on the unique benefits of on-line services, promoting their use as a *status symbol*, and indicating the services' congruence with a citizen's *lifestyle*. ... agencies could pursue *endorsements from local celebrities* or well-respected citizens in the community advocating the use of state e-Government services (emphasis added).[9]

This vocabulary clearly links to what e-government is about, the actual transactions and information exchange, or business of government, what it does daily, except that it is now to be performed online. More important, in the colonisation metaphor, is the concept of e-governmentality.[10] This idea embraces the development of self-regulation and reproduction of a governable citizen. If government is about the ability to 'structure the possible field of actions of others',[11] then the whole move to e-government must include the fostering of greater levels of e-governmentality. Whether this is by coercion (as the United States government deployed when it made many forms of welfare aid available only through a form of debit card) or by subtle marketing campaigns proposed above, the fostering of e-governmentality must work to make it seem natural; a progressive evolution that will benefit citizens through greater levels of efficiency and responsive government.

This section has explored the ideas underpinning the adoption of e-government by the Slovenian state. It is clear that e-government is an idea rooted in neo-liberal movements toward efficiency and less intrusive or obstructionist government, with a concomitant shift in power to the citizenry through technology. These ideas require the population to be ready for a move toward e-government, or that governments are willing to foster a sense of e-governmentality. The success of such efforts depends on geographic particularities – the contexts the technologies are introduced into. The next section examines that particular setting in Slovenia.

Internet usage by government and the populace

Use of the Internet by government ministries began in the mid-1990s, and intensified throughout the late-1990s, based on the perceptions of the technology by the leadership of various ministries and the government as a whole. One former Foreign Minister, Zoran Thaler, was in fact criticised for his efforts to incorporate more Internet usage into the Ministry of Foreign Affairs at a time when his critics claimed that Slovenia should be more focused upon trying to join both NATO and the European Union.[12] Slovenian Foreign Minister Zoran Thaler's view that the Internet would be a useful tool in streamlining the ministry's activities, and that it would serve to gain more friends in the international community, initially went unheeded.

It is of interest to note that the last major ministry to establish a website was, in fact, the then Ministry of Transportation and Communication. Their effort was not spearheaded by the public relations department, but by an assistant to the minister who had studied computer science, and was cognisant of the potential of the Internet as a communication tool for the publics the ministry dealt with.[13] The fact that the very ministry with competency to supervise developments facilitating the construction of information infrastructure was slow in adopting the norm of having a website demonstrates the highly contingent nature of the process.

Despite this slow start, government awareness of the possibilities increased, leading to the creation of a Ministry for the Information Society in 2000.[14] This ministry was disbanded in December of 2004 and its duties parceled out to other ministries.[15] However, during its existence, the ministry was to facilitate the development of an e-savvy society across a broad spectrum of arenas.

Today, Slovenia's government websites are highly developed, mostly serving as information sources but increasingly deploying interactive features that various browsers support. The increasing sophistication in design and the capabilities parallels the diffusion of the e-government ideology.

Slovenia's population embraces the Internet at a rate comparable to other European countries. Recent data from EUROSTAT[16] demonstrates that in several categories, Slovenian households have greater access than the EU as a whole (58 to 54 per cent) but lag behind if there are no children in the household. This bears out also in the percentage with a computer in the home (see Figures 14.1 and 14.2). In comparison to other new EU members, Slovenia is the most connected, with the highest levels of household computer penetration and Internet access of the newest

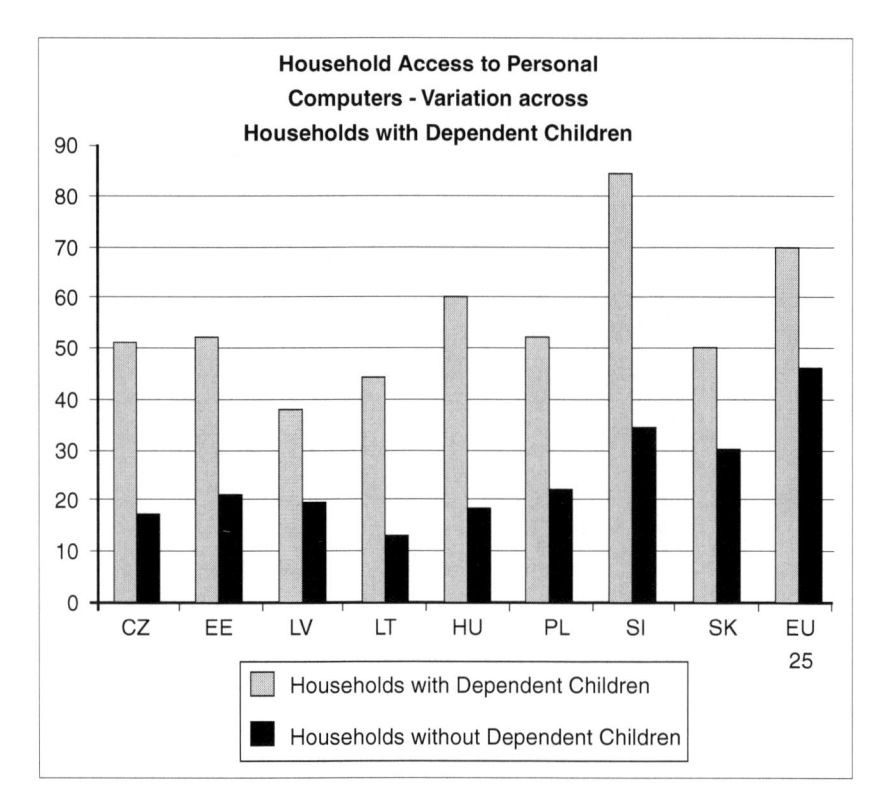

Figure 14.1 Selected countries' ICT access (2004).

Source: Demunter (2005).
CZ, Czech Republic; EE, Estonia; LV, Latvia; LT, Lithuania; HU, Hungary; PL, Poland; SI, Slovenia; SK, Slovakia.

ten members. Where the country lags is in the rollout of broadband services in the home, where it is consistently behind the previous EU members, and lagging behind Estonia[17] amongst the newest EU members. It should be noted that differences between Slovenia and the EU 25 average are not large in broadband access in relative terms. Households with children display a difference of only three percentage points, 18 per cent in the EU 25 versus 15 per cent in Slovenia. Factoring in other variables such as population densities and status as an EU Objective 1 region, the largest difference is but six percentage points.

It is clear that households with dependent children are the driving force for Internet diffusion within Slovenian society, thus constituting the need for Internet access at home for educational purposes (for the moment I ask the reader to forget the online gaming realm and the peer-to-peer illegal downloads, among the other non-educational uses children and teens have for the Internet.) A common concern of all countries developing e-government, the issue of access and bridging

Household Access to the Internet at Home: Variation Across Houses with and without Dependent Children

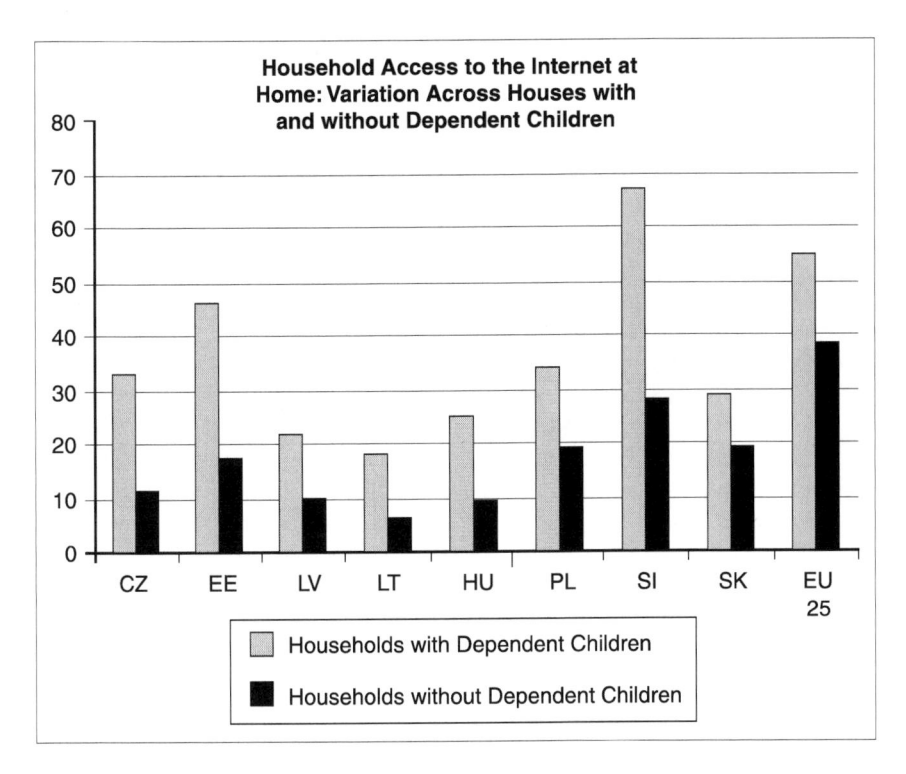

Figure 14.2 Household access to the Internet.

Source: Demunter (2005).
CZ, Czech Republic; EE, Estonia; LV, Latvia; LT, Lithuania; HU, Hungary; PL, Poland; SI, Slovenia; SK, Slovakia.

the so-called digital divide is paramount. A variety of reasons exist for not having a computer, thus obviating the need for Internet access. In the Slovenian case, respondents to surveys indicated that the top reasons for not having Internet access at home were the lack of a need for the Internet (30 per cent), the lack of skills (22 per cent), the high cost of equipment (21), the high cost of access (19 per cent) and the ability to access the Internet elsewhere (12 per cent).[18] However, even this varied by household.

This begs the question of whether Slovenia can address these gaps and even pull to even or ahead of the EU average as it clearly feels it must. In a strategy paper from the Government Centre for Informatics,[19] several of the country's characteristics suggest this will be possible. First, the country is relatively small in the European context, with the majority of the population concentrated in three statistical regions, those centring on the capital city of Ljubljana and the cities of Maribor and Celje in the northeast. Focusing efforts to upgrade infrastructure in these regions would affect approximately half of the Slovenian population. Second, the more advanced development of a service-oriented economy, with greater and greater reliance on private sector e-commerce, would likely stimulate demand for greater access, but surveys indicate that the level of use of e-services in banking is stagnant while there is an increase in shopping usage.[20] Third, greater privatisation in the telecommunications sector will likely bring in new competitors, but whether they can gain enough profit to increase access through competition remains to be seen.

Overall growth in access to and use of the Internet by Slovenia's citizens has been steady. The most recent figures show that during the first quarter of 2005, the percentage of people aged 16–74 that used the Internet increased from 37 to 47 per cent, with a full 50 per cent of the 10–74 age group using the Internet. Usage percentages climb to 77 per cent for the 16–34 demographic, 83 per cent for those 10–15 years old, but decline to 45 per cent for the 35–54 cohort. These figures represent increases over the same period in 2004.[21]

What one should take from this is that Slovenian society is using the Internet at rates comparable to other European countries, thus it should come as no surprise that efforts to roll out e-government are taking place, given perceptions that sectors of the populace are ready to embrace this new form of service. In previously admitted EU members, e-government pushes came after there had been substantial integration of ICTs into the lives of many citizens. Slovenia's efforts to foster a climate where e-government will be readily accepted and integrated into the daily lives of citizens and businesses are occurring just as more segments of society as a whole become more informatised. These concurrent processes, the greater informatisation of society and the increasing hegemony of neo-liberal approaches to government service provision serve to naturalise the process for many, despite detractors who will argue that it fundamentally changes the relationship between the state and the citizenry.

E-government overview and statistics

Slovenia's government has stated the importance of the networked information society and e-government as crucial factors in improving its standing with the European community. In keeping with the current government's official commitment to both the information society and e-government, several agencies and actors exist within Slovenia that facilitate movement toward an e-government model.

Slovenia's embrace of networked government began with the creation of the Ministry for Information Society in January of 2000.[22] In February, a policy document titled 'Strategy for e-Commerce in Public Administration for the Period 2001–4' was created, serving as a basis for the deployment, development, and creation of an electronic government through the end of 2004. e-Uprava, the central state hub for e-government services was launched in March of 2001. In December of 2004, the Ministry of Information Society was dissolved, and the election of a new government saw the creation of the Ministry of Public Administration, which assumed the responsibilities of the previous and now defunct

Ministry of Information Society. In May of 2005, the Electronic Central Register was created, allowing authorised government agencies the ability to access a centralised population register for the state.

The Ministry of Public Administration has the task of advancement and co-ordination of e-government. Within the Ministry, the Directorate for e-Government oversees the e-Government Development Section, whose job it is to monitor all aspects and stages in e-government enactment policy. The Government Centre for Informatics has the task of implementing the country's e-government infrastructure at the basic, operational level, as well as providing support for department and agency-level ventures. Founded in 2001, the Inspectorate for Personal Data Protection is a division of the Ministry of Justice. Conducting inspections and investigations in database integrity and breaches, the Inspectorate also works to set regulations for data protection measures. Of interest is the lack of centralisation of these activities. What one might conclude is that various apparatuses of the state have themselves been transformed by the need to address Internet issues within their own fields of competence, or perhaps more cynically, they are staking out strategic territory in the operations of the Slovenian state's portion of the noosphere.

The development of e-government has taken off this century. Launched in March of 2001, the state e-government portal, e-Uprava, offers services and transactional capabilities between the government, citizens, businesses, and other governmental agencies. The majority of governmental agencies (more than 1,600 LANs) are connected via a government-owned network called HKOM (Fast Communications Network). Encryption and certification are handled via a Public-Key Infrastructure, with four authorised and accredited authorities: GCI, HALCOM-CA, AC NLB, and POSTA CA. In 2005, a portal for e-procurement was to be launched, allowing for authorised governmental agencies to issue public procurement notices, as well as providing suppliers a means to reply electronically. However, this had still not occurred by November 2005.[23]

A range of services exist for Slovenian citizens, from tax information and filing, to public employment, to interaction with the state police. The e-Davki portal allows Slovenian citizens to submit and view their tax returns online. The site has experienced exponential growth, with over 23,000 citizens submitting their taxes online in 2005, representing 42 per cent growth in usage over the previous year. As the IDABC e-Government Observatory notes, this site is among the highest rated for site sophistication as measured by the functions of the site. Scores are given on a four point scale; a one represents solely online information and no interaction, a two represents the ability to download forms and interact at a minimal level within the site, a three indicates two-way interaction, not limited to the processing of forms, and those sites receiving a four are capable of full case handling, including payment functions. The latter implies the highest system development, which facilitates entire government processes being wholly conducted online.[24]

Only one other site aimed at private citizens earned the highest score, that of the Central Application Office, which handles applications to institutions of higher education. As with the e-Davki site, the entire application occurs online, greatly streamlining the process for Slovenian students.

The State Employment Service hosts and maintains several searchable databases containing job openings, and also allows for visitors to create a job profile. Profiled visitors are then eligible to receive a weekly mailing containing directed job openings. Employers are also able to view applicants in the database. The Employment Service also hosts information and forms concerning unemployment benefits.

The Ministry of Interior, which operates the Electronic Administrative Affairs website, is an exemplary case of effective e-government within Slovenia. The sites score a three out of four. Birth and marriage certificates are available for request – all handled electronically – through a centrally-maintained database called the Elektronske upravne zadeve (EUZ). Any authorised citizen with an approved digital certificate is qualified to use this service. The police also embrace ICTs. As a browser enters the English language site, they are confronted with the following quote that emphasises the use of technology:

> It is true that the law assists the power of the Police, but it is the way of communication that enables the support and co-operation of the public in enforcement of that power.[25]

This acknowledgment of communication as a vital part of police business could be read as the increasingly surveillance-heavy societies citizens inhabit, but it is clear that the police see this as a vital resource for accomplishing their goals. This is demonstrated by the fact that citizens can now report crime online and help the state apprehend suspects via the police's website, www.policija.si. This service has been available since June of 2004.

Another highly-ranked site supporting the public library system is the Co-operative On-line Bibliographic System & Services site (cobiss.izum.si.) which is sponsored by the Institute of Information Science and the Central Government. All other citizen based sites scored ones or twos in the ratings, indicating that there is much work to do in terms of the benchmarks the Council of Europe adopted in March of 2001. Much of this varies by ministry and their perception of the public they address.

The situation for business services varies depending on the service required and which ministry they must deal with. As with services to individual citizens, the range of interactivity depends on the ministry that provides the services. Taxation sites such as corporate tax payments and value added tax (VAT) score a four out of four, with these services provided by e-davki.surs.si. The sites have been in operation since 2004, and allow for the full range of ICT processing of tax processes.

Additionally, company registrations, through the Ministry of the Economy, along with the Slovenian Chamber of Commerce and Industry score the highest possible marks. Started in July of 2005, the site allows streamlined registrations using qualified digital certificates for authentication. Decisions regarding registration are likewise sent to applicants through electronic means and are too, digitally signed. Submission of statistical data between firms and the government ranks at a three out of three, indicating the submission of data is possible. The other four benchmark services are not fully interactive at the levels described above. Areas that are lacking include environmental permitting (sites post forms for download only); procurement procedures (again, forms for download) and customs declarations.[26]

Developments are not limited to the areas discussed above. The European Commission's Information Society Technology programme identifies in addition to e-Government, e-Health and e-Learning as areas for expansion of e-government services. Slovenia's forays into e-Health and e-Learning are tentative and in contrast to e-government efforts chronicled above, are in fact dominated by private sphere efforts.[27] The dominant state site is Ordinacija.net, supported by the Slovenian Ministry of Health. Aimed at the general public, the site functions as an information site, the topics ranging from locating health services across the country to the Ministry's own content on health. Surprisingly, the site is highly multilingual, including German, English, Croatian, Italian, Spanish, Serbian and French content in addition to the expected Slovenian webpages.

Development of health related sites is constrained by Slovenian law that restricts providers of health-care services' self-promotion, which directly affects not just individual doctors but public health clinics and other agencies within the state itself.

The conditions for increasing utilisation of e-government services are present in Slovenia, which enjoys a comparatively high penetration rate for personal computer ownership (58 per cent), with 74 per cent of those computer owners using the Internet. Slovenia's businesses are keeping pace with the country's citizens, with 42 per cent of enterprises of 10 or more employees using the Internet. Typical of an information society in the stages of initial growth, 78 per cent of households with Internet access still use a dial-up connection. Conversely, only 34 per cent of businesses still use dial-up and Slovenia's e-commerce market has yet to develop as rapidly as the country's Internet infrastructure. Only 9.8 per cent of households have made a purchase over the Internet, while a mere 17 per cent of businesses reported having made purchase over the Internet. In the area of interaction with public authorities and ministries via the state e-government portal, e-Uprava, 27.2 per cent of individuals report obtaining information, 16.2 per cent forms, and 6.8 per cent returned forms filled out online. Slovenia's businesses have made readier use of public authority Internet resources, with 46 per cent obtaining information, 43 per cent obtaining forms, and 36 per cent returning forms filled out online.

The usage statistics and efforts of the Slovenian state make it clear that interest in e-government is increasing, likely facilitated by government efforts to encourage the use of the e-Uprava site, as well as increased interest about the possibilities on the part of the citizenry. It remains to be seen whether this trend will increase in relation to the diffusion of the access to ICTs. One clear indicator of the trend increasing is the realisation that Slovenia's youth, and their families, are driving the demand for ICTs. Their increased usage as the current generation of children ages is inevitable.

Adoption trends by families with children indicates a greater future demand for e-government services is likely. However, this is the same segment of society that will adopt new technologies and platforms more quickly. Embracing ICT-mediated forms of governance will lead the state to commit increasing amounts of resources to serving the citizenry who embrace e-government, as technology changes, usage rates change, and expectation of the possibilities are ratcheted upward. Slovenia will face the same challenge. This presents a challenge to the state agencies to expand the platforms services are provided through. M-government is becoming a reality in many parts of Europe. (See sites devoted to the rollout of government via mobile devices such as a site from the University of Manchester's Institute for Policy Development and Management.)[28]

Conclusions

There is little doubt about the reasons e-government appears to be growing. Journalists, academics and business leaders in the computer and software industries join to become a harmonious choir singing the praises of ICTs and the potential for governments, businesses and citizens (in that order) to benefit from their use. Laying down the infrastructure, both material and social, to make e-government in any state expand necessitates policies, subsidies and a clear shift toward the embrace of e-government by government itself.

Within Slovenia, the leadership has wavered in the distant past,[29] only to follow along and attempt to get ahead of the curve again. This is made possible due to the unique geography, history and position within what Castells[30] terms the spaces of flows that link the state to others in the world system. Slovenia's position vis-à-vis Western Europe, its relative affluence among the transition states, and the legacy of the civil wars in former Yugoslavia set the stage for e-government adoption and implementation. As a small nation-state, with little clear identity in the world, any use of technology to appear open to business, efficient, modern and a safe place for capital to be invested is vital. E-government can lower the regulatory burdens on firms and citizens, in theory it can also facilitate the reallocation of scarce resources from the mundane gathering of data to the processing of it and addressing the issues of the most vulnerable populations within a society. These combine to provide tangible and symbolic benefits to Slovenia, benefits that will only reinforce, with pro-active policies, the expansion of e-government.

Notes

1 Bebler, A. (2002) 'Slovenia's Smooth Transition', *Journal of Democracy* 13(1): 127–40.
2 Austria 2006, Presidency of the European Union. www.eu2006.at/en/ (accessed January 11, 2006).
3 *The Economist* (2003) 'Why Slovenia is not the Balkans', November 20th. Available at www.economist.com/displaystory.cfm?story_id = 2206879 (accessed January 20th, 2006). See also: *The Economist* (2005) 'When Small is Beautifully Successful', October

E-government and Slovenia's multiple transitions 209

13th. Available at www.economist.com/PrinterFriendly.cfm?story_id = 5025737 (accessed January 20th, 2006).
4 Central Intelligence Agency (2005) www.cia.gov/cia/publications/factbook/rankorder/2001rank.html (accessed November 3rd, 2005).
5 CVI (Government Centre of the Republic of Slovenia for Informatics) (2004) e-uprava.gov.si/eud/e-uprava/en/sep2004-daljsa-angleska.pdf (accessed January 16th, 2006), p. 3.
6 CVI (Government Centre of the Republic of Slovenia for Informatics) (2004), p. 7.
7 See Brunn, S.D. and Cottle, C. (1997) 'Small States and Cyberboosterism', *The Geographical Review* 87(2): 240–58; see also: Purcell, D. (1999) *The Slovenian State on the Internet*. Ljubljana, Slovenia: Open Society Institute, Mediawatch Series; see also: Purcell, D. (2003) *Cyber-Slovenia: Place, Territoriality and Place-Marketing On-line*. Unpublished Dissertation, Florida State University, USA.
8 See: Arquilla, J. and Ronfeldt, D. (1999) *The Emergence of Noopolitik: Toward an American Information Strategy*. Rand Corporation, San Diego, USA. Available at www. rand.org/pubs/monograph_reports/MR1033// (accessed February 17th, 2006); see also: Castells, M. (2001) *The Internet Galaxy*. Oxford University Press. Oxford, UK.
9 Carter, L. and Belanger, F. (2004) 'The Influence of Perceived Characteristics of Innovating on e-Government Adoption', *Electronic Journal of E-government*. Available at www.ejeg.com/volume-2/volume2-issue-1/v2-i1-papers.htm (accessed November 18th, 2005), p. 17.
10 Allen, M. (2003) 'E-governance – Democracy, Transaction and Control', smi.curtin.edu.au/netstudies/docs/allen/AllenEgov2003.doc (accessed February 17th, 2006).
11 Allen, M. (2003) 'E-governance', citing Moss, 160.
12 Purcell, D. (2003) *Cyber-Slovenia*.
13 Purcell, D. (2003) *Cyber-Slovenia*.
14 Dobnikar, A. (2006) Personal e-mail communication. January 18th.
15 Ministry of Information Society (2004) www2.gov.si/mid/mideng.nsf (accessed January 11th, 2006).
16 Demunter, C. (2005) *Statistics in Focus: The Digital Divide in Europe* 38/2005. EUROSTAT. epp.eurostat.cec.eu.int/cache/ITY_OFFPUB/KS-NP-05-038/EN/KS-NP-05-038-EN.PDF (accessed November 22nd, 2005).
17 Demunter, C. (2005) *Statistics in Focus*.
18 Statistical Office of the Republic of Slovenia (2006) '29 Information Society', Vol. 6, No. 1. Available at www.stat.si/doc/statinf/29-SI-100-0601.pdf (accessed January 13th, 2006), p. 3, 9.
19 CVI (Government Centre of the Republic of Slovenia for Informatics) (2004).
20 See Cikic, S., and Vehovar, V. (2004) *e-shopping 2004*. RIS. Ljubljana, Slovenia. Available at slovenia.ris.org/main/baza/baza.php?bid=328&p1=276&p2=285 (accessed January 13th, 2006); see also: Vehovar, V. and Cikic, S. (2004) *e-banking 2004/1*. RIS. Ljubljana, Slovenia. Available at slovenia.ris.org/main/baza/baza.php?bid=334&p1=276&p2=285&p3=640 (accessed January 13th, 2006).
21 Research on Internet in Slovenia (2005) www.ris.org/uploadi/editor/1129195348SURS-gosp05.pdf (accessed November 3rd, 2005).
22 Dobnikar, A. (2006) Personal e-mail communication.
23 European Communities IDABC – E-government Observatory (2005) 'eGovernment in Slovenia', November, 2005. Available at europa.eu.int/idabc/servlets/Doc?id = 23456 (first accessed December 1st, 2005, last accessed February 16th, 2006).
24 European Communities IDABC – E-government Observatory (2005) 'eGovernment in Slovenia'.
25 www.policija.si (accessed February 15th, 2006).
26 European Communities IDABC – E-government Observatory (2005) 'eGovernment in Slovenia'.
27 Euser Country Brief: SI (2005) www.euser-eu.org/euser_countrybrief.asp? CaseID=1666&CaseTitleID=755&MenuID=112

28 University of Manchester, Institute for Development Policy and Management. www.egov4dev.org/home.htm (accessed February 16th, 2006).
29 Purcell, D. (2003) *Cyber-Slovenia*.
30 Castells, M. (1996) *The Rise of the Network Society*. Blackwell Publishers. Oxford, UK.

Further reading

Purcell, D. and Kodras, J. (2001) 'Information Technologies, Representational Spaces, and the Marginal State: Redrawing the Balkan Image of Slovenia', *Information, Communications and Society*. 4(3): 1–29.

Purcell, D. (2005) 'The Military in the Noosphere: NCT Adoption and Website Development in the Slovenian Ministry of Defense', *Information, Communication and Society*. 8(2):194–216.

Conclusions

Paul G. Nixon and Vassiliki N. Koutrakou

The chapters in this book have presented some of the core visions and realities of e-government as it manifests itself across Europe. They have illustrated how richer as well as poorer countries, bigger as well as smaller, 'old European' countries as well as 'new' ones have embraced e-government strategies, in varying ways, at different paces, yet with the same determination.

We have seen how the disparate member states of the European Union are developing systems of e-government that are remarkably similar in methods, applications and techniques but at the same time are also, sometimes, vastly different in their approach. The underpinnings of the political culture prevalent in each case state shines through, albeit in different intensities, and illustrates the crucial importance of culture and values in the implementation stage of government modernisation programmes and the effects that they can have on the lived experiences of e-government from a citizen perspective. In some ways, mirroring the threats attributed to the wider phenomenon of globalisation, we might consider those political cultures and values as being somewhat under challenge from the centralising tendency of EU-sponsored initiatives that may, at first, seem to exhibit a compelling logic towards similarity and policy homogenisation as was made apparent in Chapter two. However, as we have seen in the subsequent chapters, the reality is somewhat different with nation-states and even, at times, sub regional actors having more influence and discretion to mould the implementation of ICT based solutions to fit their own, self-determined, needs. If the nation-state is under threat from ICT inspired change we can find little, if any, evidence of it.

As Desai et al posit,[1] measuring technology achievement and its role in such applications in the network age is far from straightforward, given the vast range of technologies created and diffused, and the challenges of legislating, managing, interpreting and adapting them to satisfy different countries' imperatives and cater for local needs. The diversity is readily apparent, as one reads through the diverse country case-studies. In those countries where there is more of an established tradition of technological innovation such as Germany, the UK, France, the Netherlands and even Denmark, it is evident that initiatives are more advanced, mature, and strategies more sober and reflective. In countries where technological innovation is still relatively new, such as Estonia, Portugal, Greece, or Slovenia, there is still a sense of a 'honeymoon period', which is translated into a degree of idealism in the e-government and e-democracy initiatives launched. This creates a type of dynamism that can often overcome barriers that early adopters may have struggled with. The relative newness of democracy in some of those states fuels a long-hidden ambition to modernise at a pace that would be harder to achieve in more mature democracies. Nevertheless, we can see that across Europe there appear to be consistent expectations for the new technologies to play a significant role in revamping the government–citizen relationships, upgrading the public administration networks, and increasing transparency, efficiency and participation. To some extent, in almost every one of the countries examined, though perhaps more overtly in some than in others, these expectations are taken as a given, going unquestioned. E-government strategies tend to be characterised by a top-down technology push, treating the citizen as a customer. The creators of such systems often appear to still be reluctant to yield control of developments to more balanced two-way, let alone bottom-up driven, approaches.

Despite the patchwork of country strategies revealed in the earlier chapters, some common threads are discernible and it is of no surprise that they also coincide and form a key part of the overarching EU strategies and focus points for its sponsored programmes: the harmonisation and linking-up of local and national public administration networks within and between countries, as well as between member countries and EU institutions as with the TESTA programme and the network of national subsidiaries, the delivery of basic public services electronically through programmes to do with taxation, public procurement and other such services, as was seen in Denmark, and further, the reshaping of civil society and the public sphere at large, as shown through the e-democracy initiatives in Estonia and Greece.

The European Union forms a discreet, yet formidable overarching umbrella over the member-states' e-government strategies. Priorities such as regional rejuvenation and decentralisation via improved electronic access to administrative, medical, social, educational services even in remote parts of the continent, a reduction of the economic and social divide among European citizens, less bureaucracy and enhanced administrative efficiency in the EU's own transactions with different layers of government in member-states, a lessening of the perceived distance between the EU centre and periphery with a view to enhancing the EU's image and potentially European citizenship and identity, permeate the framework programmes co-funded by the EU that member states are able to tap into while pursuing their own strategies.[2] On a more practical note however, these programmes allow different systems to be exposed into the European melting pot, permitting lessons to be mutually learnt and the easier exchange of best practice. Of course with that exchange of best practice comes some adaptation, some re-interpretation of goals, a fine tuning of initiatives and policy implementation to take into account the specific national characteristics and the prevailing political culture.

One of the things that became evident through many of the chapters, however, was that, in practice, the level of achievement of e-government in our case countries is not necessarily always overly inspiring. Despite numerous efforts by governments, some more laissez-faire than others, accessibility to a PC is still a problem for many citizens, and even where access exists, there is not necessarily the enthusiasm to take up the opportunity to partake of the electronic services offered by authorities. It is difficult to determine which particular economic, social, or cultural parameters account for this hesitation in take-up, though of course, in the more developed countries of the EU, penetration of new technologies is comparatively more widespread than in the others. This needs to improve substantially, and for this to happen, as Lowe argues, benefits need to be shared between e-government providers and users if the projected expectations are to be met.[3] There seems to be a need, indeed almost a duty, on governments to help create the demand for online services: but what if the demand simply is not there? What then? Can we detect, for example, in the compulsory nature of online tax services such as in the Netherlands, a move to force citizens to adopt e-government even if they prefer not to?

Whilst admiring the brave new world of ICT-enabled governance we should bear in mind that the systems of such governance operate in a political world that is inhabited by human beings in both their online and offline personas. We should be careful to ensure that we do not get carried away with the potential of ICT and neglect the people for whom they are designed to provide benefits. The most important decisions in government are not technical ones but political ones.

According to Mulgan,[4] the central issue for any state when introducing any form of e-government process is whether those processes contribute to legitimation of the state. Thus, the level of creation of public value determines the level of legitimation of e-government policies and thus, the state. That level of legitimation requires the state to enlist citizen participation in e-government measures. However, that participation needs to be on a much more inclusive level than that of mere service consumers. Public value is achieved through an incredibly complex web of interactions and interdependencies including the trust relationships between states, its civil servants and citizens. It is only through continued and evolving discourse that politicians, officials and citizens can identify, mediate and prioritise public demands and ICT can clearly play a role in stimulating and facilitating that discourse both via traditional and non traditional structures.[5] Any understanding of shared value can only really be applied subsequent to that dialogue and before discussions over efficiency or productivity take place. Thus, in a system based upon e-government we can posit a shift towards service and content focused administration with an emphasis on the creation of public value.[6] The contentious area, of course, is this: who defines that public value and who determines its creation and measurement?

Fountain[7] notes that the metaphor of a 'virtual state' is increasingly being used to describe the way in which the activities, structures and processes of the state are increasingly becoming dependent on the use of digitised information and communication systems utilising ICT with which to deal with information. Such a model of e-governance may be said, on the one hand, to threaten to de-personalise the relationships between citizen and government through its reliance on technological solutions and digital interfaces. However, on the other hand it could be argued that the same technologies that could potentially depersonalise citizen government relations also have the potential to enable more specialisation and personalisation within the systems, which could improve the very same relationships that they are said to threaten. The sharing of data within and across differing ministries or departments offers the threat of abuse via a 'big brother' type enveloping state apparatus, but also potentially frees up the citizen to only have to single-key enter their data instead of repeating the same data on numerous government forms. All of this, of course, is dependent upon the creation of adequate digital signatures and identities and it is little surprise to see that much government effort in the case-study countries outlined in this volume is aimed at producing secure workable solutions to solve these somewhat thorny and often difficult issues. The notion of the virtual state enables the institutions of the state, including associated agencies and other arms-length service providers and enablers, to re-engineer the location of data, decision and policy making, services and processes. It also enables a continuous process of monitoring or benchmarking, the simplification of processes, and, potentially, the elimination of layers of bureaucracy.

Nevertheless, it must be said that the idea of ICT trimming flabby government bureaucracies can be contested. While in some senses it can eradicate processes and applications and cut some forms of red tape, it is difficult to see how it can help to eradicate bureaucracy totally. Indeed, one can argue that the technological shaping of the processes, whilst cutting some elements of red tape, also adds some others. The very nature of e-government is to utilise data across existing organisational boundaries but paradoxically through creating inter-dependence and standardisation. The virtual state is characterised as being one that is inter-sectoral, inter-agency, and inter-governmental. It is for governments to try to create new forms of organisation that can fit the needs of a modern information driven state whilst at the very least maintaining but preferably improving fundamental aspects of governance such as transparency, accountability and control based on new forms of networked relationships.

Cardoso and Lapa in Chapter 11 of this volume describe the Portuguese government's moves towards creating what Mulgan[8] views as an 'open state', which Cardoso and Lapa see as being a government system that '... reshapes itself to be less a structure that provides services or achieves outcomes directly; instead it becomes more like an infrastructure, managing complex systems with capacities for self-organisation, working together with citizens and civil society at large in the co-creation of outcomes'. This certainly entails agreements over common protocols, supporting user-friendly public systems with clear underlying rules and simpler interfaces, albeit the complexity of underlying processes.

E-government is often presented as the 'answer' to the problems of government. However, as Rawal has shown in Chapter four, this capacity for 'good' can also be subverted to become a weapon that can be used against the state. As he also demonstrates, the very strength of dependence upon ICT-facilitated e-government can leave governments open to potential cyberterrorist attack.

Moreover, ignoring the humanistic nature of government by concentrating on technological aspects such as the capacity for increased data handling can lead one to overlook the interdependencies between organisations and the technologies that they use. How ICTs are used reflects organisational form. ICTs are embedded and work within, across and between organisations. Thus, in order to comprehend ICT use in government it is also necessary to have an understanding of the forms, norms, cultures, structures, processes, and dynamics of the organisations involved. Indeed, it must be remembered that it is people who form organisations and it is they who can hinder the implementation of new organisational forms and processes, both through user or citizen resistance to change or via the reluctance of staff to embrace change.

One of the dangers of researching e-government is that one can get drawn into a trap of almost deifying e-government and giving it a status or position that it does not merit. One can be drawn into the trap of assuming that e-government, and the developing and emerging technologies that underpin it, will of themselves produce better government. It is of vital importance not to be carried away with the technological hype, the newness and the undoubted benefits that e-government has the potential to help deliver. We must remember that e-government is just government, and you can drop the 'e'! It may be useful for those involved in its creation or in examining its effects, but to the person on the street it is just government by another name, using a different technology perhaps, but still just government. E-government is just a different label to neatly attach to the tools, mechanisms and processes used by governments in their constant search to improve government citizen interactions. Exciting, of course, but no more guaranteed to raise government standards than was the introduction of the ball point pen or the telephone. It is people who raise standards, and whilst the technology facilitates those changes, without the political will to revolutionise the citizen–government interface, e-government is just yet another phase in the long history of government and administration.

Notes

1. Desai, M., Fukuda-Parr, S., Johansson C. and Sagasti, F. (2002) 'Measuring the Technology Achievement of Nations and the Capacity to Participate in the Network Age', *Journal of Human Development*, Vol.3, No.1.
2. Leitner, C. (2004) 'eGovernment in Europe: The State of Affairs', *International Journal of Communications Law and Policy*, Issue 8.
3. Lowe, C. (2004) 'Ten Steps to Massive take-up of e-Government in Europe', *International Journal of Communications Law and Policy*, Issue 8.
4. Mulgan, G. (2006) 'Reshaping the State and its Relationship with Citizens: the Short, Medium and Long-term Potential of ICTs and egovernment', in Castells, M. and Cardoso, G. (eds) *The Network Society – From Knowledge to Policy*. Washington, DC: Johns Hopkins Center for Transatlantic Relations.
5. For an example of the discourse around this topic see Michel, H. (2005) 'e-Administration, e-Government, e-Governance and the Learning City: A Typology of Citizenship Management Using ICTs', *Electronic Journal of E-government*, Vol 3, No 4, pp. 213–18; available online at www.ejeg.com
6. Millard, J. et al. (2004) 'Reorganisation of Government Back Offices for Better Electronic Public Services', available online at europa.eu.int/information_society/programmes/egov_rd/documentation/text_en.htm

7   Fountain, J. (2006) 'Central Issues in the Political Development of the Virtual State', in Castells, M. and Cardoso, G. (eds) *The Network Society – From Knowledge to Policy*. Washington, DC: Johns Hopkins Center for Transatlantic Relations.
8   Mulgan, G. (2006) 'Reshaping the State and its Relationship with Citizens: the Short, Medium and Long-term Potential of ICTs and egovernment', in Castells, M. and Cardoso, G. (eds) *The Network Society – From Knowledge to Policy*. Washington, DC: Johns Hopkins Center for Transatlantic Relations.

Index

1984 12

ADELE programme (France) 77–8, 85
administration: paperless 111–13
administrative reform: and ICT 97–9, 152–3, 166–7
Al Qaeda 51, 53–4
Ariadni scheme (Greece) 139–40
Asymmetric Threats Contingency Unit (ACTA) 55
automation: electronic service delivery 65, 72

Bangemann Report 23
banking 175
bibliographic system: on-line 206
blogging: terrorists 53
Brave New World 12
broadband 26, 68
broadband access 119; schools 156

children: uses of Internet 202
Ciencia Viva (Portugal) 156
citizens: as customers 39, 154; as democratic participants 40; as democratic supervisors 40–1; relationship with EU xxi–xxii, 30; use of electronic public services 37–8
Citizen's Portal (Portugal) 155, 164
citizenship: and e-government 33–46; and geographical territory 44; and identification 36, 41–2, 44; nature of 34–5, 43–4; particularism 43
co-operation: and ICT 95–7
Community Support Frameworks (CSF) 22
company registration: electronic 206–7
Contract with the Future 121
Counterculture: subversion of society 3–5
crime: surveillance of hot-spots 125–6
Customer Relationship Management (CRM) 42

customers: and ICT 96–9
cyber freedom: limitation of 56–7
cyber-democracy: and real world 6–11; roots 3–5
cyberactivism 49–50
cyberjihad 50
cyberspace: as counterculture 4–5
cyberterrorism 48–60; definition 49–50

danger mouse xxiv, 48–60
Danish National Board of Industrial Injuries 112
data sharing: and electronic service delivery 71, 72
democracy: and e-government 1–18; Internet xxii; and opinion polls 11
Denmark 103–18, 211; electronic pay checks 112, 116–17; electronic procurement 113; first computer 109; government computerisation 103, 109–11; healthcare 114–17; invoicing 116–17; local government 108–9; MedCom network 114–15, 116, 117; paperless administration 111–13; tax administration 113–15, 117
Deutschland On-line 92–3
Digital Cities Programme (Portugal) 158, 164
Digital Delta – the Netherlands Online 121
Digital Identification Service (Netherlands) 122–3
digital TV xxiv
dot.coms 13
duplication: reduction of 40

e-administration: France 76–9, 80–3, 84–6; satisfaction with 83
e-Citizen Charter (Netherlands) 124, 125, 127–9
e-Citizen portal (Estonia) 175

e-democracy: Estonia 173, 175–8, 180–1; France 79–80, 86; Greece 142–5; Portugal 156
e-government: advantages 12–15; balanced 40; barriers xx–xxii; benefits xx, 215; citizen-centred 40–1; citizen's needs 37; and citizenship 33–46; costs 28, 190; dangers of 12–13; definitions xix, 40, 91–2, 153; and democracy 1–18; economic incentives 105, 106, 107; and efficiency 84–5, 91, 190; EU 19–32, 37; failure rate 29; and ICT development 29–30; knowledge diffusion 105–6, 107; legislative control 13–14; and legitimation of state 213; and mobile phones 192–3; and modernisation 100, 134–5; organisational management 105, 106–7; outcomes 99, 130; purpose of 33; quality standards 125, 127–9; and real world 6–11; regulation 104–5, 107; roots 3–5; take-up 145
e-identity 41–2, 57, *see also* electronic signatures; identification; identity cards
e-procurement *see* procurement: electronic
economic incentives: e-government 105, 106, 107
educational deficiencies: and ICT use 160, 162
eEurope 2002 24
eEurope 2005 25–6
Electronic Government Action Programme (Netherlands) 121
electronic service delivery: automation 65, 72; citizen engagement 69–70; complex transactions 70–2; and cost-cutting xxiv, 64–5; and data sharing 71, 72; and exclusion xxi, 68–9; language barriers xxi, 69, 186; portals 64–5, 155; and privacy 71; and public accessibility 64–5
electronic signatures xxii; Estonia 173; France 83–4; Germany 91; legality 83–4, 91; Netherlands 122–3
electronic tax returns *see* tax administration: electronic
electronic voting 11, 72; Estonia 111, 171, 178–80, 181; France 79–80, 88; Greece 136, 142–5; ineffectiveness 180, 181; Portugal 156; security 71, 72; UK 63, 67, 69
employment service: electronic 206
English language: use on Internet 9, 17
Estonia 171–83, 211–12; e-Citizen portal 175; e-democracy 173, 175–8, 180–1; electronic identity cards 173, 175; electronic signatures 173; electronic voting 171, 178–80, 181; Internet access 174, 178; Internet banking 175; IT policy 173–5; public administration reform 172–3; Themis 177–8, 180–1; TOM project 173, 175–8, 180–1
ETA (Basque Separatist Group) 51
EU: e-government 19–32, 37; ICT investment 27; relationship with citizens xxi–xxii, 30
EU institutional architecture: and e-government 24
EURO-CITI programme (Greece) 138
European Treaty referendum 79
exclusion: and electronic delivery xxi, 68–9
executive government: and ICT 12, 13–14

facial recognition: digital 111
Framework Programmes 22
France 75–89, 211; ADELE programme 77–8, 85; e-administration 76–9, 80–3, 84–6; e-democracy 79–80, 86; European Treaty referendum 79; Internet access 75, 78, 80–1, 87; Internet voting 79–80, 88; PAGSI programme 76–7; Plan Reso 2007 77; public websites 81; reform of the state 75, 87
geographical territory: and citizenship 44
Germany 90–102, 211; e-administration 93, 94–5; federal system 94; Internet portals 91–2; Internet use 92; traditional administrative organisation 96
global economy: and domestic openness 2; and ICT 2
government: as business 39
government–citizen relationships: and ICT 212
Greece 133–51, 211–12; anachronistic bureaucracy 133–4; Ariadni scheme 139–40; e-democracy 142–5; electronic tax system 138–9, 147; electronic voting 136, 142–5; EURO-CITI programme 138; ICT development 134–5; ICT expenditure 146; Internet access 133–4, 148; KLISTHENIS programme 135; Operational Programme for the Information Society (OPIS) 140–2; Politeia project 140; SmartGov project 138; Syzefxis project 137–8; TAXIS system 138–9, 148; Trikala Digital City Project 149
healthcare: ICT 114–17, 126, 157, 164
Hezbollah 51
Hungary 184–95; broadband 186;

computer ownership 185, 186; and EU 184–5; Internet access 185–6, 187; m-government 192–3; portals 191–2

i2010 initiative 21, 26–8, 29
ICANN (Internet Corporation for Assigned Names and Numbers) 54–5
ICT: and administrative reform 97–9, 152–3, 166–7; and co-operation 95–7; confidentiality 165; crime hot-spot surveillance 125–6; and customers 96–9; and efficiency of government 119, 214; and executive government 12, 13–14; and global economy 2; good practice 25–6; and government–citizen relationships 212; healthcare 114–17, 126, 157, 164; interoperability 26–7, 109; investment in 27; lack of trust in 165; and lifelong learning 124; and modernisation 95–7; and nation-state 211; security 165; and social inclusion 66–7; training 156; and travel information 124–5
ICT development: and e-government 29–30
ICT Unit (Netherlands) 121–2, 127
ICT use: and educational deficiencies 160, 162; local government 162
identification: and citizenship 36, 41–2, 44; methods of 41–2, *see also* e-identity
identity cards: electronic xxii, 85, 153, 173, 175
Inclusive European Information Society 27–8
income: and Internet use 9–10
individual freedom: and Internet 1
information and communication technologies *see* ICT
Information and Knowledge Society Observatory (Portugal) 158
Internet: accessibility 7–10, 213; attractions for terrorists 52; democracy of xxii; and individual freedom 1; privacy 56–7, 58; regulation 49, 54–5; use by children 202; use of English 9, 17
Internet banking: Estonia 175
Internet politics: types of 4
Internet use: and income 9–10
Internet users: control of 55–6
invoicing: electronic 116–17
Ireland: e-government use 37
ISAP programme (Netherlands) 124–7
Italy: anti-terror laws and Internet 55–6

Japan: ICT investment 27

KLISTHENIS programme (Greece) 135
knowledge diffusion: e-government 105–6, 107

language barriers: electronic service delivery xxi, 69, 186
lifelong learning: and ICT 124
Lisbon Strategy 24
local government: ICT use 108–9, 162, 192; monitoring 128–9

m-government 192–3
Malaysia: Government Multipurpose Smart Card 110–11
MedCom network (Denmark) 114–15, 116, 117
Meetup.com 10–11
Mill, John Stuart: on free government 15
mobile phones: and e-government 192–3
modernisation: and e-government 100, 134–5; and ICT 95–7
Modernising Government Programme (Netherlands) 122
MSIBlast worm 49

nation-state: and ICT 211
neo-liberalism 196
Neotec initiative (Portugal) 157
Netherlands 119–32, 211; B4 Programme 122; broadband access 119; Contract with the Future 121; crime hot-spots 125–6; Digital Delta – the Netherlands Online 121; Digital Identification Service (DigiD) 122–3; digital signatures 122–3; e-Citizen Charter 124, 125, 127–9; Electronic Government Action Programme 121; healthcare 126; ICT Unit 121–2, 127; Internet access 119; ISAP programme 124–7; lifelong learning 124; local e-government 128–9; Modernising Government Programme 122; OL2000 programme 121; online tax systems 122, 213; satisfaction with government websites 119–20; travel information 124–5
'netizens' 1, 2, 4
New Left: beliefs 16; and participatory democracy 3–4
NGO-swarms 50
NHS (National Health Service) 61
noopolitik 199

OL2000 programme (Netherlands) 121
one-stop shops 97, 121
opinion polls: and democracy 11

Index

OPIS (Operational Programme for the Information Society) (Greece) 140–2
organisational interoperability 26–7
organisational management: e-government 105, 106–7

Paganini Project on Participatory Governance and Institutional Reform 22
PAGSI programme (France) 76–7
Pakistan: digital facial recognition 111
paperless administration 111–13
participatory democracy: and New Left 3–4
particularism 43
pay checks: electronic 112, 116–17
Plan Reso 2007 (France) 77
police: use of ICT 206
policy co-ordination xx
Politeia project (Greece) 140
portals: electronic service delivery 64–5, 91–2, 155, 191–2
Portugal 152–70, 211–12, 214; Ciencia Viva 156; Citizen's Portal 155, 164; Digital Cities Programme 158, 164; e-Accessibility 155; e-democracy 156; e- procurement 157–8; educational deficiencies 160, 162; electronic employment exchange 155; electronic tax returns 155; electronic voting 156; governmental organisation 159, 167; healthcare 157, 164; ICT training 156; ICT use 161; Information and Knowledge Society Observatory 158; local government 162; Neotec initiative 157; smart cards 153; Solidarity Network 155, 164; Virtual Campus 157, 164–5
Post, Emily: obsoleteness 13
power outages: as cyberterrorism 49
privacy: and electronic service delivery 71; Internet 56–7, 58
procurement: electronic 21, 113, 157–8, 205
public administration: reorganisation 97–9, 172–3
public sector modernisation: and e-government 100, 134–5

'red diaper' babies 3–4
regulation: e-government 104–5, 107
rural dwellers: disadvantages xxii

schools: broadband connection 156
security: electronic voting 71, 72; ICT 165
semantic interoperability 27
signatures *see* electronic signatures
Singaporean TradeNet 106, 108

Single European Information Space 26
SIPS (Security Intelligence Products and Systems) 55
Sixth Framework Programme *see* Paganini
Slovenia 196–210, 211–12; bibliographic system 206; broadband access 202; company registration 206–7; e-government portal 205; e-procurement 205; electronic tax returns 205; employment service 206; healthcare 207; higher education applications 205–6; Internet access 201–3, 207; Internet use 199, 201–4; police 206
SmartGov project (Greece) 138
social inclusion: and ICT 66–7
Solidarity Network (Portugal) 155, 164
Sorry Award 128
Syzefxis project (Greece) 137–8

tax administration, electronic 81, 83, 108; Denmark 113–15, 117; Greece 138–9, 147; Netherlands 122, 213; Portugal 155; Slovenia 205
tax-payers: as customers of government 2
TAXIS system (Greece) 138–9, 148
technical interoperability 27
terrorists: use of Internet 49–54
TESTA initiative 23, 137
Themis (Estonia) 177–8, 180–1
TOM project (Estonia) 173, 175–8, 180–1
trade unions: distrust of ICT 85
travel information: and ICT 124–5
Trikala Digital City Project (Greece) 149

UK 61–74, 211; constitutional arrangements 61; digital inclusion 66, 68–9; digital TV xxiv; e-government use 37; electronic service delivery 64–5, 67–9; government websites 62–3; Internet access 68; National Health Service (NHS) 61
USA: democratisation 4; e-government use 37; ICT investment 27
Virtual Campus (Portugal) 157, 164–5
'virtual state' 213–14
visa applications online 111
voting: electronic *see* electronic voting
'War on Terror' 48
weblogs *see* blogging
websites: satisfaction with 119–20; UK government 62–3
WELL: The 6, 16
Wikipedia 6, 16
Worldwide Web: and democratic debate 69–70, 72; as political tool 63

eBooks – at www.eBookstore.tandf.co.uk

A library at your fingertips!

eBooks are electronic versions of printed books. You can store them on your PC/laptop or browse them online.

They have advantages for anyone needing rapid access to a wide variety of published, copyright information.

eBooks can help your research by enabling you to bookmark chapters, annotate text and use instant searches to find specific words or phrases. Several eBook files would fit on even a small laptop or PDA.

NEW: Save money by eSubscribing: cheap, online access to any eBook for as long as you need it.

Annual subscription packages

We now offer special low-cost bulk subscriptions to packages of eBooks in certain subject areas. These are available to libraries or to individuals.

For more information please contact webmaster.ebooks@tandf.co.uk

We're continually developing the eBook concept, so keep up to date by visiting the website.

www.eBookstore.tandf.co.uk